C'est si bon!

HERITAGE RECIPES

Published by

The Young Women's
Christian Organization

of Baton Rouge, Incorporated

BATON ROUGE, LOUISIANA
1972

Proceeds from the sale of C'est Si Bon will be used for Christian work among young girls and women in the Baton Rouge area. See back of book for order blanks.

Recipes have been contributed by YWCO members, their families, and friends.

Cover design and illustrations by
NANCY HARRIS

FOREWORD

You need not be a connoisseur or a gourmet to use and prepare the fabulous assortment of recipes in C'EST SI BON.

No, all you need is a yen to serve something savoury to your loved ones and friends. Then you must follow meticulously the directions for preparing each dish incorporated in the contents of this book.

Louisiana is famous for her cuisine and the compilers of this book combed the state in an effort to get a cross-section of representative recipes from most of the area. We did not stop here, but included other states and other countries.

Those who have already tried and tested these recipes exclaim, "C'EST SI BON! C'EST MAGNIFIQUE!"

TABLE OF CONTENTS

They Rule the
World...

They Cook, Too!

FLAPJACKS SOUFFLÉ

6 eggs, separated   ½ teaspoon salt
½ cup buttermilk   ½ cup dairy sour cream
  pancake mix

Beat yolks until thick and lemon-colored. Add pancake mix, salt, and sour cream; stir just enough to blend. Carefully fold in stiffly beaten egg whites. Bake on lightly greased griddle. Serve with butter and syrup. Makes ten 4-inch pancakes.

CHET BECKWITH

DR. E. B. YOUNG'S PANCAKES
(Used when a patient could not keep food down)

One cup well-cooked mush (cornmeal). Cool enough to beat in a yoke of an egg, 2 tablespoons flour and 1 level teaspoon baking powder. Add white of an egg (whipped and folded in) Rub skillet with butter or bacon fat and cook as regular pancakes. Eat **without** syrup.

Submitted by
MRS. JESSIE COATS, SR.

SUNDAY GRIDDLE CAKES
Serves 4

2 cups 3 minute rolled oats   1 teaspoon salt
2 cups milk   2 tablespoons sugar
1/3 cup of flour   3 eggs
1 tablespoon baking powder   ½ cup Lou Ana oil

Preheat skillet to 380 degrees. If you do not have an electric skillet the heat can be estimated by dripping a small amount of water on the skillet if the water beads and dances the skillet is ready if the drops almost explode it is too hot. Heat milk in regular saucepan; pour over oats; let cool. Sift dry ingredients· Separate eggs; beat egg yolks and add to oats. Add Lou Ana cooking oil and stir in dry ingredients. Beat egg whites until stiff. Fold gently into the rest of mixture. Turn when bubbly. The skillet temperature is the critical factor.

DAN COHN

These recipes are set up as submitted by our chefs.

STEAMED EGGS

Beat two large eggs. Slowly add 1 cup of hot bouillon made with a chicken cube. Stir rapidly while adding:

¼ teaspoon salt   ¼ teaspoon MSG
1 teaspoon Lou Ana Oil

Pour this mixture into two 6 ounce size baking dishes. Add 1 tablespoon minced onion to each one and dust with red pepper. Place in suitable pot and pour in hot water to within ½ inch of the tops of the baking dishes and cover. Set pot over lowest heat so that water will never boil. Small bubbles should form on the bottom but not rise and break the surface. These will be done in about 20 minutes or when they become solid or semi-solid. Some cooks insert a tableknife and if it comes out clean, they assume it to be done. At any rate, they remain in their bath until ready to serve.

I like soy sauce with this. Excellent for breakfast.

This is a favorite that lends itself to a thousand variations. For example: add a teaspoon of sherry or make it with milk. Or add some minced ham, chicken or cooked shrimp.

FONVILLE WINANS

PO'MAN'S BREAD PANCAKES
Serves 8

4 slices dry bread   2 cups flour
3 tablespoons melted butter   1 teaspoon salt
3 teaspoons baking powder   2 eggs
3 cups buttermilk   1 teaspoon soda

Soak bread crumbs in buttermilk for a few minutes, then mix with beater. Add beaten eggs, then flour, soda, baking powder and salt. Mix well with egg beater. Add melted butter.

CHARLES NUNN

COOKING HINTS:

Grill or skillet should be well greased and hot. If pancakes are wet inside, add a little more baking powder and flour. Bread should be dry enough to crumble. Buttermilk should be fresh.

JUST PLAIN HOT CAKES
Makes 24 Medium Cakes

Sift together:

3 cups flour	2 heaping teaspoons sugar
3 heaping teaspoons baking powder	1 level teaspoon salt

Add:

½ cup Lou Ana oil	1 egg
	3 cups milk

Griddle at 350 degrees. Cut recipe to suit.

COL. TOM W. DUTTON
Spoonbill Chef

CAVIAR DIP

Beat ½ cup heavy cream until it begins to hold a shape. Stir in 2 to 3 tablespoons caviar and 1 to 2 tablespoons finely chopped onion. Put the caviar dip in the center of a serving dish and garnish with slices of hard cooked egg and small rounds of toast.

JOE GARNETT BARHAM, M.D.
Lake Charles, La.

CRAB 'N' CHIPS
Serves 4 to 6

3 tablespoons flour	1 stick butter
2 cups breakfast cream	1 teaspoon white pepper
¼ cup finely chopped green onion	dash of Tabasco
	½ lb. grated Swiss Cheese
½ cup dry white wine	1 lb. fresh crab meat
½ tsp. salt (more if needed)	2 cups crushed potato chips

Saute green onions in butter until wilted. Add flour and cream to make a white sauce. Add wine, seasonings and Swiss cheese. Stir until cheese is melted, then fold in crab meat. Top with crushed potato chips and bake at 350 degrees for 20 minutes.

ANTHONY J. DOHERTY

With this prize-winning recipe, Mr. Doherty was named state champion male cook in the annual Men's National Cooking Championship sponsored by the Potato Chip Institute International in 1969.

OXTAIL SOUP

1 small oxtail	2 quarts beef stock
1 tablespoon shortening	small bouquet garni
½ cup onions	1 teaspoon lemon juice
½ cup celery	1 tablespoon
½ cup carrots	Worcestershire sauce

Cut oxtail in ½ inch pieces, wash in cold water and wipe dry. Season with salt and pepper, roll in flour and cook 8 to 10 minutes in shortening. Transfer to soup kettle. Add onions, celery and carrots, cut real fine, bouquet garni and beef stock. Cover and simmer gently for 3½ hours. Taste for seasoning and discard bouquet garni. Skim off any grease. Add lemon juice and Worcestershire sauce and serve very hot. Bouquet garni includes celery, parsley, thyme and bay leaf wrapped in a piece of gauze and tied with a string.

RICHARD TUITE, D.D.S.

A SOUP OF FISHES

1 cup diced celery	4 tablespoons flour
1 cup diced onions	4 tablespoons butter
1 cup diced potatoes	2 tablespoons chopped
½ gal. medium oysters	parsley
2 large cans shredded	Salt, pepper, Tabasco sauce,
clams and juice	Worcestershire sauce,
5 lbs. raw shrimp	heavy cream.
2 lbs. fish meat (red	Sachet bag: pinch of
snapper, flounder	thyme, rosemary, 1 bay
filet, white fish, etc.)	leaf, 6 crushed pepper
2 cups white wine	corns, 2 cloves garlic

Par boil oysters, shrimp and fish in white wine. Sauté onions, potatoes and celery. Make roux of butter and flour. Add liquid from clams and the cooked wine from boiled fish. Add herbs tied together in cheese cloth. Simmer gently 10 to 15 minutes. Add sautéed onions, potatoes, celery and all chopped fish and add to soup until potatoes are nearly done. Add heavy cream, dash of Worcestershire and Tabasco, chopped parsley and season to taste.

(Yield: Approximately 1½ gal.)

As created and served at the City Club of Baton Rouge, Louisiana

By: C. H. BRANDT
City Club of Baton Rouge

DIP A LA DAN

2 cartons sour cream
1½ cans chopped ripe
   olives (small)
1 teaspoon garlic powder

1 tablespoon celery salt
5 Slim Jim Sausages
   (cut into slim slices)
5 drops Tabasco

Combine all ingredients. Let stand in refrigerator about 2 hours.

DAN COHN

OYSTER SOUP

1 stick butter
2 cans
   chicken broth
2 cans water
5 tablespoons flour
bunch green onions
1 teaspoon Worcestershire
   sauce

2 ribs celery
1 tablespoon soya sauce
garlic powder
   (optional)
salt
pepper
1 quart oysters
milk

Chop onions and celery extremely fine. Melt butter; add flour. **Do not brown.** Add onions and celery; sauté for 3 or 4 minutes. Add broth and water. Add Worcestershire sauce, soya sauce, salt, pepper and dusting of garlic powder. Boil gently for 20 or 30 minutes.

Add oysters and juice and milk to make the broth white. Bring to slight boil until oysters curl. Adjust seasoning.

ALLEN ANDERSON

MARYLAND CRAB CAKES
Serves 6

In a bowl combine 1 cup crumbled day-old bread with ¼ cup homemade mayonnaise, 2 teaspoons prepared mustard, a dash each of red and black pepper, and salt to taste. Work in gently 1 pound back-fin crab meat, being careful not to flake it, and shape the mixture into cakes. Heat a skillet coated with shortening and add the crab cakes. Sauté them for 3 to 5 minutes, or until they are hot and golden brown on both sides. Serve the crab cakes hot.

Submitted by RALPH SIMS

COURTBOUILLON (Gumbo Style)
Redfish or Gaspargou may be used

3-5 lb. red fish
1 gal. of water
2 cloves of garlic chopped
1 large bell pepper chopped
2 medium onions chopped
5 stalks of celery chopped
1 lemon quartered
1 lb. can of stewed
   tomatoes

1 8 oz. can tomato sauce
pinch of thyme
dash of vinegar
4 bay leaves
hot pepper sauce
green onion tops
   chopped
salt & pepper to taste
roux

Place chopped garlic, onion, bell pepper and celery in a deep pot with water. Bring to a boil and add lemon, tomatoes, tomato sauce, vinegar and seasonings. Allow to cook on slow boil for 1½ hours. Debone fish and cut into small squares; these will be used last. Place backbone and other scraps of fish in smaller pot with water and seasonings and cook down for the stock. Make a roux and add this along with fish stock to mixture in large pot. Put in bay leaves and cook for about 30 minutes or until desired consistency is reached. You may add water if necessary. Add fish squares and cook for 15 minutes. Serve in bowls over rice. Serves 6.

JOHN CONTOIS
Slidell, La.

OYSTERS BORDELAISE

Sauté 6 dozen freshly shucked and drained oysters (reserve liquor) in butter until edges curl. Season with salt and pepper. Reduce 1/10 red wine with scallions or shallots to half its original amount. Add one pint brown sauce and oyster liquor, and reduce to half.

Retire from fire and add two tablespoons butter and beat with rotary beater until fluffy.

Correct seasoning with sauce Escoffier Diable, salt and pepper.

Add oysters and **keep warm.**

Sprinkle with **diced poached beef marrow and serve.**

This dish can be served in artichoke bottoms— with pilau rice—a ring of wild rice—in a pastry shell, etc. Very excellent for cocktail party foods, served in miniature patty shells or Barquette.

By: C. H. BRANDT

As created and served at the City Club of Baton Rouge, Baton Rouge, Louisiana.

IMPERIAL CRAB, JOHN PRINCE
Serves 10

3 pounds of fresh all
   lump crab
2 cups homemade
   mayonnaise
white pepper

3 tablespoons chopped
   fresh chives (A little
   more won't hurt)
juice of ½ lemon
1 ounce imported caviar

salt to taste

Mix chives, lemon juice and caviar into the mayonnaise. Carefully go through the crab meat to make sure there is no shell. Season it with white pepper and a little salt. Put into the mayonnaise mixture. Add a little salt if needed.

Put in baking dish. Cover the top with a thin layer of mayonnaise and dust with paprika. Bake until it bubbles and browns a little on top.

Submitted by RALPH SIMS

QUICHE AUX FRUITS DE MER

One baked pastry shell (10 in.) (See recipe below)
1 small onion, thinly sliced
1 teaspoon cooking oil
4 eggs
1½ cups light cream
¼ teaspoon dry mustard
½ teaspoon basil
½ teaspoon salt

¼ lb. Switzerland swiss
   cheese, grated
½ cup diced boiled shrimp
½ cup lump crab meat
Oven temperature:
   425-350 degrees
Bake: forty-five minutes

Serving: 6 or more

Put pastry shell in freezing compartment until well chilled. Sauté onion in one teaspoon oil until transparent. Drain. Beat the eggs, light cream, dry mustard, basil and salt with rotary beater until well blended. Sprinkle half the onion in the bottom of chilled unbaked pastry shell, add half of each of the seafoods, half the cheese and half the eggs and cream mixture. Repeat in same order ending with cheese. Bake in a hot oven for 15 minutes, reduce to moderate and continue baking until a knife inserted in center comes out clean. Remove to rack. Garnish as desired. Cut into wedges. Serve immediately.

Pastry

2 cups unsifted flour
3/4 cup butter
½ teaspoon salt

3 hard cooked egg
   yolks, mashed
2 raw egg yolks

Make a well in center of flour, working either on a

table or in a bowl. Add all ingredients to well- Butter should not be ice cold, nor so soft that it is oily. Using fingertips, make a paste of center ingredients, gradually incorporating flour to make a firm, smooth ball of paste. Work as quickly as you can so the butter won't become greasy. When bowl or tabletop has been left clean, wrap the dough in waxed paper or aluminum foil and chill until firm enough to roll between sheets of waxed paper.

By: C. H. BRANDT

As created and served at the City Club of Baton Rouge, Baton Rouge, Louisiana

CRAWFISH IN PATTY SHELL

1 pound peeled crawfish tails, uncooked
1 large Creole onion, finely minced
1 clove garlic (2 if you live in South Louisiana)
About 1 teaspoon flour

Salt and pepper to taste
1 ounce dry white table wine (not Sauterne) Optional
ƒ 2 tablespoons tomato paste
1 stick (¼ pound) creamery butter

Prepared pie crust mix

Mince onion and garlic and sauté in butter until onion is soft, not brown. Add tomato paste and sauté at least 5 minutes more.

Chop crawfish tails roughly and add to above mixture. Add salt and pepper to taste. Then sprinkle flour over all and mix well. Cook about 25 minutes on low fire (20 minutes covered, then add wine, if desired, and cook 5 minutes uncovered). Serve in pie crust shells fashioned on outside of muffin tins. Bake shells before filling. Then run in hot oven until it sizzles, remove and place piece of curly parsley in middle for decoration before serving. This light dish goes well as first course with dry white wine.

Note: If too much flour used, you may end up with crawfish stew since crawfish will give off liquid- On the other hand, you may need to add a little water. Texture should neither be dry nor runny.

ERNEST GUEYMARD

RED SNAPPER MOLD
8 servings

Soften 1 tablespoon gelatin in 3 tablespoons cold water and dissolve it over hot water. Mix the gelatin with ½ cup mayonnaise, 2 tablespoons lemon juice, 1 tablespoon each of parsley and chives, both chopped, 1 tablespoon prepared mustard, and salt, pepper, and Tabasco to taste. Fold in 2 cups flaked cooked Red Snapper and 3/4 cup heavy cream, whipped. Pour the mixture into an oiled ring mold and chill it until it is set. Unmold the mousse on a chilled platter and garnish with wedges of hard-cooked eggs. Fill the center with cubed tomatoes and cucumbers mixed lightly with French dressing, and garnish with sprigs of watercress. Serve at once.

By C. H. BRANDT

As created and served at the City Club of Baton Rouge, Baton Rouge, Louisiana

BACON-BROILED SHRIMP

1 pound medium to large shrimp	1½ thin slices fresh ginger chopped very fine
bacon	¼ teaspoon garlic purée
4 tablespoons sherry	2 tablespoons honey
4 tablespoons soy sauce	2 tablespoons cornstarch
1 tablespoon bacon fat	

Peel shrimp. Wrap each one with a half strip bacon and secure with a toothpick. Place the shrimp in a shallow casserole dish, then cook in a 400° pre-heated oven for about 20 minutes or until shrimp are pink and bacon is done. (You may place these under the broiler to crisp the bacon, if desired.) Set aside and keep warm.

While the bacon and shrimp are cooking, prepare a sauce by combining: sherry, soy sauce, ginger, garlic, and honey. Heat gently to dissolve the honey. Then combine several tablespoonsful of the liquid with cornstarch and make a thin paste. Pour this back into the sauce and cook over low heat until it is thick, stirring constantly. Add 1 tablespoon bacon fat from the drippings of the shrimp to the sauce and stir in well. Serve the shrimp and sauce hot. The shrimp are dipped into the sauce to eat.

From the file of
JOHN E. UHLER

FILET OF RED SNAPPER ROQUEFORT

Cut 2 pounds filet of red snapper into 4 or 5 portions and sprinkle them with salt and pepper and the juice of 1 lemon. In a shallow pan make a bed of 4 onions, sliced, and put the fish on top. Add water barely to cover and 5 pepper corns, 3 small dried peppers, and 1 bay leaf. Cover the fish with foil, punched with holes to let the steam escape. Cover the pan and simmer the fish for 3 minutes—it should be slightly underdone. Remove the filets to individual flameproof dishes and cover them generously with Roquefort sauce. Slide each dish under the broiler until the sauce bubbles and browns slightly. Serves 4.

ROQUEFORT SAUCE

Blend together thoroughly ½ cup each of soft butter, crumbled Roquefort, and grated Parmesan, ¼ cup toasted bread crumbs, 1½ tablespoons heavy cream, 1 tablespoon lemon juice and 1½ teaspoons each of Worcestershire sauce and chopped parsley.

JOE GARNETT BARHAM, M.D.
Lake Charles, La.

POOR MAN'S CHATEAUBRIAND

3-in top round steak (or bottom round)	½ pound butter or margarine
Meat tenderizer	Black pepper (freshly
Salt	ground, if available)

Purchase round (boneless) when this cut is on sale. Cover completely with tenderizer (more than jar indicates). Rub in well. Do not pierce meat. Wrap well and freeze. Prior to cooking, allow to thaw slowly in refrigerator, approximately 24 hours. Remove from refrigerator and allow to reach room temperateure an hour or two before cooking. Light fire made of charcoal briquets ½-hour before starting to grill. When fire is a glowing red, place meat on barbecue pit. Loosen, if inclined to stick. Cook on first side for 30 minutes. Turn and cook on second side 30 minutes. (If rare meat is preferred, cook 20 minutes to a side). When "Chateau" is done, salt lightly (tenderizer has salting effect on meat), pepper, and coat heavily with softened butter or margarine. Serves 8 to 10. Good served with Bernaise Sauce.

ROY DABADIE

NOTE: Tenderizer is made from Papaya and is a good digestive agent.

BROILED SIRLOIN STEAK

4 pound sirloin,   ½ stick butter or oleo
    2 inches thick   juice of ½ lemon
salt   1 tablespoon Worcester-
garlic   shire sauce
Lou Ana cooking oil   chips off garlic clove

Rub steak with salt, garlic and Lou Ana oil liberally. Sear over hot fire on both sides then cook slowly until just pink inside. Meanwhile, prepare a sauce with butter or oleo, lemon juice, Worcestershire sauce and chips off garlic clove. Stir and heat, never allow to boil. Place steak on warm platter, slice and pour sauce over all. This mixes with the steak juices, and there's nothing better over baked potato.

DAVID I. GARRETT, JR.
Monroe, La.

SWISS STEAK
(Serves 8)

4 lb   round steak—   2 large onions, sliced thin
    2½ inches thick   1 bay leaf
1 teaspoon of salt   2 tablespoons chopped
¼ teaspoon leaf thyme   parsley
1 teaspoon marjoram   1 can (8 oz.) tomato sauce
½ teaspoon freshly   1 cup tomato catsup
    ground black pepper   ½ stick of butter
½ teaspoon monosodium   1 cup all purpose flour
    glutamate   1 cup of beef consommé
2 tablespoons melted beef   1 can (medium)
    suet or Lou Ana oil   mushrooms
             1 teaspoon oregano

Procedure

Combine flour, salt, thyme, marjoram and monosodium glutamate; divide into two (2) equal portions; spread one portion over steak and pound it into steak with a meat hammer or edge of a heavy plate until flour is taken up. Turn steak, spread the other portion on the steak and pound until all flour is taken up. Combine tomato sauce, catsup, consomme, oregano and butter; heat until the butter is melted. Brown steak on both sides in the beef suet in a Dutch oven. Add bay leaf. Cover with the sliced onions. Pour heated sauce over steak; cover lightly. Cook at 350 degrees-375 degrees for two and one-half to three hours, until done.

Drain the mushrooms; add to steak pot one-quarter hour before steak is done.

Serve with buttered noodles, fluffy rice or mashed potatoes. Garnish with chopped parsley.

A medium can of green peas, well drained, may be substituted for mushrooms.

FRED A. BLANCHE, SR.

BEEF IN A LEAF

1 pound ground beef	1 slice stale bread
½ cup rice	¼ cup milk (soak the
½ cup water (for	bread)
the rice)	head of cabbage (large
1 cup chopped onion	mustard, grape, fig,
1 tablespoon salt	collard greens, bell
1 tablespoon MSG	pepper, squash or
1 tablespoon black pepper	eggplant leaves
1 teaspoon red pepper	also do nicely).
¼ teaspoon grated nutmeg	1 can tomato juice

Carefully remove the outer green leaves down to the white leaves and trim down their spines with a sharp knife. Put these in a large pot of hot water to make them pliable. The white leaves are more tender and harder to remove, so just immerse the entire head in scalding water. This will loosen these difficult leaves and you can remove each one as it becomes relaxed.

Also give these leaves the knife treatment and allow them to rest in the hot water until pliable.

Combine the meat and everything down through the bread and milk and wrap up in the leaves, using about two tablespoons per leaf, more or less, depending upon the mood of the leaf.

Put your cabbage scraps in the bottom of a suitable pot and arrange your little goodies snugly on top. Pour on the tomato juice and add water (1½ cups should do it.) to cover. Place a plate on top, cover and simmer 1 hour.

When done, arrange the rolls on a platter. Remove the scraps and thicken the pot juice with 2 tablespoons corn starch mixed in ¼ cup water. Check seasonings. More salt or MSG may be needed. Put sauce in gravy boat. Very colorful and delicious too!

FONVILLE WINANS

BEEF AND "GOLF BALL" TOMATOES

Golf ball tomatoes are almost what the name implies. The size of golf balls, they are very hard and very green and have a taste and texture quite different than their mamas and papas. For our use they are quartered but not peeled.

1 pound flank steak	2 teaspoons sherry wine
(or any lean beef)	½ teaspoon garlic puree
1 pound "Golf Ball"	½ teaspoon black pepper
tomatoes	1 tablespoon cornstarch
½ cup slivers of onion	3/4 cup water
3 tablespoons soy sauce	1 cup raw short
2 teaspoons sugar	grained rice

soy sauce

Cut meat in small 1/8 inch slices across the grain. This is easily done if the meat is partially frozen. Sauté these slices in ¼ cup Lou Ana oil until they sort of "run out of steam." Add the quartered tomatoes and stir around for 1 minute. Cover and steam for 2 minutes. Add the onions, stir, cover, and cook another minute. Now add the sauce mixture (which you will have stirred well) all at once. Stir for 1 minute and simmer for 1 minute, covered. Cut off the fire; it is now ready to serve with steamed short grain rice which I prefer. One cup of raw rice will make three cups of cooked rice which is enough for this recipe. Don't use any salt. Use soy sauce intead.

NOTE: Many vegetables can be used in place of the tomatoes. Here are some—

Banana peppers. Deseed 3/4 pound and cut up. Sauté 1 minute ahead of meat.

Cucumbers. About 1 pound are cut in half the long way, deseeded, then cut in ¼ inch slices. Cook like tomatoes.

Bell Peppers. 1 pound. No seeds and cut into 1 inch chunks. Treat like tomatoes, after parboiling 2 minutes.

Ginger Root. (fresh) ½ cup thinly sliced and slightly fried before adding meat. It is not necessary to peel or scrape.

Celery. Several stalks are sliced diagonally in 1/8 inch thickness and after adding, are cooked like tomatoes.

FONVILLE WINANS

ONION STEAK

3 large onions cut into rings
1 flank steak cut into paper thin slivers against the grain

2 tablespoons Lou Ana oil
½ teaspoon ginger powder
2 tablespoons Soy sauce
1 teaspoon salt
½ teaspoon pepper

Heat oil and fry onion rings that have been seasoned with salt and pepper. Stir constantly. When rings are tender, turn to high heat and add meat slivers and ginger. As meat browns, add Soy sauce. Turn off heat and serve with rice.

RICHARD TUITE, D.D.S.

BRENNIG'S KIDNEY STEW

12 lamb kidneys
4 tablespoons butter
3 tablespoons finely chopped onion
¼ cup red Burgundy
1 cup beef bouillon

2 tablespoons flour
1 teaspoon Worcestershire
1/8 teaspoon paprika
1 bay leaf
3 tablespoons chopped parsley

salt and pepper to taste

Slice kidneys and saute in hot butter with the onions for about 3-4 minutes. Remove from pan onto heated platter. Add wine and stir with wooden spoon to remove any browned bits. Add flour to make paste and stir until smooth, gradually add bouillon and Worcestershire, paprika and bay leaf. Bring mixture to a boil and simmer stirring constantly for 3-4 minutes. Correct seasoning with salt and pepper and add kidneys and parsley. Allow this to continue over very low heat a few minutes and serve on toast triangles for a delicious brunch. (Heated plates are a necessity for this dish)

This dish has always been a traditional Sunday Brunch in the Brennig Family and is usually prepared by the Man of the House.

CHARLES COUDART BRENNIG, JR.
Grandson of Baron and Baroness
Benno Frederic von Brennig of
Vienna, Austria. They were known for
their distinct tastes and interests in cuisine.

STEAK WITH ROQUEFORT SAUCE

Cream 6 ounces Roquefort with 2 tablespoons cream cheese, 1 teaspoon each of Worcestershire and bottled meat sauce, and 2 drops of Tabasco. Coat a 2 pound sirloin steak with the mixture, put it in a pan, and broil it. Crush 1 garlic clove around the steak so that it mixes with the drippings. Spoon the drippings over the steak and serve immediately. Serves 2.

JOE GARNETT BARHAM, M.D.
Lake Charles, La.

UPSIDE DOWN DELIGHT

3 slices bacon	1 medium sized onion
1 green pepper, seeded	chopped
and cut in rings	2 cloves garlic, minced
12 Pimento stuffed	or mashed
green olives,	1 tablespoon shortening
sliced crosswise	1½ (10½ ounce can size)
1 can (12 ounce)	can tomato soup
whole kernel corn	2 teaspoons chile powder
Salt and pepper to taste	1 package (15 ounce)
1 pound ground chuck	cornbread mix

Brown the bacon until crisp, drain, crumble, and set aside. In a heavy 10-inch frying pan (one you can put in the oven), arrange the green pepper rings, side by side. Inside the rings, place sliced olives. Sprinkle bacon between the rings. Drain corn and spoon over top of pepper rings, pimiento sliced olives, and crumbled bacon covering completely; salt and pepper to taste. In another pan, brown the meat, onion, and garlic, adding shortening as needed. Stir in the tomato soup and chile powder. Spoon the meat sauce over the corn. Prepare the cornbread, adding ingredients as directed on package. Pour cornbread mixture on top of meat sauce. Bake in a 350 degree oven for 30 to 40 minutes. Remove from oven, cover the skillet for five minutes, then turn mixture "upside down" onto a serving platter deep enough to catch juices.

The design of the green peppers, green olives with red centers, and yellow corn will be so "pretty" you will almost hate to cut it . . . but cut in pie shaped slices and serve piping hot. You and/or your guests will be delighted with the taste sensation . · . . serves 6 to 8 . . . It is equally good (to me) served cold the next day.

CHET BECKWITH

HAMBURGER WITH ROQUEFORT

In a saucepan sauté 1 small onion finely chopped, in 2 tablespoons oil until it is transparent. Add 1 garlic clove, minced, and cook the mixture over low heat until the garlic begins to brown. Combine 1 pound lean beef, chopped, with 1 egg, 1 teaspoon chopped parsley, the onion and garlic, and salt and pepper to taste. Shape the mixture into 2 patties and make a depression in the center of each. Blend together 2 tablespoons crumbled Roquefort cheese and 1 tablespoon each of soft butter and brandy. Fill the cavities of the hamburgers with the cheese mixture and press the meat to seal in the filling. Broil the hamburgers until they reach the desired degree of doneness. Serve with Pancho sauce, Serves 2.

PANCHO SAUCE

Combine together thoroughly 3/4 cup ketchup, 6 tablespoons each of chili sauce and mayonnaise, 2 tablespoons pineapple juice, 2¼ teaspoons each of wine vinegar and dry mustard, 1½ teaspoons Worcestershire, 3/4 teaspoon horseradish, ¼ teaspoon each of monosodium glutamate and ground ginger, and 2 or 3 drops of Tabasco. Makes about 1½ cups.

JOE GARNETT BARHAM, M.D.
Lake Charles, La.

EMPRESS BEEF

1 pound flank steak cut in shoestring strips against grain	1 small can mushrooms, thinly sliced
3 tablespoons Lou Ana cooking oil	1 small can water chestnuts, sliced
3 ribs celery, cut on bias	¼ pound snow peas (look in freezer section)
1 large, white onion, thinly sliced	1 teaspoon corn starch
¼ cup water	5 teaspoons soy sauce
	½ teaspoon sugar

Brown beef in cooking oil in hot skillet. Add onions, celery, mushrooms, snow peas and water chestnuts and stir slowly for a few minutes over hot fire. Cover and simmer for 3 minutes. Stir in thickening of corn starch, sugar, soy sauce and water. Serve with rice.

RICHARD TUITE, D.D.S.

BURGUNDY GOULASH

2 tablespoons butter	¼ teaspoon caraway seeds
3 pounds beef stew meat	and crumbled,
3 large onions,	dried marjoram
chopped fine	1/8 teaspoon black pepper
2 tablespoons butter	1 bay leaf
4 teaspoons paprika	3/4 cup Burgundy
1 clove garlic, mashed	½ cup water
1 large tomato, peeled	½ pound ham, cut in
and chopped	small cubes
fresh parsley, chopped	1 cup sour cream

Heat 2 tablespoons butter in Dutch oven. Add beef and brown on all sides. Meantime sauté onions in 2 tablespoons butter until tender; add to browned beef. Stir in paprika until well blended. Add garlic, tomato, caraway seeds, marjoram, pepper and bay leaf, ½ of the wine and ¼ cup water. Cover and cook for 2 hours, stirring occasionally. Add more wine and water, a small amount at a time. Add ham and cook 1½ hours more. Just before serving, remove bay leaf and stir in ¼ cup sour cream. Serve with noodles, topping each serving with an additional spoonful of sour cream sprinkled with parsley and paprika.

RICHARD TUITE, D.D.S.

Real good served with cucumber salad and hot French bread.

BARBECUED RIBS

1 can condensed	1/3 cup vinegar
consommé	4 cloves garlic, minced
1 jar (12 ounce) orange	2 teaspoons salt
marmalade	dash of pepper
1/3 cup catsup	4-5 pounds spare ribs

For sauce, combine first 7 ingredients, just melted together, and pour over ribs. Cover and refrigerate overnight. Broil over slow coals, frequently brushing with sauce. Cook until meat is well done and nicely glazed. I serve this with Chinese hot mustard and Chinese sweet and sour sauce.

CHARLES E. BEADLES

MARINATING AND BASTING SAUCE A LA CREOLE
(For Barbecueing Steaks)

1 gal. Lou Ana cooking oil
15 oz. bottle soy sauce
4 tsp. garlic juice
8 oz. onion puree
10 oz. wine vinegar
6 oz. dry sherry wine
1 sm. can dried
   parsley flakes
   (½ oz.)

8 tblsp. salt
2 tblsp. black pepper
4 tblsp. red cayenne
   pepper
Juice of 4 lemons
4 tsp. La. Tabasco sauce
1 Coca Cola
4 medium size onions
   (chopped finely)

Mix all of these ingredients and stir for five minutes. If necessary, heat to approximately 150 degrees or until all of the ingredients are thoroughly blended. This sauce may be used for marinating steaks and various meats and may also be used as a basting sauce to maintain tenderness to meats while being grilled, barbecued or broiled.

A 36-hr. marinating period is sufficient enough for good-to-choice grade steaks and a 48-hr. marinating period is recommended for wild game meats.

J. M. Coco

ROASTED LONG ISLAND DUCKLING, HONEY SAUCE

Season a 3 to 4 pound duck with onion, celery, pinch of rosemary, salt and pepper.

Roast duckling in oven at 450 degrees to 475 degrees for one hour and 20 to 30 minutes. Drain off grease after first 40 minutes.

HONEY SAUCE: Bring one cup honey and ¼ cup vinegar to boil, let simmer for 10 minutes.

Add one teaspoon cornstarch which has been mixed with a little water, bring back to boil.

Add one ounce whiskey, juice of one lemon and ¼ cup fresh chopped mint or dissolve two tablespoons dried mint in small amount of vinegar.

Pour off fat in pan and make gravy of duck drippings. Serve gravy over rice. Pass the sauce to put over duck. Absolutely delicious!

By: C. H. Brandt

As created and served at the City Club of Baton Rouge, Baton Rouge, Louisiana

MAPLE BARBECUED RIBS

3 pounds pork ribs	3 tablespoons soy sauce
1/3 cup maple syrup	1 tablespoon sherry
½ teaspoon sugar	1 clove garlic, crushed

Cut pork ribs lengthways, then cut ribs into groups of 3 or 4. Combine the other ingredients and marinate ribs overnight in this mixture. Bake under medium heat 45 minutes then turn and cook for about 5 minutes longer, watching closely. After cooling, cut into single ribs. Wonderful for nibbling.

RICHARD TUITE, D.D.S.

ROAST TEAL DUCK

6 teal ducks	6 slices of toast
6 strips of bacon	(preferably salt rising
salt, pepper, MSG	or homemade bread)
	1 stick butter

Melt one half of stick of butter and pour some over each duck and rub into duck back and front. Season buttered ducks well inside and out with salt, pepper and MSG. Wrap a strip of bacon around the middle of each duck and secure it with a toothpick. Put a small lump of butter inside each duck and put the ducks and the remainder of the stick of butter in a roasting pan. Pour ¼ cup of water into roasting pan dripping some over each bird. Put ducks in oven (pan uncovered) and roast at 425 degrees for 45 minutes to one hour, basting occasionally with juice in bottom of pan.

While ducks are cooking, brown toast slowly in moderate oven. Place one duck on each piece of toast and pour drippings in roasting pan generously over each serving so that drippings soak into toast. Serve with cranberry sauce.

ROBERT KENNON, JR.

DUCK, SAUCE PIQUANTE

4 ducks—skin the ducks and remove all fat, cut ducks up like chicken, you may remove large pieces from bones. Dust each piece on each side with red pepper, black pepper, salt, and flour.

Use black iron pot, cover with oil. Cook ducks,

turning till they are brown and flour sticks to pot. Add oil if needed.

Cut up 2 large white onions, add, and cook till brown.

Dilute 1/3 can of tomato paste up to 1 glass of water—Add. Stir regularly with wooden spoon to prevent sticking and burning. Cook 2 hours adding water or wine as needed to maintain volume.

Cut into 1 inch lengths, one pound of sausage and parboil for about 1 hour to reduce fat, and drain.

One-half hour before ducks are done add this sausage, 1 can of mushrooms, chopped tops of bunch of shallots, and 1 hat full of parsley chopped finely (size 7 hat). Show the parsley to the guests so they will believe it—use this much.

Serve with rice.

GEORGE H. JONES, M.D.

CHICKEN JAMBALAYA
Serves 6

1 3-lb. broiler, disjointed	2 tsp. salt
½ cup butter	¼ tsp. pepper
1 large onion, chopped	½ tsp· monosodium
1 cup celery, chopped	glutamate
3 cloves garlic, minced	1½ cups water
1 No. 2 can tomatoes	2 cups uncooked rice
1 4-oz. can mushrooms, sliced	1 tsp. gr. onion tops, chopped
Evangeline hot sauce	1 tblsp. fresh parsley,
1 green pepper chopped	chopped

Melt butter in large heavy skillet or Dutch oven. Salt and pepper chicken parts and brown in butter. When brown, remove from the skillet and set aside. Pour off about ½ of the butter in skillet. Add onions, green pepper, celery, and garlic and sauté until tender. Stir in tomatoes and mushrooms. Cook slowly 20-30 minutes. Season with hot sauce, salt, pepper and monosodium glutamate. Add water and rice, bring to a boil, stir once. Return chicken pieces to skillet. Cover. Reduce heat and cook for 45 minutes. Just before serving, stir onion tops and parsley into rice.

J. M. COCO

DOVES IN CREAM

10 to 12 doves
1 medium onion, grated
1 tablespoon salt
1 tablespoon freshly
    ground black pepper

½ teaspoon thyme
½ cup chicken stock
½ cup of sherry
1 cup of heavy cream
1 pony of brandy

½ cup clarified butter

Dry doves inside and out with paper towel. Combine salt, black pepper and thyme; rub seasoning inside and outside the doves. Sauté doves in butter until brown. Remove doves to covered casserole. Add onion, chicken stock to butter in frying pan. Cut fire, add sherry, pour over doves. Cover casserole, bake in oven at 350 degrees. Baste frequently until done. Remove doves. Finish sauce with the cream; heat until it thickens a little (do not boil) ; add brandy. Pour sauce over birds. Serve on hot platter.

Garnish with parsley, slices of lemon.

FRED A. BLANCHE, SR.

LOUISIANA CHICKEN SAUCE PIQUANTE

2 chickens, approx.
    3 lb. each
3 cupsful Lou Ana
    cooking oil
    or shortening
4 cloves garlic
    finely chopped
1 bunch shallots

3 sm. cans tomato
    sauce
1 cup finely chopped celery
1 cup finely chopped
    bell pepper
salt, red pepper and
    black pepper (to taste)
3 lb. onions

Measure cooking oil or shortening and pour into a large cast-iron pot. Cut chickens into serving-size pieces and season with salt, red pepper and black pepper and brown in cooking oil or shortening. Remove chicken from pot and place in a pan.

Brown onions and garlic in oil or shortening, then add chickens. Pour tomato sauce over the chickens and add finely chopped celery and green shallots. Add enough water to cover all of these ingredients and lower the flame. Stir about every 10 minutes. You may add approximately 1 cup of flour to thicken the gravy as desired.

About 1 hour before the chicken becomes tender,

add Bell pepper. If you find that there is too much oil or shortening, skim up before serving. This will serve approximately 12 people. Serve with Louisiana rice.

J. M. Coco

GREEK BARBECUED CHICKEN

Chicken halves
Salt and black pepper
Oregano
1 stick oleo or butter
   per chicken

Crushed, fresh mint
1 clove of garlic (crushed)
   per 2 chickens
Juice of ½ lemon
   per chicken

Chopped parsley

Sprinkle salt, black pepper and oregano over chicken halves. Prepare a sauce of remaining ingredients. Cook chickens preferably in a covered, cast iron Charbroiler. Brown both sides before basting starts. Add wet hickory chips to charcoal. Giblets are especially good with this recipe.

Submitted by GARNER MOORE

BARBECUE SAUCE FOR CHICKENS
Serves 18

4 large white onions
   (chopped)
3 cloves garlic (pressed)
1 pint Lou Ana oil
½ lb. margarine
½ cup vinegar
Juice of three lemons,
   hulls of two
1 teaspoon salt

1 small bottle
   Worcestershire Sauce
Dash hot sauce
Generous dash
   powdered allspice
2 level tablespoons catsup
   or chili sauce
Drop or two of liquid
   "smoke" (optional)

Sauté onions and garlic in oil until clear; add all other ingredients and simmer until blended. Approximately 20 or 30 minutes.

This is basting sauce, for use while chickens are being barbecued, a little too oily to be used as a serving sauce.

ROY DABADIE

PAELLA A LA VALENCIANA

3 2½ lb. frying chickens	½ doz. chopped fresh
olive oil	tomatoes
2 large onions,	2½ lbs. shrimp
finely chopped	½ gal. oysters
2 lbs. rice, saffron	6 only lobster tails
hot water or broth	2 cans mussels
2 cloves garlic	

Cut each chicken into 8 pieces—use gizzards. Brown in a skillet with oil. When pieces are nicely browned, season with salt and pepper and put aside. Leave gizgards in oil and sauté onions and garlic with them. Add rice and stir it in oil for several minutes or until it turns slightly yellow. Season with salt, pepper and saffron. Pour water or broth over rice to cover and let it cook down. Add chicken pieces, tomatoes and additional liquid if necessary. When rice is just beginning to tenderize, add raw shrimp (peeled) and then oysters. Cook until shrimp and oysters are tender. At this time boil lobster tails—shell them and keep hot. Serve in chafing dishes. Use lobster tails cut into 3 pieces to decorate top or rice . . . . also, add julienne of pimientos and peas. Serves 20, or more.

By: C. H. BRANDT

As created and served at the City Club of Baton Rouge, Baton Rouge, Louisiana

CHICKEN LOUISE

Cut a three to four pound chicken into serving pieces and sauté them with one tablespoon chopped shallots in a skillet in ¼ cup butter until they are golden brown on both sides. Add 1 cup sherry and cook the mixture for 3 minutes. Add 1 cup light cream, 2 drops of Tabasco, a dash each of monosodium glutamate and salt, and a beurre manie made by kneading together 1 tablespoon each of butter and flour. Cook the mixture for 20 minutes, or until the chicken is tender. Arrange the chicken on a heated platter. Cook the sauce over high heat until it is reduced to the desired thickness. Swirl in ¼ cup cold butter, pour the sauce over the chicken, and serve immediately. Serves 4.

JOE GARNETT BARHAM, M.D.
Lake Charles, La.

CHICKEN DIABLE

3 pound fryer   2 teaspoons MSG
2 teaspoons black pepper   2 teaspoons salt
1 teaspoon garlic powder

Set oven regulator to maximum. Cut chicken into 12 or 14 parts (all parts are small because they are going to be cooked fast). Skin the chicken if you are counting calories. Mix seasoning together (I put it in a salt shaker). Instead of salt and garlic powder, you may use 1 tablespoon garlic salt. Lay a piece of foil in a 1 inch deep baking dish, so you won't mess up the pan and have a hard time cleaning it. Lay the chicken pieces thereupon and "dust" generously with the "Chik-Mix" (seasoning). Turn the pieces and dust again (you may have a little left over). Quickly slip the chicken into hot oven and set your time for 15 minutes. It'll sure be done by then, a bit crispy in spots and succulent on the inside. If your oven is real hot, the chicken might be done in 10 minutes.

FONVILLE WINANS

Note: This dish is the "specialty of the house."

BAKED BEANS

Serves 4-5

1 can B & M baked beans (1 lb., 3 oz.). Discard lump of fat

Add:
4 tablespoons cane syrup (or more)
2 tablespoons Worcestershire Sauce
2 teaspoons (heaping) prepared mustard
Dash seasoned salt

2 tablespoons (heaping) tomato catsup
1/4 teaspoon Tabasco
Dash celery salt

Chopped:
2 large white onions
2 green onions and tops
1 large bell pepper
4 ribs celery and tender leaves

Mix well; place in casserole; cover with semi-cooked and drained bacon strips Bake in slow oven (approx. 250 or 300 degrees) for 1 or 1½ hrs. Larger quantities should be baked longer.

ROY DABADIE

SAUTÉED CABBAGE

4 strips bacon
½ cup chopped onions
½ cup green onions
2 tablespoons chopped
    bell pepper
6 cups shredded cabbage

1 teaspoon salt
2 tablespoons sugar
¼ teaspoon Tabasco
¼ teaspoon black pepper
1 teaspoon caraway seed
2 tablespoons pimiento

1 teaspoon Accent

Fry bacon. Saute in bacon fat the onions, green onions, and bell pepper until onions are transparent. Then add cabbage. Add seasoning, crumbled bacon and chopped pimiento for color. Do not overcook.

RICHARD TUITE, D.D.S.

CAMP SPOONBILL JAMBALAYA

4 Mallard ducks or
    3 chickens
3 medium onions,
    chopped

1 large can tomatoes
¼ cup catsup
Salt, cayenne pepper, and
    Tabasco to taste

2 cups rice

Cook rice and game separately. Brown onions, add tomatoes and catsup. Cook until forms a puree. Add cooked rice and game or chicken that has been stripped from bones.

COL. TOM DUTTON
Spoonbill Chef

Col. Dutton's comment; This is a foolproof recipe and can be varied at will.

BAKED LIMA BEANS

1 pound large, dry
    lima beans
½ pound bacon, cut up
1 large, dry onion,
    chopped

½ bell pepper, chopped
1 small can pimiento
1 tablespoon brown sugar
¼ cup catsup
1 clove garlic

Pick over and wash lima beans. Cover with water, add garlic, and cook for 45 minutes. Sauté bacon, onion and bell pepper. Remove from fire and add mashed pimiento, brown sugar and catsup. Add above ingredients to limas which have been drained (but save pot liquor to add to beans from time to time while baking). Add salt and pepper to taste. Place in buttered casserole and bake at 250 degrees for two to three hours—adding the saved pot liquor to beans while baking—as needed. Delicious with baked ham and green salad.

NORMAN SAURAGE, JR.

PAIN TERRIFIQUE

2 loaves French bread,
   split lengthwise
2 sticks oleo, softened
½ teaspoon
   garlic powder

1 dash oregano
1 teaspoon parsley flakes
Yellow mustard
1 bunch green onion tops
Sesame seed

Put butter or oleo, garlic, oregano and parsley in bowl and blend with fork. Spread each half of bread generously with garlic butter. Then spread on yellow mustard to cover all; sprinkle on chopped green onions tops and smooth in with back of spoon. Cover all with sesame seed. Slice bread diagonally and wrap in aluminum foil.

Heat in oven and serve. OR, freeze for future use.

HUBERT N. WAX

MR. NICK'S CHILI

2 lbs. beef, coarse ground
2 medium onions, chopped
2 garlic cloves, crushed
1 teaspoon cumin
   powder or seeds

1 oz. jar of chili powder
Flour
Dash monosodium
   glutamate, salt
   and pepper to taste

Put all ingredients in large pot. Sprinkle with flour. (The thickness depends on amount of flour). Cover with water and bring to boil. Stir and break up any big pieces of meat with spoon. Let simmer for 1 hour (the longer the better). If it gets too thick add water and continue to cook little longer. Ready to eat or cool and put in freezer. May add canned chili beans or canned crowder peas if desired.

R. C. KEMP, M.D.

SLOPER'S SPINACH

1 package chopped frozen spinach	½ teaspoon salt
	¼ teaspoon pepper
1 can cream style corn	¼ cup Italian bread
¼ cup minced onion	crumbs
3 tablespoons butter	4 tablespoons Parmesan
1 teaspoon vinegar	cheese, grated

Sauté onions in butter. Mix with corn, spinach, vinegar, salt and pepper. Put in buttered baking dish, cover with bread crumbs and Parmesan cheese and dot with butter. Bake at 400 degrees for 15 or 20 minutes.

DAVID C. HUMPHREYS

TEXAS BAKED ONIONS

1 medium size onion	1 tablespoon Worcester-
2 tablespoons brown sugar	shire sauce
	1 pat butter

Place onion in tin foil. Sprinkle brown sugar on top of onion. Place butter pat on top of the onion and sugar. As the onion is being wrapped in the foil, pour worcestershire sauce on onion. Twist foil around onion and place in charcoal coals, or place in 375 degree oven for 1 hour. (1 onion per serving.)

ROBERT E. PATTERSON
Irving, Texas

POTATOES SYMPHONY

Peel and dice any quantity you wish of Irish potatoes. Peel and chop 2/3 of same quantity by volume of white onions and 2/3 of same quantity of chopped bell peppers· Bacon drippings sufficient to smother. Salt, pepper and paprika to taste.

Melt drippings in heavy saucepan. Add potatoes, onions and bell peppers. Stir making sure they don't stick. Add salt, pepper (black, white and/or red) and paprika. Cook until done. Garnish with chopped parsley and serve. (This is delicious)

HOMER BELANGER

SUPPER CLUB CHILI

½ cup Lou Ana Oil
3 large onions (chopped)
2 green peppers (chopped)
4 ribs celery (chopped)
5 pieces minced garlic
Salt to taste
Black pepper

4 to 5 pounds
  ground meat
1 large can tomato paste
1 quart water
5 tablespoons paprika
4 tablespoons
  chili powder

1/8 teaspoon red pepper

Sauté onions, green pepper and celery in oil. Add meat and garlic and cook slightly (until greyish in color). To this mixture add water and cook fast for 15 minutes or until desired thickness. Add salt and pepper to taste. Add other ingredients and let simmer for about 30 minutes. This is best when allowed to "age"—make ahead and refrigerate or freeze.

STERLING GLADDEN, JR.

PISOLÉ

4 cups cubed cooked pork
2 cans chili without beans
2 cans hominy, drained
2 cups chopped onions
2 cups chopped celery
1 chopped bell pepper
  (optional)
1 clove garlic

1 can tomatoes (small)
1 cup grated cheddar
  cheese
Salt, pepper and red
  pepper to taste.
A pinch of chili powder
  and a dash of Tabasco
  may be added

Sauté onions, celery and bell pepper in oil in heavy iron pot. Add pork (left over roast may be used) and brown. After brown add seasonings and tomatoes. Simmer about 15 minutes. Add the 2 cans of hominy which have been drained and rinsed. Stir and blend over low fire for 15 minutes then turn into buttered casserole and top with grated cheese. Run in oven 30 minutes before serving. Serve over hot, buttered cornbread.

(This is wonderful for football game suppers).

THOMAS BRYAN PUGH III

TAMALE PIE

½ pound ground pork
1 pound ground beef
1 cup chopped onion
½ cup chopped bell
   pepper
2 teaspoons chili powder
½ cup yellow corn meal,
   with 1 cup of water

Dash of monosodium glutamate
Black pepper and salt
   to taste
1 #303 can of peeled
   tomatoes
1 can whole kernel corn
1 cup of chopped ripe
   olives

½ cup chopped celery

Sauté meat and then add all of the other ingredients and cook until done. Place meat mixture in a baking dish and cover with cooked cornmeal. Cook in oven at 350 degrees for 1 hour uncovered. Add sharp cheese on top and let melt.

ED. HEMPHILL
Monroe, La.

TEXAS CHILI

3 lbs. coarse ground lean
   beef (never veal)
¼ cup olive oil
1 quart water
2 bay leaves*
8 dry chili pods or
   6 tbs. chili powder
3 teaspoons salt
6 tablespoons corn meal

10 cloves finely chopped
   garlic
1 teaspoon ground comino
1 teaspoon oregano or
   marjoram
1 teaspoon red pepper
½ teaspoon black pepper
1 tablespoon sugar
3 tablespoons flour

When olive oil is hot, in 6-quart pot, add meat and sear over high heat, stir constantly until gray (not brown), it will then have consistency of whole-grain hominy. Add one quart water and cook (covered) at bubbling simmer 1½ to 2 hours. Then add all ingredients except thickening. Cook 30 minutes longer at same bubbling simmer. Further cooking will damage some of the spice flavors. Now add the thickening previously mixed in cold water. Cook five minutes to determine if more water is necessary (likely) for your desired consistency. Stir to prevent sticking after thickening is added. In case too much fat was left in meat, it will show on top after spices are added. Skim off most before thickening is added. Too much suet in chili produces unpleasant backfires. You'll find out how much to keep by experience.

* Add bay leaves with water at start and remove after fifteen or twenty minutes.

CHET BECKWITH

UNBELIEVABLE HOLLANDAISE

1 small skillet	1 lemon
1 stick butter or oleo	2 egg yolks

Slightly beat 2 egg yolks, mix with juice of one lemon and pour into cold skillet (that preferably has been in ice box for 30 or 40 minutes.) Add 1 stick of butter or oleo and put on **low** fire. Move the stick of oleo or butter around and around as it slowly melts—as soon as it melts the mixture will start thickening and when at desired consistency remove and serve over poached eggs or vegetables or whatever! It is so good I could just eat it with toast, or without anything.

CHET BECKWITH

POTATO SALAD

4 large Idaho Russet baking potatoes	1 pint oil made into mayonnaise (ingredients: 1 egg, 2 tablespoons lemon juice, 1 teaspoon each salt, sugar, dry mustard, ¼ teaspoon cayenne pepper)
2 bay leaves	
8 hard boiled eggs	
8 tender ribs celery (chopped)	
1 large can pimientos	
4 teaspoons prepared mustard	
½ cup (or more) chopped parsley	1 small onion, grated
	1 large bell pepper (optional)

Peel and cube potatoes. Boil until tender in salted water with bay leaves. Chill. (Water proportions—3 cups water, 2 teaspoons salt). Mash hard-boiled eggs in salad bowl. Sprinkle with seasoned salt. Add cayenne pepper to taste, mustard, mayonnaise, and onion juice. Blend well. Add chilled potato cubes, pimientos and parsley. Mix and chill. Just before serving, add chopped celery and ½ of bell pepper, chopped. Sprinkle with paprika and garnish with remaining half of bell pepper, sliced in rings.

ROY DABADIE

JOHN'S SALAD

1 head of lettuce	1½ cups of mayonnaise
2 cloves of garlic	½ cup of chili sauce
(Use garlic press or	2 oz. bottle of stuffed
chop fine)	olives chopped

Mix mayonnaise and chili sauce, add garlic and chopped olives. Stir well and chill in refrigerator. Break lettuce or cut into quarters and pour dressing on top. Serves 4.

JOHN CONTOIS
Slidell, La.

BUTTERMILK DRESSING

½ teaspoon garlic powder	1 pint buttermilk
1 teaspoon onion powder	½ teaspoon monosodium
2½ tablespoons parsley	glutamate
2 teaspoons salt	½ teaspoon pepper
1 pint mayonnaise	

Blend all ingredients. Let stand in open bowl overnight in refrigerator. Will thicken. Keeps 3 weeks in refrigerator.

McVEA OLIVER
Monroe, Louisiana

ARTICHOKE SALAD

6 large artichokes	2 tablespoons home-made
2 (or more) tablespoons	mayonnaise
finely minced green	1 teaspoon paprika
onion	2 tablespoons French
1 tablespoon parsley	dressing (using French
Salt and white pepper	olive oil and lemon
to taste	juice)

Cut off ¼ or 1/5 of artichoke from top, then boil until tender (about 45 to 50 minutes). Drain. Then remove leaves and the choke. For six servings, save 42 of best leaves. Scrape pulp from remaining leaves, combine in wooden bowl with the six bottoms (sometime called heart), chop and mash well. Then add all other ingredients and mix well. Add more mayonnaise or French dressing if texture dry. Cover bowl and marinate in refrigerator overnight.

Meanwhile, prepare more French dressing, add paprika, place in cups or low glasses and stand leaves up in cup to marinate overnight in refrigerator.

Remove from refrigerator about hour before serving. To serve, place full ice cream scoop of artichoke mixture in middle of salad plate and place about seven leaves around plate, wiping leaf with tissue if dressing has spread to top of leaf. Decorate top of salad with bit of mayonnaise and paprika, or with two long strips of pimiento and then the mayonnaise and paprika· If more substantial salad desired, ring base of artichoke pulp with about four boiled shrimp which have been marinated in French dressing and paprika, and for good measure, place one shrimp on top. Can serve as beginning course at dinner with home-made buttered Melba toast made from French bread. A plague on your house if you don't use creamery butter. Serves six.

ERNEST GUEYMARD

SPAGHETTI SALAD

1 lb. package smallest spaghetti (vermicelli —long, not curly kind for soup)
½ lb. New York State sharp cheese (cut into very small cubes)
1 can (small or large) pimientos (chopped and drained)
1 white onion (grated)
1 large bell pepper (chopped)
2 teaspoons leaf tarragon (pounded in mortar with pestle)
Cayenne pepper to taste
Mayonnaise to mix (approximately 1 cup: ½ homemade; ½ bought real mayonnaise)
Juice 1 large lemon

Break spaghetti into pieces. Cook as follows: Place into 12 cups boiling water to which 8 teaspoons salt have been added. Boil 2 minutes, stirring constantly, remove from fire, cover and let stand 10 minutes. Stir well and drain in colander. When cool, place in mixing bowl. Add lemon juice, grated onion, tarragon, cayenne, pimiento, bell pepper, cheese and mayonnaise. Taste· Add more mayonnaise and salt if needed. Chill. Keeps indefinitely in refrigerator. Serves 8 to 10.

Excellent served with sliced homegrown tomatoes.

ROY DABADIE

CHRYSANTHEMUM SALAD

Pull out the petals from 3 large chrysanthemums, 2 yellow and 1 mauve. Combine ½ cup white wine vinegar with 1 teaspoon each of honey and chopped fresh tarragon and the juice of 1 lemon and marinate the petals in the mixture for 30 minutes. Drain the petals, reserving the marinade, and mix them with ½ pound lettuce, a bunch of watercress, and 4 large pimiento stuffed olives, sliced. Make a dressing of ½ cup olive oil, 3 tablespoons of the reserved marinade, and salt and pepper to taste. Toss the salad with the dressing just before serving.

JOE GARNETT BARHAM, M.D.
Lake Charles, La.

A DESSERT OF LEMONS, NICOLE
Serves 8

3 doz. lady fingers, separated	Juice of 2 lemons
1 tablespoon butter	3 egg whites, beaten stiff
1 teaspoon cornstarch	½ pint whipping cream
½ cup sugar	¼ cup confectioner's sugar
3 egg yolks, slighty beaten	¼ teaspoon salt
1 cup milk	1 teaspoon rum

Place butter, cornstarch, ½ cup of sugar, egg yolks and milk in the top of a double boiler over boiling water. Cook slowly, stirring occasionally, until the mixture is thick and smooth. Add lemon juice, and stir. Remove from the heat, and allow to cool down some. While still warm, fold in the beaten egg whites.

Line the bottom and sides of a deep casserole dish with halves of lady fingers, and rounded sides out. Spoon in a thick layer of the sauce, cover with a layer of lady fingers, and alternate the two until all ingredients are used up. Place in the refrigerator, and harden for 12 hours.

Before serving, whip confectioner's sugar, salt and rum into the whipping cream until stiff. Top the chilled cake-sauce mixture in the casserole dish with whipped cream and serve.

By: C. H. BRANDT

As created and served at the City Club of Baton Rouge, Baton Rouge, Louisiana

LE GATEAU DES NOIX OR WALNUT CAKE

3 sticks butter
2 cups sugar
6 egg yolks, lightly beaten
3/4 cup milk
1/4 cup brandy
1 teaspoon vanilla

3½ cups flour
½ teaspoon salt
2 cups coarsly chopped
    walnuts
6 egg whites
1 teaspoon cream of tartar

½ cup Grand Marnier

Cream butter and sugar until smooth, then mix in egg yolks. Mix milk, brandy, and vanilla. Sift flour and salt. Stir these two mixtures alternately into the butter and egg mixture, then add walnuts. Beat egg whites until foamy, add cream of tartar, and beat until they form definite peaks. Fold into batter gently, but thoroughly. Pour mixture into a 10-inch tube pan that has been oiled, lined with brown paper, and oiled again. Bake in a 275 degree oven for 2½ to 3 hours, or until it tests done. Cool on wire rack about 30 minutes, then remove from pan and cool completely. Before you serve the cake, peel paper off carefully, sprinkle with confectioner's sugar. Heat ½ cup of Grand Marnier slightly, pour over cake, set aflame, and serve with whipped cream.

J. C. STOVALL, M.D.

COFFEE TOASTAIRE

Serves 6

1 egg white
1 tablespoon dark
    instant coffee
½ teaspoon salt
2 tablespoons sugar

¼ cup sugar
1 teaspoon vanilla
1/8 teaspoon almond extract
¼ cup toasted (slivered)
    almonds chopped

1 cup whipping cream

Combine egg whites, beaten stiff but not dry, with coffee and salt. Add 2 tablespoons sugar gradually, and continue beating until stiff and satiny. Beat cream, gradually adding ¼ cup sugar. When stiff, add vanilla and almond extract. Fold into egg white mixture. Add nuts, saving a few to sprinkle on top. Pour into fancy paper cups and freeze.

NORMAN S. SAURAGE, JR.

FUDGE PIE
9 inch pie shell

Semi sweet baking
   chocolate—2 squares
3 eggs
1 cup sugar

¼ cup flour
½ cup butter
½ cup, or more pecans
1 teaspoon vanilla

¼ teaspoon salt

Melt 2 squares semi-sweet baking chocolate in double boiler. Beat 3 eggs, add 1 cup sugar which has been mixed with ¼ cup flour to the eggs and mix. Add mixture to the melted chocolate, then melt ½ cup butter and add with ½ cup pecans, 1 teaspoon vanilla and ¼ teaspoon salt. Pour into pie shell which has been baked for 3 to 5 minutes, and bake in 275 degree oven for 30 minutes or until set. Cool. This is so good, you won't believe it!

CHET BECKWITH

DEWBERRY JELLY

4 cups dewberry juice   3 cups sugar

Boil ripe and some semi-ripe dewberries until all juice is rendered. Mash and strain through jelly bag. To 4 cups juice add 3 cups sugar. Over very low heat stir mixture until sugar is dissolved. Divide evenly into 2 pans and boil rapidly until it strings from fork. Pour into ½ pint jars and seal with parafin.

Mayhaw jelly same as above.

DICK MORNHINVEG

CHET'S PRALINES

MIX WELL:
2 cups sugar
1 3/4 cups sweet milk
1/3 teaspoon soda   in
   "dutch oven" or some-
   thing deep because it
   foams up while cooking.
   Cook over medium heat
   until hardball forms

when dropped in water. Stir occasionally while cooking to prevent sticking to bottom of container.
Take off stove and add:
1 tablespoon butter
1 cup pecans
1 teaspoon vanilla

Mix well and return to stove and cook one-two minutes more. Remove from stove and whip until starts to thicken. Drop spoonfulls on wax paper, and drop **fast** because it hardens quickly once it starts. By the time you have dropped the last one, the first one you dropped is usually ready to pick-up. These are the greatest pralines you have ever eaten. Do not cook on a rainy day, they **will not** harden.

CHET BECKWITH

BEEFSTEAK TARTAR
2 People

½ lb. lean boneless beef, preferably beef tender-loin, or top or eye round, ground 2 or 3 times.
2 teaspoons salt
2 tablespoons freshly ground black pepper
2 tablespoons capers, thoroughly drained

2 tablespoons finely chopped onions
2 tablespoons finely chopped fresh parsley
8 flat anchovy filets, thoroughly drained
Dark bread
Butter
Dash of Tabasco and Worcestershire sauce

2 egg yolks

The beef and other ingredients are combined at the table to individual taste. Serve beefsteak tartar with dark bread and butter.

HUBERT CONRAD,
Manager Baton Rouge
Country Club

CRAWFISH CARDINAL
2-4 People

1 lb. peeled crawfish tails
1 pint cream sauce seasoned with Tabasco,
½ cup brandy

Worcestershire sauce and the juice of two lemons
½ cup sauterne

Heat 3 tablespoons of butter in pan. Add crawfish tails. Cook for 5 minutes. Add ½ cup of brandy and ½ cup Sauterne Wine. Simmer everything for 5 minutes more. Add cream sauce. Serve with pilaf rice and sprinkle with chopped parsley.

GEORGE RUPPEINER,
Chef of Baton Rouge Country Club

SPATZLE TINY DUMPLINGS
To make about 4 cups:

3 cups all-purpose flour	1 cup fine dry bread
1 teaspoon salt	crumbs (optional)
¼ teaspoon ground nutmeg	¼ pound (1 stick)
4 eggs	butter (optional)
1 cup milk	

Mix together well sifted flour, ½ teaspoon of the salt and the nutmeg. Break up the eggs with a fork and beat them into the flour mixture. Pour in the milk in a thin stream, stirring constantly with a large spoon, and continue to stir until the dough is smooth.

Bring 2 quarts of water and remaining ½ teaspoon of salt to a boil in a heavy 4 to 5 quart saucepan. Set a large colander, preferably one with large holes, over the saucepan and with a spoon press the dough a few tablespoons at a time through the colander directly into the boiling water. Stir the Spatzle gently to prevent them from sticking to each other, then boil briskly for 5 to 8 minutes, or until they are tender. Taste to make sure. Drain the spatzle thoroughly in a sieve or colander and transfer them to a deep heated serving dish and pour ¼ pound melted butter over them.

HUBERT CONRAD,
Manager Baton Rouge
Country Club

SHRIMP GEORGE
Serves 8

Cooked, peeled and deveined shrimp—2 pounds	1 tablespoon horseradish
Sauce:	Dash of Tabasco
1 pint mayonnaise	Dash of Worcestershire
1/3 cup ketchup	sauce
¼ cup brandy	Dash of MSG
	Shreaded cocoanut

Put shrimp on shredded lettuce. Cover with George Sauce. Sprinkle with coconut.

GEORGE RUPPEINER,
Chef of Baton Rouge Country Club

Soups

CHICKEN-OYSTER-FILÉ GUMBO

½ cup Lou Ana oil
5/8 cup flour
1-4 pound stewing chicken, cut up
1 pint, or more, oysters in juice
1 onion chopped

1 clove garlic chopped
1½ quarts water
1 heaping tablespoon file
½ cup dry sherry (optional)
Salt and pepper to taste

Heat oil in large pot, stir in flour gradually and continue to stir until roux is a rich dark brown. Add chopped onion and cook until soft, but not brown. Add water gradually, stirring until smooth. Season to taste and add garlic. Allow mixture to come to a boil then turn heat to simmer for 10 minutes. Then add the cut up, raw chicken, bring to a boil, then again turn to simmer until chicken is cooked. (You may want to remove bones from chicken). Add the dry wine, if desired, and just before serving, add the oysters with juice and let simmer until oysters just curl. Turn off heat and add the filé. Stir and serve at once over a mound of cooked rice. Serve with a tossed green salad, French (garlic) bread and a dash of hot green peppers chopped for those who like the peppers.

MRS. RHEA N. WATTS,
Solitude Plantation

When I have a buffet dinner where there are a number of guests, I like to pass the gumbo in large cups or mugs just before the dinner is served.

CORN SOUP

Small chuck roast or soup bones and brisket
1 large onion (chopped)

Large can tomatoes
1 rib celery (chopped)
6-8 ears fresh corn cut from cob

Put meat in Dutch oven filled with water. Let boil. Skim off foam. Add large can of tomatoes, onion, and celery. Let simmer as you do vegetable soup. In black iron skillet smother cut corn in little LOU ANA oil until tender. After soup has simmered about an hour add corn and simmer another half hour. Serves 4-6.

MRS. W. V. LARCADE
Crowley, La.

BORSCH

1 good size soup bone	1 clove garlic
with meat	1 onion, sliced
8 or 10 cups water	1 carrot
1 bay leaf	1 bunch beets and stems

Boil soup bone in water to which bay leaf, garlic, onion and carrot have been added. When done skim off fat and drain. While soup bone is cooking, boil beets until tender. Reserve about 1 quart liquid in which beets are cooked and add to strained beef broth. To soup stock add:

2 onions, diced	1 tablespoon vinegar
1 potato, diced	1 teaspoon sugar
3 ribs celery, diced	1 cup shredded cabbage
1 can tomatoes	(later beets thinly
1 can consommé	sliced or diced)

Salt and pepper to taste

Cook all vegetables in stock until done—about 40 minutes. About 10 minutes before serving, add cabbage. Cut meat off bones and add to soup. Serve in deep soup bowls with a dollop of soup cream, and on the side serve a hot, salted, boiled Irish potato sprinkled generously with parsley and chives. Warm, buttered brown bread is excellent with this.

MRS. GLENN E. LASKEY
Ruston, La.

Comment: This recipe was given to me while traveling in Russia. It is a welcome variation from regular vegetable soup and is quite delicious.

GAZPACHO SOUP
Serves 20-25

10 cups peeled, diced	3 cups canned tomato
ripe tomatoes	juice
3 peeled cucumbers	5 tablespoons olive oil
½ cup diced green	4 tablespoons vinegar
peppers	Salt and pepper to taste
½ cup chopped onion	Tabasco

1 bud garlic

Pulverize all in blender.

MRS. TED DUNHAM

GAZPACHO (Cold Tomato Soup)

½ cup olive oil
4 tablespoons lemon
  juice
6 cups tomato juice
2 cups beef broth
½ cup finely-minced
  onion
2 tomatoes cubed

2 cups finely-minced
  celery
1/8 teaspoon Tabasco
2 teaspoons salt
¼ teaspoon pepper
2 green peppers
  finely chopped
2 cucumbers diced

Croutons

Beat oil and lemon juice. Stir in tomato juice, broth, onions, green pepper, tomatoes, celery, Tabasco, salt and pepper. Taste for seasoning. Should be well chilled—at least 3 hours. Serve cucumbers and croutons separately.

MRS. RALPH M. FORD

BLACK BEAN SOUP

2 cups (1 pound)
  black beans
1 pound ham, with
  some bone
½ stick butter
2 ribs chopped celery
1 chopped bell pepper
2 medium onions,
  chopped
¼ cup chopped parsley
1 cup tomatoes

½ cup diced carrots
2 bay leaves
Paprika
¼ teaspoon red pepper
2 tablespoons tarragon
  vinegar
1 teaspoon sugar
1 tablespoon
  Worcestershire sauce
½ cup wine—Madeira
1½ teaspoons salt

Cover beans with 2½ quarts of water. Soak 3 hours or more. Drain and add 8 cups cold water. Cover and simmer 1½ hours with the ham—(smoked), with bone and skin preferably. Sauté the celery, green pepper and onions. Add 1 tablespoon flour and some water. Stir frequently. Add parsley, tomatoes, carrots, bay leaves, red pepper, and paprika to sauté and cook for 30 minutes. Then add all to beans and simmer, covered, for 2-3 hours or until beans are real tender. Discard bone. Put through blender. Add vinegar, Worcestershire, wine and salt. Reheat. Serve with lemon slices. Garnish with chopped, or grated, hard boiled egg whites.

MRS. ATWELL E. CHAMPION

APRICOT SOUP

1 pound dried apricots	¼ cup heavy cream
3 fresh peaches, peeled and sliced	¼ cup tapioca
	½ sup sugar

Soak fruit over night in water and sugar. Cook until soft and put through sieve. Heat soup to boiling point. Stir in cream and tapioca gradually. Cook stirring constantly until soup is thick and creamy.

Serve hot or chill in refrigerator

MRS. TED DUNHAM

CHARLESTON OKRA SOUP
Serves 6

1 large onion	2 cups hot water
1 pound sliced okra	3 beef bouillon cubes
1 can spaghetti sauce (or seasoned tomato sauce)	2 bay leaves
	Salt and pepper
	Fresh basil leaves

2 pieces cut up bacon

Sauté bacon until brown, add onion (chopped) stir until transparent. Add okra, spaghetti sauce, hot water, bouillion cubes, bay leaves and seasonings. Simmer 3 hours or longer. Serve with cornbread sticks.

MRS. DAVIS FOLKES
St. Francisville, La.

SAUERKRAUT SOUP

1 can Sauerkraut, chopped	1 cup sour cream
1 can Sauerkraut juice	¼ cup water
4 slices bacon	Salt
2 chopped onions	Red pepper
½ pound smoked sausage	Worcestershire sauce
1 tablespoon flour	Fresh ground black pepper

Bring to a boil sauerkraut and juice. Then simmer. Fry bacon and add onions until transparent. Add sausage and seasoning to sauerkraut mixture. Mix flour and water and add to soup. Serve hot with sour cream spooned on top.

MRS. ELWOOD ANDERSON

ANDALUSIAN COLD "SOUP-SALAD"
Serves 6

1 quart tomato juice, or the sieved pulp of fresh or canned tomato
Enough croutons, or sippets, of butter fried bread
2 or 3 hardboiled eggs
1 small fine minced cucumber
1½ teaspoons Worcestershire

1 mild onion chopped very fine
1 teaspoon dry mustard
1 lime or lemon sliced thin
1 clove well crushed garlic
1 lemon or 2 limes, juice
2 tablespoons olive oil
1 sweet green pepper chopped fine
1 dash or so Tabasco
Salt & hand-ground black pepper

Work egg yolks and olive oil into smooth paste in wood salad bowl. Add crushed garlic, seasonings, lemon juice; then work tomato pulp in, add cucumber, green pepper. Stir briskly. Chill in ice 3 hours . . . Cut egg whites into strips, put on bottom soup bowls with chopped pepper, thin slice lemon and possibly 3 strips scarlet pimento. Pour in soup, add 2 ice cubes to each bowl; dust on hot croutons. Consume with dry white, chilled wine.

MRS. RALPH SIMS

A form of gazpacho, I consider this one of the best hot weather soups around.

CLAM CHOWDER

1 to 2 cans minced clams (round, flat cans)
1 large, white onion

3 cups raw, cubed Irish potatoes
1 quart hot milk

Lightly brown onions in a little bacon fat. Place a layer of potatoes in the bottom of a deep, heavy, aluminum pot, or iron Dutch oven, then a layer of clams. Sprinkle with a little flour, salt and pepper. Repeat. Add 2½ cups of boiling water. Let cook slowly about 25 or 30 minutes or until potatoes are tender. Then add hot milk. Let the clam mixture get hot through, but never let it come to a boil—barely let it simmer. When ready to serve, taste for salt and pepper. Add a generous pat of butter.

This, with a green salad, makes a wonderful meal.

MRS. ROBERT B. WALLACE

LETTUCE SOUP—(MEXICO)
(And don't pass this one up)

2 to 4 cups Romaine lettuce
    chopped very fine
1 cup water
2½ cups chicken stock
½ cup cream or
    evaporated milk

1 tablespoon chopped
    onion
1 tablespoon butter
Nutmeg
Salt
Pepper

Croutons for garnish

Cook lettuce and water in pressure cooker for 5 minutes (or in a regular pan with a small amount of water until lettuce is tender. Heat onions in butter and add to the lettuce mixture. Do not throw away the water. Add remaining ingredients and bring to a boil. Lower heat immediately and simmer 10 to 15 minutes. Serve with browned buttered croutons. Serves 6.

Submitted by:
MRS. ROBERT C. KEMP

MOCK TURTLE SOUP

½ pint red beans
1 tablespoon butter
1 medium onion chopped
1 clove garlic minced

A dash of Tabasco
1 tablespoon lemon juice
1 cup sherry
2 hard boiled eggs

Salt and pepper to taste

Cover beans with water and boil until tender. Put thru sieve, saving the water in which they were cooked. Brown flour in butter and add to the beans and water (Should make 1½ quarts) Add the seasonings and the lemon juice, and let simmer gently for an hour. Add wine and serve with chopped hard boiled eggs on top. Better still, make mock turtle eggs instead of chopped hard boiled eggs.

MOCK TURTLE EGGS

Mash the yolks of hard boiled eggs with a little butter. Add a beaten raw egg, then mold in the shape of turtle eggs. Either drop these in boiling water for 2 minutes, or roll in flour and sauté in butter. Add a dash of cayenne.

Submitted by:
MRS. GRAHAM BIENVENU
with permission of the family of
Natalie Scott

CURRY SOUP

1 apple, grated or chopped
1 small white potato, grated or chopped
2 tablespoons onions, finely chopped
1 rib celery, using the leaves, chopped fine
2 cups chicken stock
2 cups milk
Salt and pepper to taste
1 teaspoon curry

Mix well. Heat and serve. Serves 4.

MRS. GEORGE H. REYMOND

NEW ENGLAND CLAM CHOWDER

2 cans clams minced
¼ pound salt pork
1 medium onion
½ stick butter
1 quart milk
1 medium Irish potato

Dice pork into small pieces, fry in sauce pan over low heat until fat is rendered and pork is slightly brown. Reserve the pork croutons. To rendered fat, add chopped onion and cook until onions are translucent. Add clams and broth. Add potato (small diced). Add butter and cook covered over moderate heat until potato is tender. Add milk, salt and pepper to taste, and remember that the fat from the salt pork is salty. Heat, but do not boil (it may curdle), then serve with a few pork croutons in each plate.

MRS. ROBERT C. KEMP

TERRAPIN SOUP
(or soft shell turtle)

1 pint terrapin meat
1 quart chicken stock
2 tablespoons butter
1 tablespoon arrow root flour or plain flour
2 hard boiled egg yolks
1 cup hot cream
¼ cup Madeira or sherry
Salt and pepper
Pinch of mace

Simmer meat in stock for half hour (or until tender). Mix flour and butter and heat. Add hot cream and mashed egg yolks. Add meat and stock. Must be two cups of stock. Let simmer a moment and turn off heat. Add wine and serve.

MRS. GEORGE M. SIMON, JR.

LENTIL SOUP

3 pounds of soup meat
1 pound lentils (dried)
1 bunch green onions
4 to 6 ribs celery
1 large potato

Salt annd pepper
1 large onion (chopped)
1 tablespoon
   Lou Ana oil
1 tablespoon flour

Boil soup meat until done in 4 quarts water. Let broth simmer down to 2 quarts. Lift off fat from broth before adding to lentil soup. In the meantime pick the black lentils and discard them. Wash good lentils and drain. Cover with 3 quarts cold water and boil for 2 hours. Add beef broth. Cut green onion and celery in small pieces. Peel and dice potato and add to lentil soup, boil for about 45 minutes. Sauté large onion in oil until light brown. Add flour and stir until smooth adding a little of the soup and stir slowly until it is like cream sauce. Add this mixture to soup 10 minutes before serving. Slice soup meat and serve with the soup. A few slices of smoked sausage or smoked meat will add to flavor.

MRS. ERICH STERNBERG

TURTLE SOUP

2 pounds turtle meat
4 quarts water
2 large spoons
   Lou Ana oil
2½ large spoons flour
2 large onions chopped
½ cup bell pepper
   chopped
½ cup celery chopped

1 can tomato paste
Salt and pepper to taste
1 teaspoon whole cloves
1 teaspoon whole
   allspice
1 tablespoon
   Worcestershire sauce
¼ cup lemon juice
1 cup sherry

Boil turtle in water for 1 hour. Make roux with oil and flour. In the roux, sauté onions, pepper and celery, then the tomato paste and fry until brown. Add turtle meat and stock. In a cloth, put cloves and allspice and tie it, then add it to the soup. Add Worcestershire and lemon juice and cook for 1½ hours. Add the sherry and cook another half hour. All of this should be done on a low fire. Serve with mashed hard-boiled eggs on top.

MRS. OMER HEBERT
Plaquemine, La.

FRENCH ONION SOUP

18 med. size onions   6 slices toasted
(red or yellow)   French bread
8 cups rich beef broth   6 heaping tablespoons
¼ cup good olive oil   Parmesan cheese
2 tablespoons sugar   Salt and pepper to taste

Slice onions on the bias to avoid rings. Cook very gently in olive oil in heavy skillet until they are "melted" and clear. Season with salt and pepper and sugar.

Meanwhile trim lightly toasted bread rounds to fit individual earthenware bowls. Portion out the onions and their juices equally in the bowls. Discard some of the onion pulp if necessary, but save every drop of the juices.

Heat beef broth and fill the bowls almost to the top. Heap a tablespoon of cheese on the top of each, cover and bake 15 minutes in preheated 375 degrees oven.

Of course, this soup does not have to be baked, the toast and cheese may be baked a few minutes then added to the soup in any type of soup bowl.

This is a delightful dish to serve to anyone suffering with stomach disorders of most types. You must of course, delete the pepper and cheese.

MRS. DANIEL HENDERSON

TURTLE SOUP

1½-2 pounds turtle meat—   Paprika
preferably snapper—   Celery salt
no fat   Tarragon
1 bay leaf   Oregano
1 3/4 cups chopped celery   Marjoram
2 cups chopped onions   Lemon peel
½ cup chopped   Worcestershire sauce
bell pepper   Kitchen Bouquet
1 small can tomatoes   1 cup green onions—
½ can hot tomatoes   chopped
3 cans tomato sauce   Parsley
12 allspice   3 shredded hard-boiled eggs
Sherry wine

Cut turtle in small pieces, salt and pressure cook 15 minutes with the bay leaf. Sauté onions, bell pepper and celery in chicken fat. Simmer with the rest of the ingredients, adding water as needed. Reserve green onions and parsley until last half hour, and eggs and wine until just before serving.

MRS. OUDREY GROS
Belle River, La.

CRAWFISH BISQUE
Serves 8-10

1 water bucket (2½ gallons) crawfish	½ box salt

Put live crawfish in boiling water to cover and pour in salt. Leave 20 minutes. Then wash, scald and clean them. Peel tails and clean out heads, reserving the fat. Fill heads with the following stuffing:

All the tails, chopped or ground 1 large onion, chopped	½ cup green onion tops 2 tablespoon parsley 1 small clove garlic

3 slices stale bread

Cook seasoning in bacon fat until limp, then add bread and tails, cooking a few minutes more. Save a portion of the dressing for the soup part of the bisque. With remainder, stuff heads, roll them in flour and fry until brown in hot fat.

GRAVY FOR BISQUE

2 heaping kitchen spoons of bacon fat 1 heaping kitchen spoon flour 1 large onion	2 cloves garlic 3 bay leaves ½ cup green onions 2 tablespoon parsley 2 quarts water

Make a roux with bacon fat and flour. Stir constantly and when dark brown, add onion and garlic (chopped very fine) and cook until onion is limp. Add water and simmer for half an hour. Add bay leaves, green onions and parsley. Add stuffed heads and dressing left. Simmer another half hour, then skim fat and serve—6 heads to one serving.

From the file of
LAURANCE MOUTON SIMON
St. Martinville, La.

READY ROUX

1 cup Lou-ana oil	1 onion (chopped)
1½ cups plain flour	2 pods garlic (crushed)
1 bell pepper (chopped)	1 stalk celery (chopped)

Heat oil to simmer temperature. Slowly add flour stirring constantly. Reduce heat and stir until mixture is golden brown. Remove from fire and add all vegetables. Return to low heat and stir until vegetables are transparent. Remove from fire and let cool. Put into jars and store in refrigerator. It will keep indefinitely. This roux is good for stews, gumbo, soups, gravies or casseroles when needed.

CONSTANCE GUILBEAU
Sunset, La.

ROUX—OVEN METHOD

Place 2 tablespoons Lou Ana oil and 2 tablespoons flour in a skillet and place in 450 degree oven. Brown for 15 to 20 minutes, stirring once or twice. Just flour can be used to make roux this way, eliminating the oil.

MRS. LOWELL MOORE
Jennings, La.

TURKEY GUMBO FILÉ

Turkey carcass and left over meat	Salt and pepper to taste
½ pound raw shrimp (peeled and deveined)	2 quarts water
1 link pork sausage	3 tablespoons bacon drippings
1 onion chopped	3 tablespoons flour
2 ribs celery chopped	½ bell pepper chopped
½ tablespoon dry parsley	2 bay leaves

Reserve large meaty pieces of turkey. Pick all meat off carcass. Boil carcass in 2 quarts water. Discard bones and reserve water. **Boil** some of the grease out of sausage, drain and slice into small pieces.

Make a dark roux of bacon fat and flour, stirring constantly. Sauté celery, onion, bell pepper in roux until soft. Fry sausage along with seasonings. Add shrimp, stir until pink. Add water in which carcass was boiled. Add bay leaves and parsley, salt and pepper to taste. Simmer about 30-45 minutes. Add turkey meat.

Serve in soup bowls over a spoonful of rice. Sprinkle prepared gumbo filé (½ teaspoon) over top if desired. Do not cook filé in pot.

MRS. P. CHAUVIN WILKINSON
Poplar Grove Plantation

SEAFOOD GUMBO

3 kitchen spoons bacon fat
3 kitchen spoons flour
2 bunches green onions
2 stalks celery
1 large can tomatoes
6 pounds shrimp
1 quart oysters
Monosodium glutamate

6-9 crabs (boiled & broken in pieces)
2 pounds fresh okra or 3 packages frozen okra
Parsley
Salt, pepper, hot sauce, Worcestershire and kitchen bouquet

Make a good, dark brown roux with the bacon fat and flour. Sauté celery and green onions together. Add shrimp and cook a few minutes until they become pink. Add tomatoes and okra and cook 5 minutes. Add 1½ to 2 quarts of hot water, then the roux, vegetable mixture, seasonings and the crabs. Let cook for about 45 minutes. Twenty minutes before serving, add oysters and cook until edges curl. Serve over cooked rice. Serves 8 to 10.

MRS. MALCOLM BRIAN, JR.

OYSTER SOUP

6 dozen oysters
1 bunch green onions
1 quart milk
1 quart half and half
1 box salt free crackers
3 stalks celery

4 tablespoons chopped parsley
1 dash Tabasco
1 dash Worcestershire sauce
1 stick oleo

Sauté chopped onions and celery in oleo. Roll crackers into fine crumbs and add to celery and onions. Drain oysters and cook in skillet until they curl, drain and set aside. Add milk and half 'n half to celery mixture. Add parsley, Tabasco and Worcestershire and heat thoroughly, but do not boil. Add oysters and let entire soup heat for two minutes. Correct seasonings. Serves 6.

MRS. PAUL MARKS

CHICKEN-OKRA GUMBO
Serves 8

1 young hen or large fryer	2 medium-sized tomatoes, cut
Lou Ana cooking oil	1 large bell pepper
2 pounds okra	1 large onion
Salt and pepper to taste	2 quarts water

Cut chicken into pieces and salt, pepper and flour in paper bag. Fry until golden brown in deep oil, then set aside, leaving only about ¼ cup of oil in pot. Cut okra into ¼ inch circles and return to drippings in pot along with tomatoes, bell pepper and onion. Cook until okra stops roping, stirring often. Add salt and pepper to taste and about 2 quarts of water. Return chicken to pot and cook on a slow fire for about 1½ hours. Turn fire off and let stand; this improves the flavor. When ready to serve, place a spoonful of steamed rice in each plate of piping hot gumbo.

MRS. CHARLES SCOTT

CORN CHOWDER

One large pot	3 large onions, finely chopped
½ pound bacon, finely chopped	
	2 cans frozen Cream of Shrimp soup, thawed and undiluted
3 medium large Irish potatoes, peeled and cubed	
2 boxes raw shrimp, peeled, devined and coarsely chopped, or 1 pound shrimp from market, same procedure (10 ounce size for frozen raw shrimp)	3 cups boiling water
	3 cans whole kernel corn, drained (10 oz. size)
	1 quart of milk
	Seasoning to taste (salt, red and black pepper)

Sauté bacon until crisp, drain on paper toweling. If there is lots of bacon fat pour most of it out. Cook onion in same pot with remainder until limp. Add cubed potatoes and three cups boiling water. Cook slowly until potatoes are about half done. Add shrimp soup, shrimp, corn, bacon and milk. Cook on moderate heat for a few minutes and then add seasoning, as desired. Be cautious about salt as shrimp soup is salty. Continue cooking until potatoes are soft. Correct seasoning if necessary. Makes four quarts and freezes very well. To reheat use double boiler. Served with a tart dressing green salad, French bread and a dry white wine, I think it makes a grand meal.

KATHERINE BRES
Brusly, La.

FORCE MEAT BALLS FOR SOUP

1 cup cooked veal or
  chicken minced fine
½ cup bread crumbs
  (fine)

4 hard cooked egg yolks
1 tablespoon milk
½ teaspoon flour
2 whole eggs

Add milk to hard cooked egg yolks and mash into a smooth paste. Add to cooked meat, bread crumbs and flour, mix well and blend together with the 2 whole eggs. Flour hands well and roll mixture into small balls. Drop into soup or bouillon about 20 minutes before serving.

MRS. ROY FIELD

COURTBOUILLON

1 4-5 pound red snapper
  or red fish
2 full kitchen spoons flour
2 full kitchen spoons bacon
  or Lou Ana oil
2 cups onion, chopped
4 cloves garlic

red pepper browned
  with flour
Salt to taste
2 quarts fish stock made
  from head and back
  bone of red snapper
  after fileting

1 small can tomato paste

Filet red snapper and cut into large pieces about 1½ inch thick. Brown flour with pepper slowly in fat stirring constantly until dark brown. Add onions and garlic and brown slightly and add tomato paste. Cook slowly until this makes a thick paste. When the oil begins to separate from this paste it is done. Add fish stock, stirring until smooth and let simmer for 20-30 minutes. Add more water if it is too thick. Fifteen minutes before serving add fish and let simmer.

Serve with hot crusty French bread. This is a fish soup not a sauce to be served over rice. If desired add ice cream scoop of rice to soup bowl as it is served.

MRS. LYTTLETON T. HARRIS

SHE CRAB SOUP

2 cups or 1 pound white   1 small white onion,
    crab meat   chopped fine
½ cup or ¼ pound   1 quart milk
    crab roe   1 pint breakfast cream
4 tablespoons butter   Pinch white pepper
2 teaspoons flour   Pinch mace
       ½ cup sherry (optional)

Soften onion in butter in heavy pot. Remove from heat and add flour. Slowly add milk, being careful not to let it lump. Put back on heat, let come to a simmer and add crab meat, roe, pepper and mace. Cook slowly for 20 minutes. Add pint of cream, stirring well. Remove from heat and add wine. If sherry is not used, I like a full teaspoon of Worcestershire sauce and a pinch of rosemary. Serve with croisants, other hot rolls or croutons (home made).

CROUTONS

Sauté small squares of bread (stale) in butter until crisp and pale brown on all sides. Float on top of soup just before serving.

MRS. GEORGE M. SIMON

BOUILLABAISSE
Serves 8

2 fresh lobsters (or 4   2 tablespoons parsley,
    small lobster tails)   chopped
2 pounds speckled trout   1 large carrot, chopped
3 pounds red snapper   2 cloves garlic, crushed
4 dozen oysters   ½ teaspoon saffron
4 dozen shrimp   1 bay leaf (optional)
2 dozen scallops   4 cups tomatoes, canned
4 green onions, chopped   including juice
1 cup onion, chopped   1 tablespoon salt
2 quarts water   ¼ teaspoon red pepper
       ½ cup olive oil

Cut lobster, trout and red snapper in one inch thick slices. Heat olive oil in large pot, add onions, carrot, green onions and garlic and cook until softened or light brown. Add tomatoes, parsley, bay leaf, saffron, salt and pepper Then add water, lobsters and scallops. Cook 15 minutes. Add trout, red snapper, and shrimp. Cook

10 minutes more, add oysters and cook 3 minutes and remove from heat.

THE EDITORS

Serve at once over French bread which has been cut in thick slices and brushed with garlic and olive oil and toasted. Parmesan cheese sprinkled on bread before toasting is good.

CORN AND SHRIMP SOUP

1 tablespoon bacon fat	2 quarts peeled,
1 tablespoon flour	fresh shrimp
2 onions, chopped fine	6 ears fresh corn
1½ quarts water	2 tomatoes
Salt, black and red pepper	

Brown flour and onions in bacon fat. Add shrimp and corn cut from the cob, and tomatoes. Add water and cook on low heat for 1½ hours. Season to taste.

MRS. WILLIAM SLACK

Salads

"WANT MORE" SALAD DRESSING

2 cloves garlic grated
2 small onions grated
¼ cup ketchup
¼ cup chili sauce
1 cup mayonnaise
Lemon juice and
    salt to taste

½ cup Lou Ana oil
1 teaspoon Worcestershire
    sauce
1 teaspoon black pepper
1 teaspoon prepared mustard
1 teaspoon paprika &
    dash Tabasco

Mix all together and shake well. Good on green salads or fish, shrimp, etc. Will keep in refrigerator for a week or longer.

THE EDITORS

MAYONNAISE

1 egg yolk
1 full teaspoon prepared
    mustard
3 heaping teaspoons
    catsup

1 teaspoon Worcestershire
    sauce
½ teaspoon salt
¼ teaspoon red pepper
1 teaspoon vinegar

3 cups Lou Ana oil

Mix all ingredients together and beat well in electric mixer. Beat in 1 tablespoon oil at a time, holding mixing bowl in one place (not allowing to turn) until 6 tablespoons have been added. Then add larger amounts of it, still not allowing bowl to move until mixture is smooth. Beat well after each addition. Continue until 3 cups of oil have been used. Then beat thoroughly for several minutes. This will never separate unless it is put too close to freezing compartment of refrigerator. This mayonnaise should be thick enough to cut with a knife. It does not take over 10 minutes to make.

MRS. E. S. GIRAULT
Monroe, La.

LIZZY'S FRENCH DRESSING

1/3 cup vinegar
¼ cup Beau Monde
1 teaspoon black pepper
1 tablespoon salt

1 cup Lou Ana oil
1 tablespoon parsley flakes
¼ teaspoon red pepper
1 teaspoon garlic powder

Shake well and store in refrigerator. Makes 1 pint.

MRS. W. T. BAYNARD

ROUQUEFORT OR BLEU CHEESE DRESSING

1/3 cup red wine
  vinegar
1 teaspoon black
  pepper, coarsely ground
2/3 cup Lou Ana oil

4 ounces bleu or
  Roquefort cheese
  (grated)
1 teaspoon salt

Combine all ingredients and store in refrigerator. Toss with crisp salad greens.

MRS. R. GORDON KEAN

SOUR CREAM DRESSING

2 tablespoons minced onion
1 tablespoon butter
1 tablespoon flour
1 teaspoon sugar

1 teaspoon salt
1 teaspoon vinegar
3/4 cup or more of
  sour cream

Soften onion in butter. Add flour, sugar and salt. Slowly stir in cream and cook until it thickens. Add vinegar. Mushrooms or 1 cup grated cheese may be added. Serve over green beans or asparagus.

THE EDITORS

FOOL-PROOF HOME MADE MAYONNAISE

1 quart Lou Ana oil
4 egg yolks
1 hard boiled egg yolk

1 teaspoon yellow mustard
Salt and red pepper
2 tablespoons vinegar

Put egg yolks in small bowl of electric mixer. Add mashed yolk of hard boiled egg. Put on medium speed and mix well. Add oil very slowly and when it begins to thicken, add rest of ingredients. The secret of this is the hard boiled egg yolk. It also helps to have the oil cold.

MRS. RALPH PERLMAN

ROQUEFORT DRESSING
(makes about 1 quart)

1 small can evaporated milk
3 tablespoon lemon juice
1 pint mayonnaise

1 garlic button, minced
2 large wedges blue or
  Roquefort cheese

Whip evaporated milk and lemon juice until stiff in mixer. Set aside. Blend remaining ingredients together until well blended. Fold in whipped evaporated milk, adding salt or other seasonings as desired. A dash of Tabasco is good in this. Store in refrigerator—will keep well for several weeks.

MRS. THOMPSON TALIAFERRO
Lafayette, La.

POPPY SEED DRESSING I

¼ cup sugar	1½ teaspoons onion juice
1/3 cup vinegar	or grate little onion
1 teaspoon salt	very fine
1 teaspoon powdered	1 cup Lou Ana oil
mustard	1½ teaspoon poppy seed

Mix dry ingredients and vinegar in mixmaster. Add onion juice and oil gradually, beating constantly. Add poppy seed last. Good with avocadoes, grapefruit and orange sections.

MRS. ROBERT L. PETTIT

POPPY SEED DRESSING II

1 cup honey	2 tablespoons prepared
1 cup white wine vinegar	mustard
1 cup pure fresh	2½ cups Lou Ana oil
lemon juice	5 tablespoons poppy seed
1 teaspoon salt	

Mix in order listed. Blend in electric blender until oil disappears. One medium size onion, finely grated, may be added if desired. Good on fruit salad.

THE EDITORS

HEALTH DRESSING

2/3 cup Lou Ana oil	1 tablespoon lemon juice
3 tablespoons sugar	½ teaspoon grated onion
1/3 cup catsup	1/3 cup vinegar
3/4 teaspoon salt	

Combine all ingredients in a jar and shake well. Makes about 1 1/3 cups.

MRS. ORDA MCKENZIE
Natchitoches, La.

FRENCH DRESSING

1 cup Lou Ana oil
1/4 cup vinegar
2 tablespoons lemon juice
½ cup catsup

1 teaspoon salt
2 tablespoons onion juice
Red pepper and
  garlic to taste

¼ cup sugar

Mix in order given. Good for any vegetable or fresh fruit salad.

MRS. EUGENE FLOURNOY
Monroe, La.

GOLDEN GLOW DRESSING

1 can Cheddar Cheese
  soup
½ cup mayonnaise
2 tablespoons lemon juice

1 teaspoon grated
  onion juice
2 dashes Tabasco sauce
2 tablespoons vermouth

Mix together and serve on any mixed green or vegetable salad. One small clove of crushed garlic may be added.

MRS. LEWIS S. DOHERTY, II

ORANGE-HONEY DRESSING

¼ teaspoon paprika
½ teaspoon dry mustard
1 teaspoon salt
3 tablespoons
  lemon juice

2 tablespoons cider
  vinegar
3 tablespoons frozen
  orange concentrate
1 cup Lou Ana salad oil

½ cup honey

Combine dry ingredients. Add honey, lemon juice and orange concentrate. Blend well. Beating constantly, slowly add oil. Beat 5 minutes longer at medium speed. Chill.

Submitted by
MRS. CORBIN OWEN

CLUB DRESSING

1 cup vegetable oil
½ cup sugar
1 cup vinegar
2 cups catsup

2 teaspoons salt (more
  or less, to taste)
2 tablespoons onion juice
2 pods garlic

Combine ingredients in order given, mix until well blended. Pour in fruit jar and place in refrigerator. Let stand at least 24 hours before using. Remove garlic pods. This dressing is a very good substitute for salad dressing or mayonnaise when making sandwiches.

MRS. ESTELL GORDON CURRIE

BOILED DRESSING

½ tablespoon salt   few grains cayenne
1½ tablespoon sugar   ½ cup vinegar
½ tablespoon flour   2 eggs
1 teaspoon mustard (dry)   3/4 cup milk

1 tablespoon butter

Mix dry ingredients in top of double boiler. Add vinegar and beaten eggs, add milk and butter. Cook until thick.

From the file of
MRS. ESTELLE LEWIS CORBETT

AVOCADO DRESSING

½ cup orange juice   2 teaspoons mayonnaise
½ lemon (peeled and   1 avocado peeled
    seeded)   and cubed

½ teaspoon salt

Put orange juice, lemon, salt and mayonnaise in blender and blend at low speed. Add avocado and run at low speed until smooth. Yields about 1¼ cups.

THE EDITORS

SALAD MIXTURE

1 10 oz. jar salad olives   1 teaspoon garlic salt
1 2½ oz. jar capers   ½ teaspoon salad herbs
2 cups of finely chopped,   1 teaspoon salt
   raw carrots   ½ cup vinegar and
4-5 cups of finely chopped,   lemon juice
   celery   ½ cup Lou Ana oil

½ cup olive oil

Mix well and let stand for several hours in container.

THE EDITORS

HONEY DRESSING FOR FRUIT SALAD

1½ cups sugar
2 teaspoons dry
   mustard
2 teaspoons salt
3 tablespoons onion
   juice

1 cup Lou Ana oil (never
   olive oil)
2/3 cup tarragon
   vinegar
Add pinch of mace,
   cardamon, nutmeg

1 cup pure, dark honey

Mix sugar, mustard, salt and vinegar. Add onion juice and beat well in mixer. Add oil slowly alternating with honey and beating well. When thick seal in small jars. Never refrigerate until after jar is opened for use. Always stir before serving. Makes about 4 half pint jars.

This makes a good poppy seed dressing: add 2 teaspoons poppy seed and ¼ cup Lou Ana oil to 1 cup of dressing.

MRS. MARTHA WATTS GUTHRIE

ENGLISH PEA SALAD

1 can tiny English
   peas, drained
½ cup celery hearts
1 cup sharp cheese
1 pimiento, drained
½ cup pecans

4 tablespoons
   India relish
Salt and pepper
   to taste
Mayonnaise

Chop celery, cheese & pimiento to size of peas. Mix all ingredients, adding enough mayonnaise to hold together. Pack lightly into pyrex custard cup, then invert on lettuce leaf to serve.

MRS. P. C. ARMISTEAD

COLD SLAW

1 head very fresh, crisp
   cabbage
1 green pepper
1 onion
2 pimientos

Dressing:
1 part Lou Ana oil
2 parts apple vinegar
3 parts sugar
Lots of salt to taste

Chop cabbage in wooden bowl. Chop other ingredients, add to dressing, and toss cabbage in mixture thoroughly. Refrigerate 24 hours in uncovered dish. Make enough dressing to cover the slaw.

THE EDITORS

CAESAR SALAD FOR FOUR

6 cups mixed salad greens
(endive, watercress,
romaine, etc.)
1½ cups croutons
6 tablespoons French
dressing
Juice of 1½ lemons
1½ teaspoons garlic oil

1½ teaspoons
Worcestershire sauce
1 clove garlic
4 tablespoons grated
Parmesan cheese
1 one-minute egg
1 tablespoon freshly
ground pepper

2 tablespoons olive oil

Put 1 clove garlic in 2 tablespoons olive oil and let stand for 2 to 4 hours. Use about 1½ teaspoons of this in dressing, along with French dressing, lemon juice, garlic oil, and Worcestershire sauce. Mix well. In a large bowl, toss the salad greens well, add the croutons, egg, the beaten mixture over all. Add freshly ground pepper and the Parmesan cheese and serve immediately·

MRS. JAMES W. MC LAURIN

CUCUMBER ASPIC
(Serves 14)

4 tender cucumbers
½ cup vinegar
1 teaspoon salt
1 teaspoon sugar
3 envelopes gelatine
3/4 cup water

3 3-oz. packages
cream cheese
1 can pimiento chopped
4 green onions chopped
2 tablespoons milk
or cream

Peel and slice cucumbers. Liquefy a few slices at a time in the blender. Add sugar and vinegar and enough water to make 4 cups liquid.

Bring half the liquid to a boil while the gelatine softens in 3/4 cups of cold water· (divide the gelatine in two cups) Soften the cream cheese with the milk and stir till smooth. Dissolve the gelatine in very hot liquid and then add remainder of cucumber liquid and cream cheese.

Put in refrigerator and when it begins to set stir in pimiento and green onions and pour in lightly oiled mold. Unmold after several hours on a bed of lettuce. Serve with tomato wedges and mayonnaise.

MRS. I. H. RUBENSTEIN

TOMATO ASPIC
Serves 8

4 cups tomato juice
3 tablespoons gelatine
Juice of 1 lemon
2 teaspoons Worcestershire
  sauce

Grated onion to taste
1 large avocado
½ cup finely minced celery
½ cup finely minced bell
  pepper

1 teaspoon salt

Soak gelatine in 1 cup tomato juice, then dissolve in 3 cups hot tomato juice. Add onion, lemon, salt and Worcestershire. Place in refrigerator and when it is partly congealed, add avocado, cut in bite size pieces, celery, and bell pepper. Return to refrigerator until firmly set.

THE EDITORS

STUFFED CABBAGE SALAD

1 medium-size cabbage
½ cup sour cream
1 cup celery
½ cup shredded carrots
3/4 cup halved grapes
2 quartered tomatoes

2 tablespoons wine
  vinegar
2 tablespoons sugar
½ to 1 teaspoon salt
¼ cup chopped parsley
2 hard-boiled eggs

Wash cabbage thoroughly and scoop out centermost part with sharp knife, leaving a good solid edge· Shred the cabbage fine and add all the ingredients except the eggs and tomatoes. Pile mixture into cabbage shell. Garnish with quartered eggs and tomatoes, and serve cold.

MRS. LEWIS O. WHITE

COLORFUL CAULIFLOWER SALAD
Serves 4

1 medium size raw
  cauliflower
1 small jar stuffed
  olives

3/4 cup sharp cheese
  chunks
Tangy salad dressing
  (Recipe below)

2 medium size tomatoes

Clean cauliflower and cut flowerets from main stalk in adequate size pieces for salad. Put small, tender leaves in salad, also. Peel tomatoes, cut into wedges; add to salad with cheese cut in chunks. Slice enough stuffed olives to make a good color contrast. Toss with dressing.

TANGY GARLIC DRESSING

1 teaspoon sugar
1½ teaspoons salt
1 teaspoon dry mustard
Dash of red pepper
1 tablespoon
    Worcestershire sauce

1/8 teaspoon paprika
½ cup vinegar
1 cup Lou Ana salad oil
1 tablespoon
    grated onion
½ teaspoon cornstarch

3 cloves garlic

Blend dry ingredients in saucepan. Stir in vinegar and bring to a boil, stirring constantly. Simmer 5 minutes. Cool. Add Worcestershire, grated onions and salad oil. Add garlic. Refrigerate for 4 hours before serving, and remove garlic before serving. Makes 1½ cups.

MRS. LEWIS O. WHITE

TOSSED GREEN SALAD

Dressing:

1 large clove of garlic
    crushed
1 tablespoon Rocquefort
    cheese mashed

1 teaspoon mustard
2 tablespoons lemon
    juice
3 tablespoons olive oil

Mix well in large salad bowl

Add:
1½ teaspoons salt

3/4 teaspoon black pepper
1 teaspoon oregano

In this dressing, marinate:

½ cup chopped bell pepper
1 cup chopped celery
1 avocado chopped

1 large tomato chopped
    and drained
¼ cup parsley

Refrigerate. Tear Romaine lettuce into large dish towel to be well drained and crisp. Refrigerate. At serving time, put lettuce on top of marinated vegetables and toss.

MRS. FRANK GRIGSBY

BUTTERBEAN SALAD

2 packages frozen baby
   lima beans
2 tablespoons
   Lou Ana oil
2 teaspoons salt

2 tablespoons
   chopped parsley
2 tablespoons vinegar
1 garlic toe, pressed
2 teaspoons sugar

1 cup sour cream

Cook beans in unsalted water. Drain and add other ingredients. Toss lightly. Cover and chill in refrigerator several hours, preferably overnight.

MRS. RICHARD ODOM
Cheneyville, La.

SALADE NICOISE
(4 servings)

2 tomatoes, cut in quarters
1 sliced green pepper
1 sliced cucumber
2 chopped endives
7 sliced radishes
1 celery heart chopped
   or sliced
1 sliced onion

1 can black olives
1 can tuna fish (in oil)
3 anchovies (or 4)
1 sliced hard-boiled egg
a pinch of parsley
Olive oil, vinegar, salt,
   pepper, and mustard.
Mix together well

Mix all ingredients, except the anchovies, in a salad bowl, with dressing. Place the anchovies on top of the salad. If desired, the tomatoes and egg slices may be arranged on top as well.

H. S. H. PRINCESS GRACE DE MONACO

TART POTATO SALAD

3 cups boiled potatoes
4 hard cooked eggs
1 cup celery, chopped
¼ cup apple cider
   vinegar
1/3 cup Lou Ana salad oil

1 tablespoon sugar
2 teaspoons prepared
   mustard (full)
¼ cup sweet pickle
¼ cup dill pickle
½ teaspoon celery seed

salt and pepper to taste

Boil potatoes (new ones, if possible) until fork penetrates. Do not cook until mealy. Cut in rather large chunks. Crumble egg yolks, chop egg whites, finely, and add all other ingredients. Toss as green salad.

From the file of
LAURANCE MOUTON SIMON

MYSTERY SALAD

3 regular packages
  raspberry jello
3 1-pound cans
  stewed tomatoes
6 or 8 drops Tabasco

1 pint commercial
  sour cream
1 tablespoon creamed
  horseradish
½ teaspoon salt

½ teaspoon sugar

Dissolve jello in 1¼ cups of hot water. Chop the tomatoes up well and add jello and Tabasco. Pour into 12-cup mold. When congealed, turn out on platter and fill center with sauce made of sour cream, horseradish, salt and sugar.

JO ANN HACKENBERG,
Submitted by
MRS. ROBERT B. JENNINGS

OLD FASHIONED PERFECTION SALAD

2 cups finely shredded
  cabbage
½ cup chopped
  green pepper

1 cup chopped celery
¼ cup diced pimiento
1/3 cup sliced stuffed
  olives

First, mix 2 envelopes gelatine, ½ cup sugar and 1 teaspoon salt. Add 1½ cups boiling water to dissolve gelatine. Then add 1½ cups cold water, 1 cup vinegar and 2 tablespoons lemon juice. Chill partially, then add other ingredients.

Mold this in an oblong mold and then decorate with carrot rolls, ripe olives on top and around lettuce leaves. A very tasty salad with roasts, ham, etc.

MRS. CHARLES MYER

BEET AND JELLO SALAD

1 package lemon gelatine
1 cup beet juice
1 jar shoestring or
  cubed beets
3 tablespoons
  lemon juice

3 tablespoons vinegar
¼ teaspoon salt
¼ cup finely
  chopped celery
1 tablespoon finely
  chopped green onions

Pour 1 cup of hot beet juice over gelatine and stir until dissolved. Add other ingredients. Put into individual molds. Serve on lettuce with mayonnaise. This jello is also good if you use pecans and omit the onions.

MRS. ALDRICH STROUBE

SAUERKRAUT SALAD

1 large can sauerkraut
1 large chopped onion
2 chopped bell peppers
3/4 cup chopped celery
1 large jar chopped
   pimento

Drain sauerkraut and cut fine. Add other chopped vegetables, then cover with this:

DRESSING

½ cup Lou Ana oil
1 cup sugar
2/3 cup cider vinegar
½ cup water

Mix well and blend into above sauerkraut. Leave in refrigerator, well covered, for one or two days before using to allow it to marinate. Wonderful on lettuce leaf with pork or ham. Even if you don't like sauerkraut, you'll like this.

MRS. GEORGE T. TATE
Alexandria, La.

ASPARAGUS SALAD MOLD
Serves 7 or 8

3/4 cup sugar
1 cup water
½ cup white vinegar
2 tablespoons gelatin in
   ¼ cup water
1 can green asparagus
   cut up
1 cup celery chopped fine
½ cup pecans chopped
2 pimentos chopped
Juice of ½ lemon,
   or to taste
2 tablespoons grated onion
Salt and pepper to taste

Simmer sugar, water and vinegar a few minutes. Add softened gelatin to hot liquid. When mixture begins to jell, add other ingredients and chill until firm.

MRS. L. M. DAVIS

GERMAN POTATO SALAD

Medium size
   Irish potatoes
3 or 4 slices bacon,
   chopped
¼ cup vinegar
1 medium onion
   coarsely cut
1 tablespoon flour
Sugar, salt & white
   pepper to taste

Boil potatoes in salted water, drain, peel while warm. Fry the bacon, remove from skillet and set aside. In hot bacon fat, wilt the onions, add the flour, sugar salt and white pepper to taste, then add ¼ cup vinegar, and bring to a boil. Pour over sliced potatoes and garnish with celery seed and 2 finely chopped hard boiled eggs. Keep warm until served.

MRS. B. N. SWEENEY
Rayne, La.

GOLDEN RICE SALAD

1½ cups raw rice
4 chicken boullion cubes
3 cups salted water
¼ cup Lou Ana oil
2 tablespoons vinegar
1½ teaspoons salt
1/8 teaspoon pepper
1 cup ripe olives

2 chopped dill pickles
¼ cup chopped pimiento
1 small onion minced
½ cup mayonnaise
2 tablespoons
    prepared mustard
2 hard boiled eggs,
    diced, (optional)

1½ cups sliced celery

Cook raw rice, salted water and boullion cubes 20 minutes. Blend salad oil with vinegar, salt, pepper and mustard and pour over hot rice. Toss and set aside to cool. (Cook 1½ cups of raw rice in 3 cups salted water and 3 bouillon cubes to get the 4½ cups of cooked rice). Add remaining ingredients, toss, and chill thoroughly before serving.

MRS. LOWELL MOORE
Jennings, La.

AVOCADO MOUSSE

2 tablespoons plain
    gelatine dissolved
    in 3 tablespoons
    cold water
1 package lime gelatine

1 cup ripe, mashed
    avocado
½ cup home made
    mayonnaise
1 cup cream, whipped

2 cups hot water

Dissolve gelatin mix and lime gelatine in the hot water. When partially congealed, stir in the remaining ingredients, pour into molds greased with mayonnaise and allow to set in the refrigerator. Unmold on crisp salad greens. You may fill the center of the mold with fresh strawberries, grapes, pineapple and orange sections. Serve with mayonnaise mixture that has grated orange peel and a dash of curry added.

MRS. WILLIAM SLACK

ASPARAGUS MOUSSE
Serves 8

4 eggs	2 cans white
2 lemons	asparagus tips
½ pint whipping cream	1 tablespoon
2 tablespoons butter	plain gelatine
2 tablespoons flour	Salt and paprika

Heat butter in double boiler. Stir flour into this. Beat eggs well and pour into the butter mixture, stirring constantly. Add half the asparagus juice and cook until thickened. If this should lump, strain. Dissolve gelatin in ¼ cup hot or cold water. Add lemon juice and seasoning to gelatine. When completely cool, add whipped cream. Now, add this to the egg mixture. Grease a regular loaf pan with oil and line with asparagus tips, pour part of the mixture over this layer of tips, and repeat layers until all is used. Chill for at least six hours. Unmold and garnish with black olives and lettuce.

From the file of
MRS. LEE HERZBERG

VEGETABLE SALAD

1 can asparagus	½ pint cream, whipped
½ can small English peas	Salt
2 whole pimientos	Pepper
4 egg yolks	Gelatine (1 envelope to
1 tablespoon flour	2 cups liquid)
1 lemon (juice)	

Save juice from peas and asparagus and heat. Add to beaten egg yolks and flour and let cook until thick. Remove from fire and add to gelatin which has been softened in ½ cup cold water. Add remaining ingredients. When cool fold in whipped cream and place in refrigerator.

THE EDITORS

GOLD AND GREEN SALAD (PAPAYA)

1 papaya	½ teaspoon each salt,
1 cup Lou Ana salad oil	dry mustard &
1/3 cup tarragon vinegar	instant minced
¼ cup sugar	onion
1 tablespoon lime juice	4 cups mixed salad greens
¼ teaspoon paprika	

Cube papaya, reserving seeds. Put salad oil, vinegar, sugar, lime juice, paprika, salt, mustard and onion in blender and blend thoroughly. Add 1½ tablespoons papaya seed to blender and blend until seeds are size of coarsely ground pepper. Chill. Combine cubed papaya and greens. Toss lightly with desired amount of dressing. NOTE: To peel papaya, let ripen at room temperature. Dunk in boiling water for 1 minute, then drop into ice water. With tip of paring knife, pull away peel.

MRS. M. F. MAGRUDER

SWEET AND SOUR BEAN SALAD

2 cans whole, small
    green beans
1 can red beans
1 can wax beans (all
    thoroughly drained
    and as dry as possible)
2 medium white or
    purple onions, (sliced
    in rings)
4 ribs tender celery
    (sliced, not chopped)
1 small green pepper
    (chopped)
1 can mushrooms
    (drained)

1 can pimiento peppers
    (sliced and drained)
½ can toasted slivered
    almonds, add just
    before serving.

Dressing:
1½ cups sugar
½ cup oil (olive
    or Lou Ana)
1 cup wine vinegar
1 teaspoon salt
½ to 1 teaspoon
    red pepper

Bring above to boil slowly. Pour over bean mixture while still hot. Chill thoroughly before serving.
Good with smoked meats, fried chicken, roast, etc.

MRS. ROY DABADIE

BEAN AND CARROT SALAD

1½ cups sugar
1¼ cups water
1¼ cups vinegar

6 tablespoons Lou Ana oil
2 cans string beans
2 cans small carrots

1 thinly sliced onion

Put sugar and vinegar in saucepan and heat until sugar is dissolved. Put beans, carrots and onion in bowl and add vinegar, water and oil. Mix well and place in refrigerator to chill. Serve on chopped lettuce with diced tomatoes and riced hard boiled egg. Add more beans and carrots to solution as needed.

MRS. WILLIAM A. GOTSCHALL

BEAN SALAD

1 #2 can whole beans	3 pimentos, cut or jar
1 #2 can English peas	of pimiento pieces
4 strips of celery	1 onion, sliced and soaked
1 green pepper	in vinegar

SAUCE

1 teaspoon salt	½ cup Lou Ana oil
1½ cups sugar	1 teaspoon water
1 cup salad vinegar	

Mix ingredients (do not heat) for sauce. Mix vegetables and pour sauce over them. Let stand overnight. Drain for 3 hours before serving.

MRS. EDWARD L. SIMON

MARINATED GREEN BEANS

2 cups vertical pack	½ cup finely chopped
green beans	celery
1 cup olive oil	Garlic salt
¼ cup lemon juice	Onion salt
Salad herbs	

Drain green beans and put into glass type bowl. Sprinkle over garlic salt, onion salt, salad herbs, and celery. Mix olive oil and lemon juice and pour over. Let marinate several hours or overnight, turning frequently.

THE EDITORS

GREEN BEAN SALAD I

1 sliced onion	¼ cup olive oil &
4 boiled potatoes	Lou Ana oil combined
sliced thin	2 tablespoons vinegar
2 No. 2 cans green beans	

Mix and marinate for several hours

MRS. J. CLIFTON HILL

GREEN BEAN SALAD II

Cold cooked green beans   2 hard boiled eggs
French dressing   1 teaspoon prepared
1 cup celery   mustard

Chives to taste

Marinate cold beans for several hours in French dressing. Cut celery fine, lengthwise. Mix with chopped whites of eggs, chives and yellows of eggs that have been mashed and combined with mustard and small amount of French dressing. Serve over green beans.

Mrs. L. W. Brooks

BROCCOLI SALAD I

1 package frozen   Dash Tabasco sauce
   chopped broccoli   2 tablespoons
1 tablespoon gelatine   Worcestershire sauce
¼ cup cold water   2 hard cooked eggs, diced
1 can consomme   1 small jar pimiento,
1 large package   chopped
   cream cheese   3/4 teaspoon salt
½ cup mayonnaise   ¼ teaspoon black pepper

2 tablespoons lemon juice

Cook broccoli in salted water as directed on package until tender. Drain. Dissolve gelatin in cold water and add hot consomme. Blend the softened cheese with mayonnaise. Add all seasonings, then the eggs and broccoli. Lastly add the gelatine mixture and mold in individual molds.

Mrs. Sam B. Short

BROCCOLI SALAD II

2 packages chopped   1 tablespoon lemon rind
   broccoli   1 cup creamed
1 envelope unflavored   cottage cheese
   gelatine   3/4 cup mayonnaise or
¼ cup water   ½ cup sour cream

1 can consommé

Cook broccoli. Soak gelatine in water and dissolve in hot consommé. Add all other ingredients, pour into mold and refrigerate.

Mrs. Charles Kennon

BROCCOLI SALAD MOLD
Serves 6

1 package (10 ounce) frozen, chopped broccoli
1 can (10½ ounce) beef consommé
1½ package plain gelatine in ¼ cup water
2/3 cup mayonnaise

1 tablespoon garlic or plain vinegar
1 teaspoon horseradish and a dash garlic juice
Salt, pepper, Worcestershire and hot sauce to taste

2 tablespoons lemon juice

Cook broccoli according to directions. Do not over-cook. Heat consomme and add softened gelatin, lemon juice and vinegar. Chill until syrupy. Beat with rotary beater, or automatic on low speed. Add mayonnaise and beat again. Add broccoli and seasoning. Pour into 3-cup mold or into 6 custard cups, and chill until firm.

MRS. L. M. DAVIS

SPINACH SALAD
Serves 9

3 boxes frozen spinach
3 hard boiled eggs (chopped)
1½ can pimientos (minced)
Mayonnaise

1½ green peppers (chopped)
3 tablespoons chopped onion
3/4 cup chopped celery
Lemon juice

Thaw spinach, combine all ingredients and toss. Refrigerate until served

MRS. T. J. SINGLETARY

CHICKEN SALAD

2 cups cooked chicken
1 envelope gelatine
½ cup cold water
2 tablespoons lemon juice
2 teaspoons horseradish
1 cup chopped celery

2 tablespoons minced onion
2 teaspoons prepared mustard
1 cup mayonnaise
½ teaspoon salt

½ teaspoon curry powder

Soften gelatine in cold water and dissolve over hot water. Add lemon, salt, curry, horseradish, mustard and mayonnaise and mix well. Add rest of ingredients and let set and chill.

ELENA H. HULINGS

CREAM OF TOMATO SALAD
Serves 10-12

2 envelopes gelatine
½ cup cold water
1 can tomato soup
½ cup water
1 cup sliced stuffed
   olives
1 cup diced celery
1 8-ounce package
   cream cheese

2 tablespoons grated
   onion
2 teaspoons salt, Tabasco
1 large can artichoke
   hearts, washed and
   drained (Shrimp or
   crab can be substituted
   for artichokes)
1 cup mayonnaise

Soak gelatine in ½ cup cold water. Heat tomato soup and ½ cup water until very hot. Add to gelatine. Add rest of ingredients (cream cheese very soft, like mayonnaise). Too rich for large servings. Add horse radish and seasonings to mayonnaise to serve on salad.

MRS. WILSON TREGRE
Shreveport, La.

MOLDED CHICKEN SALAD

1 6-pound chicken
4 cups celery,
   chopped fine
¼ cup chopped parsley
1 tablespoon
   Worcestershire
1½ cups mayonnaise
2 hard boiled eggs

2 envelopes unflavored
   gelatine
1 small bottle stuffed
   olives
3 bay leaves
1 tablespoon onion salt
A few celery leaves
   chopped fine

Salt to taste

Cover chicken with water, add bay leaves, celery leaves, onion salt and salt to taste. Cook until meat falls off the bones. Strain and put aside 4 cups of the liquid. Cut chicken in fine pieces, add celery, 1 chopped egg and mayonnaise to which the Worcestershire sauce has been added. Heat the strained liquid and add gelatine to it. Mix and stir well into the chicken mixture. Grease a mold and line the bottom with the other chopped egg and the sliced stuffed olives. Pour the well mixed chicken mixture into the mold. Let stand in the refrigerator over night. Turn out on platter and garnish with lettuce.

MRS. SARGENT PITCHER, SR.

SPINACH-SHRIMP SALAD

1 large avocado	1 pound (12 cups) spinach
3 oranges, sectioned	2 cups cleaned and
(Remove pulp)	cooked shrimp

1 tablespoon orange juice

Wash and drain spinach, tear in pieces. Peel and slice avocado and sprinkle with orange juice. Toss all together with orange-French dressing:

ORANGE FRENCH DRESSING

2/3 cup Lou-Ana Oil	½ teaspoon grated
½ cup frozen undiluted	orange peel
orange juice	¼ teaspoon salt
1 tablespoon vinegar	¼ teaspoon dry mustard

Dash of hot pepper sauce

Combine all ingredients in screw-top jar and shake well. Chill. For variation, add poppy seeds to dressing.

MRS. R. O. RUSH

MOLDED FISH SALAD

4 cups flaked fish	1 teaspoon
1 cup chopped celery	Worcestshire sauce
¼ cup chopped	Saffron (tip of coffee
dill pickle	spoon)
¼ cup chopped	1 teaspoon salt
sweet pickle	1 package unflavored
4 hard boiled eggs	gelatine

12 drops Tabasco

Simmer fish in 1 quart of water until fork penetrates or fish flakes. Remove skin and bones and cool. Mix with above ingredients. Reserve stock.

PREPARATION OF STOCK

To gelatine add ½ cup cold water. Dissolve in 1¼ cup hot fish stock. Season to taste with salt, 4 drops Tabasco and ½ teaspoon Worcestershire sauce. Remove 3/4 cup of above seasoned stock and add saffron to color yellow.

In bottom of fish mold place slices of 1 hard boiled egg. Use pimiento or slice of stuffed olive for fish eye. Pour in the ½ cup saffron stock and set mold in refrigerator until stock jells. Then spoon salad on top and pour remaining mixture of stock jell over salad. Keep overnight in refrigerator before serving.

MRS. GEORGE SIMON

Note: In making salad, toss, do not stir, to keep fish from getting mushy. This same recipe can be used with shrimp, chicken or crab meat.

SHRIMP SALAD SUPREME

1 cup boiled shrimp
  chopped
3/4 cup chopped celery
1 chopped pimiento
1½ teaspoon grated
  onion
Salt to taste

1 small bottle stuffed
  olives, sliced
1 tablespoon gelatine
3/4 cup mayonnaise
2 hard boiled eggs,
  chopped
Juice of 1 lemon

Soften gelatine in 2 tablespoons cold water, dissolve over hot water. Add mayonnaise, lemon juice and salt. Pour over other ingredients. Mix well and pour in mold or molds.

MRS. NORMAN S. SAURAGE, JR.

This recipe came from the old Majestic Hotel in Lake Charles, La. which was known for its delicious food.

CELERY SOUP AND TUNA MOLD

1 10½-ounce can cream
  of celery soup
2 envelopes unflavored
  gelatine
1 cup cold water
1 3-ounce package cream
  cheese, softened

1 cup mayonnaise
3 stalks celery,
  chopped
¼ cup onion, chopped
1 7-ounce jar pimientos,
  drained and diced
1 7-ounce can tuna, flaked

Heat undiluted soup. Soften gelatine in cold water. Stir gelatine into soup over low heat until dissolved. Cool. Blend cream cheese into mayonnaise. Toss together celery, onions, pimientos, and tuna. Mix with mayonnaise. Stir in gelatin mixture and pour into lightly oiled 1½ quart mold. Chill until firm.

MRS. CONVILLE HOBGOOD, SR.
St. Francisville, La.

CUCUMBER RING WITH LOBSTER
OR ALASKA KING CRAB

1 large cucumber
1 flat can crushed
   pineapple and the
   juice
1 3-ounce package
   lemon Jello

1 teaspoon plain gelatine
1 heaping tablespoon
   sugar
Juice of one lemon
Paprika
Salt

Soak teaspoon gelatine in ¼ cup cold water. Dissolve Jello in 1 cup boiling water, add plain gelatine and mix. Add all other ingredients and season to taste. Pour into ring mold and refrigerate several hours before unmolding. Fill with lobster or King crab salad and garnish.

SALAD

2 cups crab or lobster
1 cup celery, chopped
4 hard boiled eggs
White pepper and salt

½ cup home made
   mayonnaise
Capers
Lemon pepper Marinade

Mix all together and place in cucumber ring.

MRS. JOHN S. FOX
Monroe, La.

CONGEALED EGG SALAD

2 tablespoons unflavored
   gelatine
¼ cup cold water
½ cup juice from olives
   and gherkins
½ cup small gherkins, cut
½ cup stuffed olives, cut
8 hard cooked eggs, cut

¼ cup lemon juice
½ teaspoon sugar
1½ cups mayonnaise
½ teaspoon salt
   (or more)
Tabasco to taste
Worcestershire
   sauce to taste

Soak gelatine in cold water. Dissolve in hot olive and gherkin liquor. Add all other ingredients and pour into mold to congeal. Serve on lettuce leaves with cold, sliced corn beef, tomatoes, rye bread and ice tea or beer.

MRS. JOE DURRETT
Monroe, La.

CHICKEN AND LOBSTER SALAD

3 cups cooked
　chicken breast
1 cup lobster
　(or crab meat)
French dressing
3 hard boiled eggs

1 cup chopped celery
1 cup mayonnaise
2 tablespoons chili sauce
2 tablespoons chopped
　chives
½ cup whipped cream

Dice chicken and lobster. Marinate in French dressing with chopped egg whites and celery about an hour.

To prepare the dressing mash the egg yolks and blend into the mayonnaise with the chili sauce, chives and a little salt. Fold in whipped cream.

Mix salad with dressing and serve on a bed of lettuce.

MRS. THEODORE L. DANIELSON

LOBSTER AND MACARONI SALAD
Serves 8-10

1 pound shell shape
　macaroni (cooked in
　salt water and
　drained)
1 bunch green onions
　chopped (tops
　included)
3 shredded carrots

1 small bunch parsley,
　chopped fine
1 whole onion, grated
1 can lobster meat
1 can crab meat
1 rib celery, chopped fine
3/4 bottle chili sauce
Almost 1 pint mayonnaise

Mix all ingredients with macaroni. This can be made ahead of time.

MRS. NORMAN S. SAURAGE, JR.

SUNSHINE SALAD
Serves 8-10

1 (3-ounce) package
　orange gelatine
1 (8 3/4-ounce) can
　crushed pineapple
　and juice

1 cup hot orange juice
1 can whole segment
　Mandarin pieces
　(no juice)
3/4 cup sour cream

Dissolve gelatin in hot orange juice. Add other ingredients and mold. Serve with poppy seed dressing or celery seed dressing.

MRS. BERLIN E. PERKINS, JR.

BING CHERRY SALAD I
Serves 18-20

1 No. 2 can Bing cherries, seeded and drained
1 No. 2 can crushed pineapple, drained
2 cups juice and water
1 package black cherry gelatine
1 cup celery, finely cut
1 package raspberry, cherry, or strawberry gelatine
2 bottles Coca-Cola
2 small packages cream cheese
½ cup flaked coconut (optional)
1 cup nuts, chopped

Heat fruit juice to boiling, pour over the gelatine. Stir until dissolved. Add Coca-Colas, chill until slightly thickened. Break up or beat cream cheese and add to nuts and fruits. Fold into gelatine, chill until firm. Amounts of pineapple, cherries, cream cheese and nuts may be varied to taste.

MRS. ROBERT E. BARROW, JR.
St. Francisville, La.

BING CHERRY SALAD II

2 packages cherry gelatine
2 scant cups black bing cherry juice— plus water
Seeded cherries from large can of black bing cherries
2 cups dark port wine
1 cup chopped pecans

Drain cherries, seed and cut in half. Measure juice and add enough water to make 2 scant cups. Heat and pour over gelatine, stirring until completely dissolved. Add 2 cups port wine and when cool add cherries and nuts. Pour in molds or pan and place in refrigerator until jelled. Serve on lettuce with mayonnaise.

MRS. WILLIAM A. GOTSCHALL

CRANBERRY-TOKAY SALAD
Serves 8-10

2 cups raw cranberries, ground
2 cups raw cranberries, halved
1 cup Tokay grapes halved and seeded
1 cup toasted pecans
½ pint whipping cream
2 cups sugar

Day before serving: Prepare cranberries as above; cover with sugar. Do not stir! Refrigerate overnight. Prepare grapes.

Next day: Toast pecans lightly in moderate oven (no salt). Whip cream. Drain cranberries and combine with other ingredients.

MRS. FRANK M. HEROY, JR.

HOLIDAY RIBBON SALAD
Serves 24

2 3-ounce packages
   lime gelatine
1 3-ounce package
   lemon gelatine
½ cup miniature
   marshmallows
1 1-pound 4-ounce can
   crushed pineapple

1 8-ounce package
   cream cheese
1 cup heavy cream
   whipped
1 cup mayonnaise
2 3-ounce packages
   cherry gelatine
1 cup pineapple juice

Water as directed

Dissolve lime gelatine in 2 cups hot water, then add 2 cups cold water. Pour into a 14 X 10 X 2 inch pan. Chill until partly set. Dissolve lemon gelatine in 1 cup hot water in top of double boiler. Add marshmallows, which have been cut in small pieces, and stir to melt. Remove from heat and add 1 cup drained pineapple juice and the cream cheese. Beat until well blended and stir in pineapple. Cool slightly. Fold in whipped cream and mayonnaise. Chill until thickened, then pour this over the lime gelatine. Chill until almost set. Dissolve cherry gelatine in 2 cups of hot water. Add 2 cups of cold water. Chill until syrupy. Pour over pineapple layer. Chill until firm. Colors may be changed by using different flavors of gelatine.

MRS. A. J. ALFIERI

STRAWBERRY SALAD

1 large strawberry
   gelatine
1 cup boiling water
1 tablespoon gelatine
   (dissolve and add
   to gelatine mixture)

1 large package frozen
   strawberries
1 large can crushed
   pineapple
1 cup nuts
3 mashed bananas

1 pint sour cream

Mix all together. Spread half of it in large pyrex dish. Let set a while. Spread 1 pint sour cream over the jello mixture. Let this set a while. Spread remainder of jello mixture over the sour cream, and let set. Good with chicken and ham.

MRS. WM. R. SMITH

FLUFFY ORANGE SALAD

1 3-ounce softened
  cream cheese
1 5-ounce jar pimiento
  cheese spread
1 16-ounce can sliced
  peaches
2 tablespoons mayonnaise

1 11-ounce can Mandarin
  orange sections,
  drained
1 13-ounce can pineapple
  tidbits, drained (1 cup)
1 cup tiny marshmallows
1 cup whipping cream

Beat together cream cheese, cheese spread and mayonnaise. Drain and cut peaches, reserving ¼ cup liquid. Beat reserved syrup into cheese mixture. Fold in fruits and marshmallows. Whip cream and fold into fruit mixture· Chill at least 6 hours, or overnight.

MRS. WILLIAM SLACK

STAINED GLASS SALAD OR DESSERT

1 package (3 ounce)
  lime gelatin
1 package (3 ounce)
  strawberry-banana
  gelatine
1 package (3 ounce)
  raspberry gelatine
3 bananas

2 packages unflavored
  gelatine
1 can (No. 2) drained,
  crushed pineapple
1 cup pineapple juice
¼ cup sugar
1 package black cherry
  gelatine

1 pint whipping cream

To each package of lime, strawberry-banana and black cherry gelatin add ½ package softened * gelatine. Dissolve each flavor separately in 1 cup boiling water· Add to each 3/4 cup cold water. Pour each into a separate square cake pan. Let congeal at room temperature. ** Chill. Cut into ½ inch cubes and store in refrigerator until ready to use. Make syrup of pineapple juice and sugar, pour over raspberry gelatine and ½ package softened gelatine and stir to dissolve. Place in refrigerator until thick but not congealed. Whip cream. Fold in raspberry gelatine. Fold in gelatine cubes, drained crushed pineapple and sliced bananas. Pour into bundt cake pan, angel food cake pan or a 10-cup mold oiled with Lou Ana salad oil.

Variation: Also delicious when omitting pineapple and bananas.

*—To soften gelatine add ¼ cup tap water to each package of unflavored gelatine.

**—By allowing gelatine to congeal at room temperature it will not melt when served.

MRS. GRAHAM O. PEAVY

ORANGE GELATINE MOLD
Serves 8-10

3 small packages orange
  gelatine
2 cups boiling water
1 orange
1 lemon
3 tablespoons sugar
1 teaspoon grated
  lemon rind
1 teaspoon grated
  orange rind
1 teaspoon almond
  extract

4 tablespoons Port
  or Sherry
1 large can grated
  pineapple
1 jar (8-ounce)
  Maraschino cherries
  sliced in 4 parts
¼ cup stuffed olive
  juice water
½ cup stuffed olives
  sliced
½ cup slivered almonds

Pour 2 cups of water over the packages of orange gelatine, add 3 tablespoons sugar, and let stand until cool. Add olive juice water, grated orange and lemon rind. Cut lemon and orange in half and use a sharp knife to remove the segments of each, then squeeze the balance of the juice into the mixture, along with crushed pineapple and juice, sliced cherries and juice, olives and slivered almonds. Add last the almond extract and wine. Pour into well oiled ring mold or individual molds, chill until firm, and serve.

MRS. C. HUBERT BANTA

Meats

SPICY BARBEQUE SAUCE

2 small cans
    tomato sauce
1 cup bacon drippings
½ cup Lou-Ana oil
½ cup water
1 small bottle
    Worcestershire sauce
1 tablespoon Hickory
    Smoke sauce

1 teaspoon black pepper
Red pepper to taste
1 tablespoon salt
1 tablespoon hot sauce
1 teaspoon horseradish
1 teaspoon celery salt
1 lemon—juice and rind
Add garlic and onions
    if desired

1 tablespoon vinegar

Mix all ingredients together and cook over low heat for about 40 minutes. It is a good sauce to broil raw shrimp in and then chill for hors d' oeuvres.

MRS. WILLIAM B. BATES

CHERRY SAUCE FOR HAM

2 cans pitted Bing cherries
2 tablespoons corn starch

¼ cup water
½ cup brown sugar

Juice of one lemon

Mix corn starch in ¼ cup cold water. Heat two cans of cherries, add the corn starch and water mixture and stir in the brown sugar and lemon. Cook, stirring constantly, until thick. Serve hot over hot baked ham.

MRS. CHARLES CROOK

MOLDED MUSTARD DRESSING

1 cup homemade
    mayonnaise
½ pint heavy cream,
    whipped
8 drops Tabasco

1/3 cup prepared
    mustard
1 envelope unflavored
    gelatine
½ teaspoon salt

Dash pepper

Soften gelatine in cold water; stir over low heat until dissolved. Cool. Add mustard and seasoning to mayonnaise. Stir in gelatine. Chill in refrigerator until slightly thickened. Fold in whipped cream and pour into one quart mold. This is excellent with roast beef, ham or chicken. Can be poured in small molds and used as garnish for cold ham, etc.

THE EDITORS

PEPPER STEAK ROAST
Serves 6

1 beef chuck roast (about 3 lbs.) cut about 2 inches thick	2 tablespoons lemon juice
Instant unseasoned meat tenderizer (follow directions on the bottle)	½ cup bottled Italian salad dressing
	1 small box Peppercorns (crack well)

Pierce meat deeply with fork. Mix Italian dressing and lemon juice and pour over meat. Chill. Turn meat several times and marinate for at least 8 hours. When ready to grill, remove meat from marinade, sprinkle meat with tenderizer, crush peppercorn with rolling pin. Place ½ on each side of steak. Place on grill about 6 inches above hot coals, grill turning once, 15 minutes for rare or until done as you like it. Carve into ¼ inch thick slices.

MRS. HEIDEL BROWN

BURGUNDY WINE GRAVY
AND YORKSHIRE PUDDING
FOR STANDING RIB ROAST

6 tablespoons roast beef drippings	Pepper to taste
¼ cup unsifted all purpose flour	2 cans (10½ oz. size) condensed beef bouillon
½ teaspoon salt	½ cup Burgundy wine

Place beef drippings in pan. Stir in flour, salt and pepper to make a smooth mixture, stirring until all the brown bits are dissolved. Bring to a boil, then reduce heat and simmer for about five minutes. Taste for seasoning.

YORKSHIRE PUDDING

1 cup milk	½ teaspoon salt
1 cup all purpose flour (sifted first)	2 tablespoons roast beef drippings

2 whole eggs

In a medium size bowl, beat eggs until fluffy. Add milk. Continue to beat until smooth. Mix flour and salt. Pour egg and milk mixture over the dry ingredients and whip with a spoon until smooth. Pour beef drippings into a 10-inch pyrex plate, tilt around to coat the bottom and sides. Pour in batter and bake 25-30 minutes at 425 degrees. Serve immediately. Serves 6. (Looks like a souffle.)

MRS. ROBERT B. WALLACE

EYE OF THE ROUND ROAST

3 to 4 pound eye of the
  round roast
1 cup chopped left-over
  ham
Salt and pepper
½ cup Lou-Ana oil

1 pod garlic (crushed)
1 tablespoon chopped
  onion
1 can petit pois peas
1 small can mushrooms
  stems and pieces

Slit roast lengthwise to make cavity. Combine garlic, onion and ham. Fill cavity and tie or skewer together. Salt and pepper roast thoroughly and sear well in hot fat in Dutch oven. Add ½ cup water and bake in 250 degree oven until done to taste. Three hours for very well done—2½ hours for medium pink. Add drained peas and mushrooms 20 minutes before roast is done. Slice roast fairly thin on platter. Spoon a serving of peas and mushrooms over each slice, garnish and serve.

MRS. CHARLES GARRETSON
Monroe, Louisiana

SAUERBRATEN
Serves 6

4 pounds rump of beef
Salt and pepper to taste
Flour
2 tablespoons shortening
2 onions
½ cup vinegar
1 cup water

2 tablespoons lemon juice
  (fresh, frozen, or
  canned)
3 bay leaves
3 whole cloves
2 tablespoons catsup
6 ginger snaps

Sprinkle meat with salt, pepper and flour. Brown the surfaces in heated shortening. Add sliced onions, vinegar, and all remaining ingredients except ginger snaps. Cook to a boil, then reduce heat, cover tightly and cook slowly for 2½ to 3 hours, or until beef is tender when tested with a fork. During the last 30 minutes of cooking, stir crumbled ginger snaps into gravy. Cut meat in slices. Serve with gravy. This goes well with rice, potatoes, or noodles. It has lots of gravy.

MRS. RUDOLPH E. KRAUSE
Lake Charles, La.

SLOW ROASTING

For a delicious taste treat, convenience and variety, try slow roasting:

Brush tender cut beef roast with oil and place on rack in pan and place in an oven 150 degrees F. and allow it to remain for 24 hours. Salt and pepper roast during the last hours of cooking. Garlic or other seasoning may be added to the oil with which the roast is brushed, if desired. Meat will be juicy and tender and slice beautifully. This roast will be medium rare. For well done roast and less tender cuts, set thermometer at 160 degrees F.

Pork, veal, tenderized ham or home-cured ham, venison, lamb, chicken and turkey may be cooked in the same manner using the following temperatures:

Hen 185 degrees
Duck, young 185 degrees
Goose, young 185 degrees
Ham,
    home cured 170 degrees
Ham,
    tenderized 155 degrees
Lamb 160 degrees
Pork 170 degrees
Turkey 185 degrees
Veal 185 degrees
Venison—may be treated
    much the same as beef

Turkey may be stuffed during last few hours of cooking. Cavity, meantime, may be filled with seasoning of your choice, such as onion, celery etc.

MRS. MELVIN D. ROBINSON

POT ROAST

1 top sirloin or top round roast	1/3 cup red wine
1 large onion	Salt and pepper to taste
½ cup water	Flour, garlic & Lou-Ana oil

Stuff roast with garlic, then rub roast generously with salt and pepper, then flour. Cover bottom of Dutch oven with small amount of fat, then brown roast on all sides. Add water and wine, cover, and cook about 30 minutes to the pound If necessary, add water and wine when needed.

MRS. J. W. ANDREE

LOUISIANA GOVERNORS' STEAK
(As prepared by Jesse Anderson for eight former governors in the mansion in Baton Rouge, Louisiana)

Into an iron skillet drop a piece of fat cut from the steak about the size of an almond and with the tines of a fork, grease the entire surface of the skillet. Turn heat on high and heat to smoking point. Place steak— either T-bone or sirloin or porterhouse— on skillet unsalted, and immediately place an old fashioned flat iron (can be bought in antique stores) on steak. This weight causes the brown, crisp, delicious seal which prevents juices from escaping. In one or two minutes, when brown, turn steak and replace iron to seal other side. Turn fire down to medium. Cook several minutes and turn once more, using your own timing according to whether you prefer rare, medium, or well done meat. Remove to hot plate and salt. Then place a slice of butter on steak and sprinkle with chopped parsley, adding freshly ground black pepper, if desired. Serve immediately.

Note: I find that the best buy in the meat department is porterhouse steak because it will serve two— the filet for the lady and the sirloin strip for the man of the house!

MRS. SAM H. JONES
Lake Charles, La.

BEEF TENDERLOIN (MARINADE)

1 beef tenderloin	½ cup Worcestershire
Lou Ana oil	sauce
½ cup soy sauce	¼ cup lemon juice
Sliced onions	Pepper

Rub beef tenderloin on all sides with oil and cover top with sliced onions. Place in marinade made of remaining ingredients. Cook 45 minutes to an hour in 350 degrees oven, turning several times, and basting with marinade.

MRS. ANDREW P. GAY
Plaquemine, La.

BARBECUE ROAST BEEF

Barbecue sauce:
1 medium onion chopped
2 tablespoons vinegar
1 tablespoon prepared
    mustard
2 teaspoons sugar

2 teaspoon dry mustard
1 teaspoon chili powder
½ teaspoon salt
½ teaspoon paprika
Few drops Tabasco
3/4 cup ketchup

¼ cup water

Put in sauce pan and simmer 5 minutes. A 5-pound "Eye of Round" or your choice cut. Marinate the roast in the sauce for 48 hours, turning often, and keep in refrigerator. Wipe meat dry and brown in small amount of fat on all sides, in an open roast on top of stove to seal juices in. Pour over the marinade, and cover. Start in cold oven at 325 degrees, cook for 2½ hours. Serve hot or cold.

MRS. MARVIN STUCKEY

STEAK IN WINE
Serves 3

1 pound sirloin steak
½ stick butter
1 teaspoon black pepper

1 teaspoon salt
1 cup red wine
    (any kind)

1 medium onion

Cut steak in bite size pieces. Chop onion very fine. Saute steak and onion until brown. Add wine. Cook on high heat 20 minutes and serve. (Leftover steak is also good to use in this recipe.)

MRS. WILLIAM T. BAYNARD

GRILLADES

1 veal round, thinly sliced
    (about 1½ pounds)
1 medium onion, chopped
3 or 4 pods garlic,
    chopped very fine

2 tablespoons parsley,
    minced
1 small green pepper
1 1-pound can whole
    tomatoes

Salt and pepper to taste

Brown meat in small amount of Lou-Ana oil. Remove meat and cook onions, pepper and add garlic last, since it cooks faster. Do not brown. Return meat to skillet, add tomatoes, salt and pepper, and enough water to cover meat. Simmer, tightly covered, until tender.

Good with grits for breakfast, or rice for lunch or dinner

From the files of:
MRS. MARGUERITE ANDREE
New Orleans, La.

DAUBE GLACÉ

10 pounds beef round or boneless chuck
1½ cups pepper vinegar
¼ cup cooking oil
6 small-medium onions, quartered
2 stalks celery with tops
6 carrots, halved
4 bay leaves
Pinch thyme

Salt, pepper, cayenne to taste
4 oz. sherry wine
3 packages gelatine (unflavored)
4 hard boiled eggs, sliced
2 lemons, sliced
Horseradish sauce:
½ pint whipped cream with wet horseradish to taste, folded in.

1 dozen cloves

Put daube in pan and pour pepper vinegar over it. Salt to taste and allow to soak overnight or up to 24 hours, turning once. Drain meat, reserving marinade and brown in cooking oil in large pot. Cover with water (add beef bouillon cube if boneless roast is used), add onions, carrots, celery, bay leaves, thyme, cloves, black pepper, cayenne and pepper vinegar marinade. Simmer 4-5 hours, or until meat is tender, on top of stove. Remove meat, strain liquid and measure. Three pints of liquid are necessary for a 10 pound roast. If too much, reduce by boiling down. If too little add water. Then add sherry, bring to boil and add gelatin, pre softened, in small amount of water. Taste for correct seasoning of salt and red pepper.

Remove all fat, bone, tendons from meat and break into chunk size pieces. Meat should be so tender that knife is hardly necessary.

In bottom of large mold (vegetable crisper of refrigerator is right size) arrange sliced hard boiled eggs and lemon slices, place meat evenly over surface, pour liquid gently over whole and jell in refrigerator. Any grease in liquid will rise to top and can be easily removed when firm. Unmold onto large platter, decorate with parsley or other greens and serve with horseradish sauce in side dish.

MRS. GORDON KEAN

HUNGARIAN VEAL CHOPS
Serves 4

4 veal chops 1 to 1½ inch thick
Salt & pepper
2 tablespoons olive or or Lou Ana oil
¼ cup chopped onions

½ cup sliced raw carrots
1 cup fresh tomatoes or sliced canned
1/3 cup dry sherry
1 cup sliced mushrooms
2 tablespoons butter

1 tablespoon parsley

Sprinkle chops with salt & pepper, brown in oil with onions, add carrots, tomatoes and sherry. Cover and simmer slowly for 1 hour. Saute mushrooms in butter and add parsley to chops. Cook another 5 minutes and serve with a green vegetable dressed with butter and Parmesan cheese.

MRS. BENTON HARELSON

ROAST LEG OF LAMB
Serves 12

1 small (5 lb.) leg of lamb, trimmed
3 tablespoons lemon juice
2 cloves garlic, minced
½ cup dry Vermouth

1 tablespoon curry powder
2 teaspoons salt
¼ teaspoon pepper
2 onions sliced

Sprinkle the lamb with the lemon juice. Mix the garlic, curry, salt and pepper to a paste; rub into the lamb. (If possible, season the day before the lamb is to be roasted. Fasten it up in a plastic bag so the curry odor won't be all in your refrigerator). Place leg in a roasting pan; arrange onions around it. Roast in a 400 degree oven for 30 minutes. Drain off fat. Add Vermouth, reduce heat to 350 degrees. Roast 1½ hours longer or until lamb is tender, basting frequently. Add a little water when needed. Serve hot.

MRS. HARRY M. BRIAN
Rayville, La.

ROSEMARY LEG OF LAMB
Serves 12

6 or 7 pound leg of lamb
3 garlic cloves
3 teaspoons dried rosemary
2 tablespoons olive oil

½ teaspoon salt
¼ cup finely chopped parsley or dried parsley flakes

Finely chop and mash garlic (garlic press does nicely.) Mix garlic, salt, parsley, rosemary and oil. With small sharp knife, make 6 or 7 incisions in the heaviest section of the meat. Into these incisions press the garlic, rosemary, parsley mixture. Spread remaining mixture over surface of meat. Sprinkle entire roast with salt and black pepper.

Roast the lamb in a moderately slow oven (325 degrees) basting frequently with water or light stock, for 2½ hours, or until the meat is tender but still faintly pink inside. If you don't want it to be pink, cook it 3 hours. Remove meat to heated platter and garnish with fresh parsely.

MRS. WARREN MUNSON

CURRY SAUCE FOR LAMB
Serves 6-8

3 pounds lamb shoulder	¼ cup Lou-Ana corn oil
2 tablespoons minced onion	¼ cup chicken broth
2 tablespoons curry powder	¼ cup dry, white wine
	1 teaspoon salt

Tabasco to taste

Cut lamb into cubes, place on skewers and broil 15-20 minutes. Fresh mushrooms and green peppers may be used alternately with lamb on skewers. Baste with sauce and serve over cracked wheat or brown rice cooked with ½ stick of butter added to water. This precludes the need for a gravy.

THE EDITORS

ORANGE-CURRY PORK ROAST

4-6 pound pork loin roast	2 cans frozen orange juice. Add 1 cup water for each can.
Unpeeled oranges cut in wedges	
	4 tablespoons soy sauce
Sauce:	2 tablespoons curry powder
2 tablespoons salad oil	

Have butcher loosen backbone from ribs but leave attached. Cut chops to within one inch of backbone in 1 to 1¼ in. chops. In each slit insert a wedge of orange, peel side out. Insert meat thermometer. Bake in oven at 350 degrees. Baste with sauce every 15 minutes.

MRS. R. O. RUSH

GRILLED PORK LOIN

5-7 pound pork loin	2 tablespoons minced
¼ cup Lou-Ana	green onions
corn oil	2 teaspoons chili
½ cup orange juice	powder
2 tablespoons	2 teaspoons grated
minced onion	orange rind
Tabasco to taste	2 teaspoons salt

Buy rib end of loin and place on spit so it will balance. Rotate on low fire 35-40 minutes per pound. Baste with sauce as it cooks.

THE EDITORS

PORK CHOP MAJESTIC

6 center cut pork chops	1 cup boiling water
with filets—3/4	2 large onions, sliced in
inch thick	thin rings
Seasoned bread crumbs	6 tablespoons sherry
1 chicken bouillon cube	¼ cup soy sauce

1 tablespoon sugar

Sprinkle garlic salt on pork chops, coat them with seasoned bread crumbs and brown in bacon fat in skillet. Dissolve bouillon cube in boiling water and add to chops, along with the other ingredients. **Simmer** covered for an hour, turning once. If desired, thicken sauce with a little flour before serving with rice.

MRS. LYTTLETON T. HARRIS

DELICIOUS PORK CHOPS

6 pork chops, one	1 tablespoon chopped
inch thick	fresh dill or
Salt and pepper to taste	1 teaspoon dried
1 tablespoon (or more)	dill seed
chopped onion	1½ cups sour cream

1 tablespoon melted butter

Saute chops in melted butter until brown and tender. Season with salt and pepper and sprinkle with onion. Cook until onion is soft and done. Remove chops to a hot platter—Add dill and sour cream to the pan and blend thoroughly. Heat well but do not boil. Serve sauce over chops.

MRS. DEAN MOSELY

PORK PACQUET

6 pork chops (lean)   Onions
Raw rice   Bell peppers
           Fresh tomatoes

Brown pork chops and season with salt and pepper. Place each pork chop on square of double aluminum foil, top with ring of bell pepper. Fill bell pepper ring with uncooked rice, top with tomato and onion slices. Season again lightly with salt and pepper. Seal individual servings tightly in foil and bake at 325 degrees for 1½ hours. A meal in a pacquet.

MRS. CHARLES P. MANSHIP JR.

HAM CROQUETTES

2 cups ground or finely chopped lean baked ham
3 chopped green onions
1 small can chopped mushrooms (coarsely)
2 eggs slightly beaten with two teaspoons milk or water

2 teasp. prepared mustard
Cracker crumbs
1 cup thick white sauce, made as follows:
3 tablespoons butter or oleo
4 tablespoons flour
1 cup milk
NO SALT—Ham is salty

Melt butter and smooth flour in at low heat. Gradually add milk, stirring constantly till thick and smooth. Cook long enough to lose the taste of raw flour.

Mix ham, onions, mustard and mushrooms well, add most of the white sauce and blend well. Add more white sauce, but no more than is necessary to bind it together. Press the mixture down on a platter and let stand in refrigerator for at least two hours.

When nearly ready for dinner, shape mixture into individual croquettes, (egg shape), roll in cracker crumbs, then in the egg mixture, then in the cracker crumbs again. Drop in two inches of hot fat and fry to a golden brown, then drain on paper towels.

Salmon croquettes may be made with this recipe but omit mustard and add salt to taste. Be sure to remove the skin and bones from cheaper brands of salmon.

MRS. ROBERT BARRY

SWEET AND SOUR SPARE RIBS

4 or 5 pounds spare ribs   Soy sauce

Brush ribs with soy sauce and bake in medium oven until brown and crisp—about 1 hour and 15 minutes. Cut into serving portions and put on platter with the following:

SAUCE

1 cup sugar	3 tablespoons soy sauce
1 cup vinegar	1 green pepper sliced
1 tablespoon corn starch	in thin strips

Bring to a boil and add the corn starch mixed with a little cold water, stirring until thick and transparent. Serve over rice.

MRS. GEORGE LOCK PARET
Lake Charles, La.

HAM BAKED IN DOUGH

Use any ham—whole, half, canned, boneless or bone in.

4 cups flour	2 tablespoons dried
1 cup brown sugar	mustard
2 tablespoons ground	1 teaspoon black pepper
cloves	Pickle juice, apple cider
2 tablespoons cinnamon	or pineapple juice

Add enough juice to dry ingredients to make dough that can be floured and rolled. Cover fat part of ham with rolled dough. Put in a cold oven and bake at 325 degrees, 20 minutes per pound. Baste every 20 or 30 minutes. Remove dough to cut and serve. This is especially good served hot.

MRS. C. J. FREELAND
Crowley, La.

VEAL BIRDS

Veal cutlets	Egg
Package of herb dressing	Golden mushroom soup
Green onions	Cooking oil or bacon fat
Salt and pepper	

Add hot water, egg and chopped green onions to dry herb dressing to moist consistency. Season veal cutlets both sides. Place generous amount of dressing in center of each cutlet, fold cutlet over dressing and tie with string. Brown stuffed cutlets in fat in heavy skillet or dutch oven, add 1 can Golden Mushroom Soup undiluted. Cover and simmer for 1¼ hours or until very tender. Pour the gravy over veal birds when serving.

MRS. FRANK JONES

HAM ROLLS IN SOUR CREAM SAUCE

2 cans cream of
  mushroom soup
2 cups creamed cottage
  cheese, sieved
½ cup finely chopped
  green onion
1 teaspoon dry mustard

½ teaspoon salt
1 pint sour cream
2 eggs, slightly beaten
1 package chopped
  spinach, cooked and
  drained
24 slices cooked ham

Combine soup and half of sour cream in bowl. Set aside for sauce. Combine remaining sour cream and onions, cottage cheese, eggs, spinach, mustard, salt. Mix well. Spoon about 2 tablespoons on each slice of ham. Roll up. Place in shallow baking dish. Cover with sour cream sauce. Bake at 350 degrees for 25-30 minutes.

MRS. GEORGE WALKER, SR.
Monroe, La.

MEAT LOAF
Serves 6-8

1½ pounds ground beef
1 cup seasoned Italian
  bread crumbs
1 package dry
  onion soup
1 egg slightly beaten
2 tablespoons
  parsley flakes
1 can cream of celery soup

1 cup grated
  Romano cheese
2 tablespoons
  Worcestershire sauce
½ to 3/4 cup milk
  (enough to make
  mixture soft enough
  to shape into loaf)
Dash of Tabasco

Mix all ingredients well, shape into loaf. Place in pan and bake in preheated 350 degree oven for about 30 minutes. Mix together ¼ cup of milk, 1 tablespoon parsley flakes, and 1 can "Cream of Celery" soup. Pour this sauce over meat loaf and continue cooking approximately another 60 minutes.

MRS. ROBERT E. BARROW, JR.
St. Francisville, La.

PARMESAN CHEESE MEAT LOAF
Serves 4

½ to 3/4 pound ground
   chuck or shoulder
1 teaspoon salt
1 teaspoon Accent
½ teaspoon black pepper
1/3 cup finely chopped
   onion
1 teaspoon Worcestershire
   sauce

1 beaten egg
1 medium size ripe
   tomato (finely
   chopped)
2 or three tablespoons
   grated Parmesan
   cheese
Finely crushed
   cracker crumbs

Mix all ingredients well, using enough cracker crumbs to make mixture of good consistency to handle and shape into a loaf. Bake in a 350 degree oven for about 45 minutes.

MRS. BEN BOGARD
Ruston, La.

STUFFED HAM

1 well shaped lean ham
1 teaspoon pepper
1 teaspoon allspice
1 teaspoon celery seed
1/3 cup ham juice
1 teaspoon cinnamon

1 cup onions
   chopped fine
Pinch of mustard
½ stick butter
1 quart stale biscuit
   crumbs ground up

½ teaspoon cloves

Have butcher remove bone from ham. Wash thoroughly and tie with string before boiling several hours until well cooked. Set off fire and let cool in water in which it was boiled. When cooled, untie, and stuff with above ingredients which have been mixed. If necessary, soften dressing with a little vinegar. Retie and bake in slow oven until light brown. When cold, remove strings and slice.

JEWELL MOORE

DAUBED HAM

1 12 to 18 pound
   fresh ham
1 large onion
1 bell pepper
4 tender pieces
   of celery

½ cup parsley
1 teaspoon black pepper
½ teaspoon red pepper
2 well beaten eggs
2 cups bread crumbs
1 tablespoon salt

Steam a 12 to 18 pound fresh ham in salted water with an onion until almost done. Remove skin. With a sharp knife cut out cones 2 inches deep and 1 inch in diameter, leaving about 1 inch between cones. Put removed ham through a food chopper with the remaining ingredients (except bread crumbs). Moisten two cups bread crumbs with ham broth. Add all ingredients and mix well. Stuff in hollowed out places. Stick allspice in spaces between dressing. Place in roaster and bake, adding enough broth to keep moist. Bake slowly about 1½ hours or until brown. Serve hot or cold with "chow chow".

Mrs. D. O. Willis
St. Francisville, La.

KIDNEY STEW

2 pounds baby beef or
    calf kidneys (must
    be bright red—
    not dark)
1 large dry onion
    chopped fine

½ cup fresh bell pepper,
    or ½ package of
    frozen bell pepper
1 teaspoon salt
½ teaspoon lemon pepper
1 teaspoon garlic powder

1 tablespoon butter

Cut kidneys into small pieces, discarding all fat. Saute finely chopped onion and bell pepper until soft. Add chopped kidney, turn fire very low under tightly covered pot and cook slowly until tender—about 2 hours or more. Freezes well.

Mrs. Henry George Mc Mahon

FILET GOULASH
Serves 8

4 beef filet steaks
1 stick butter
2 onions, sliced
6 peeled, fresh tomatoes
Salt and pepper to taste

1 pint box fresh, sliced
    small mushrooms
1 large green pepper,
    sliced fine
1 pod garlic, chopped fine

Paprika

Slice filets in thin, ribbon-like slices. Brown in butter and add other ingredients. Cook in skillet on top of stove, add small amount of water and do not cook very long. Serve over rice.

Mrs. George Lock Paret
Lake Charles, La.

GREEK STEW
Serves 6

3 pounds beef stew
   meat cut into 1½
   inch cubes
Salt and freshly ground
   black pepper
½ cup butter
2½ pounds small, peeled
   onions (size of golf
   balls)
1 can (6 ounce)
   tomato paste

1/3 cup red table wine
   (preferably Burgundy)
2 tablespoons red wine
   vinegar
1 clove garlic, minced
1 bay leaf
1 small cinnamon stick
½ teaspoon whole cloves
¼ teaspoon ground cumin
2 tablespoons ground
   raisins

1 tablespoon brown sugar

Season meat with salt and pepper. Melt butter in iron Dutch oven or heavy kettle with cover. Add meat and coat with butter but do not brown. Arrange onions carefully over meat. Mix together the tomato paste, wine, vinegar, sugar and garlic. Pour over meat and onions. Add bay leaf, cinnamon, cloves, cumin and raisins. Cover onions with a plate to hold them in tact. Cover kettle and simmer for 3 hours. Do not open pot or stir. As you serve the stew, stir the sauce gently to blend. Serve with sesame seed bread (should be "sopped" in the sauce), green salad and a red wine.

MRS. HEIDEL BROWN

BARBECUED BITS A LA SANTA FE
Serves 6-8

1 clove garlic,
   finely minced
½ cup Lou-Ana oil
½ cup catsup
¼ cup lemon juice
1 tablespoon vinegar
½ teaspoon salt
¼ teaspoon black pepper
½ cup onions,
   finely chopped

½ teaspoon oregano
½ teaspoon prepared
   mustard
½ cup bottled barbecue
   sauce, milk type
2 teaspoons meat
   tenderizer
3 to 4 pounds boneless
   meat, cut into 1½
   inch cubes

Mix all ingredients except meat. Simmer over low heat for 10 minutes. Cool. Put meat in shallow pan and cover with cooled sauce. Cover pan and let marinate in refrigerator at least 6 hours. Remove meat from pan, place on skewers and broil over charcoal about 15 or 20 minutes. Turn meat every 2 or 3 minutes, basting occasionally.

If you like, alternate the meat on skewers with onions, green peppers or squash·

MRS. JACK CLAYWORTH,
Santa Fe, New Mexico

SEVEN-HOUR STEW

4 pounds boneless
   beef brisket
1 cup Burgundy
1½ cups water
6 tablespoons minute
   tapioca
2 small bunches carrots
   (scraped)
3 bay leaves

2 large onions, chopped
1 can tomato sauce and
1 can water
1 bunch green onions,
   chopped
Salt and red pepper
   to taste
1 rounded tablespoon
   brown sugar

Cut beef into desired sizes; bite-size pieces are nice. Put everything except carrots in a Dutch oven. Cover tightly· Bake in oven for 30 minutes at 350 degrees. Lower oven to 250 degrees and bake 7 hours. Add carrots last hour of cooking. This stew freezes well. Just reheat. It must cook 7 hours originally to be browned correctly.

GERTRUDE STANTON
Crowley, La.

MEAT PIE

1 tablespoon Lou-Ana oil
2 tablespoons flour
1 pound ground
   beef chuck
1 pound ground pork
Salt and pepper to taste

6 green onions chopped
3 tablespoons
   chopped parsley
½ teaspoon
   Worcestershire sauce
Dash of Tabasco

Make a roux of flour and oil, add other ingredients, and cook thoroughly. Let cool before placing in pie dough. You may make your own favorite pie dough or use the frozen ones—1 for the bottom and 1 for the top. Punch holes in the top shell or dough. Bake in preheated 400 degree oven for 30 or 40 minutes, or until golden brown.

MRS. RATCLIFFE ANDERSON

GOULASH
Serves 4

1 pound veal and	Salt to taste
1 pound beef	1 teaspoon paprika
1 onion	1 cup strained tomatoes

12 very small potatoes

Cut veal and beef into one inch squares and brown in hot fat with onion. Salt to taste and add paprika. To browned meat add drained tomatoes. Simmer until tender. Half an hour before serving, add very small potatoes. If goulash gets too thick, add juice from tomatoes.

MRS. HUGH A. NEAL

MOCK CHOW MEIN

2 tablespoons Lou-Ana oil	2 chicken bouillon cubes
½ garlic pod minced	1 large green pepper diced
2 cups, or more, left over roast pork and a little gravy	1½ cups celery diced
	2 tablespoon cornstarch
½ cup chopped onion	2 teaspoons soy sauce
	2 cups water

In shortening, cook onions and garlic until soft. Add pork roast cut into small pieces. Mix 2 chicken boullion cubes in boiling water, cook for a few minutes, then add to pork. Then add green pepper and celery. Cover and cook slowly for a little while. Mix cornstarch and soy sauce (or Worcestershire) in ¼ cup cold water. Add to meat and cover, cook until thickened, and season to taste. Serve over hot noodles.

MRS. RICHARD MORNHINVEG

BARBECUED BEEF TURNOVERS
Serves 6

Make a 2 crust recipe for pastry and store in refrigerator while making this sauce.

3 cloves of garlic	½ teaspoon dry mustard
½ green pepper	½ cup catsup
1 small onion	½ cup cold water
2 tablespoons butter	2 tablespoons vinegar
2 tablespoons brown sugar	2 teaspoons Worcestershire sauce
2 cups chopped leftover roast beef	¼ teaspoon black pepper

½ teaspoon Tabasco

Chop garlic, pepper and onion finely and cook in

skillet with melted butter until wilted. Add remaining ingredients and cook slowly for 15 minutes. Put 2 cups chopped leftover roast beef in bowl and add enough sauce to moisten well. Preheat oven to 400 degrees. Roll pastry on floured board to thickness 1/8 inch. Cut into 9 inch squares and put mound of filling in center of each. Brush edges with water, then fold into triangles and seal edges together with a fork. Bake on cookie sheet for 15 to 20 minutes or until browned. Serve with remaining sauce over top.

(This is an excellent way to use up left over roast beef).

MRS. ROY A. WALLACE

ENGLISH STEAK AND KIDNEY PIE

3 pounds round steak
1 large kidney
1 large onion

Flour for dipping
Salt and pepper to taste
Cold stock or brown gravy

Trim fat from meat. Skin and core kidney. Cut meat and kidney into small pieces. Dip in flour seasoned with salt and pepper. Lay lightly in deep 3 quart baking dish. Add sliced onion and half fiill with stock or gravy.

RUFF-PUFF PASTRY

4 cups flour
3/4 cup lard
3/4 cup oleomargarine

1 teaspoon salt
3/4 cup cold water
1 egg

Sift flour and salt in bowl. Add shortening in pieces the size of a small marble. Gently toss to a fine paste with cold water. Turn onto floured board and press into oblong shape. Roll in one direction only. Fold in thirds. Seal edges by pressing lightly. Half turn. Repeat until there have been three turns, then double over and roll out a little larger than baking dish. Wet rim of dish. Cut off strips of pastry the width of rim and lay on rim. Wet again and cover with pastry. Trim and mark edges. Cut hole in center. Brush lightly with beaten egg. Roll out trimmings and decorate top. Bake in 450 degree oven for 15 minutes. Reduce heat to 350 degrees and cook for an additional hour.

MRS. MAXWELL SIMMONDS

DRY HASH

1 pint chopped,
    cooked meat
	½ teaspoon garlic salt
	    or 3 pods of dry garlic

1 pint chopped, boiled potatoes	2 teaspoons salt 5 tablespoons butter
½ pint broth	1 large onion
1 teaspoon Creole herb blend	Red Pepper to taste Green onions & parsley

Chop onions fine and saute in butter. Add meat, then all other ingredients. Put in pyrex baking dish and bake in moderate oven for about 1 hour.

MRS. OMER HEBERT
Plaquemine, La.

STUFFED TUFOLI
(Italian)

TOMATO SAUCE

1 cup chopped onions	1 cup beef stock
2 cloves garlic	or water
1½ tablespoons olive oil	3 tablespoons tomato paste
1 can (#303) Italian style tomatoes	1 bay leaf ¼ tablespoon salt
¼ teaspoon oregano	1/8 teaspoon pepper

Saute onions and garlic in olive oil on low burner until golden, stirring frequently. Add tomatoes, beef stock, tomato paste, bay leaf, salt and pepper. Simmer uncovered for 2 hours adding water if necessary. Add oregano and simmer 15 minutes. (about 2½ cup yield)

STUFFING

1 large green pepper,
    minced
	1 cup grated
	    Parmesan cheese

1 stalk celery, minced	¼ cup minced parsley
4 cloves garlic, minced	2 hard-cooked eggs,
¼ cup olive oil	minced
½ pound ground beef	1 cup bread crumbs
1/3 pound ground lean pork	2 eggs well beaten 1½ teaspoons oregano

1 package (10 oz.)
    frozen chopped
    spinach, thawed
	Salt and pepper
	12 ounces tufoli
	    (size 29)

1 large onion, minced

Saute onion, pepper, celery, and garlic in olive oil until tender; add ground beef and pork. Cook, stirring constantly, until lightly browned. Add spinach, cheese, parsley, and hard-cooked eggs. Continue cooking until meat is brown and mixture is well blended. Add bread crumbs, eggs, and oregano. Season with salt and pepper. Cook until mixture is firm.

Cook tufoli in boiling water (salted) about 12 minutes, or until tender, but firm, drain. Stuff with meat mixture and arrange in baking dish. Cover with tomato sauce and bake in 350 degree oven for 20 minutes. Yield: approximately 42 stuffed tufoli.

MRS. GILBERT MUNSON

BEEF AND GREEN PEPPERS

1 pound beef shredded	2 cups green peppers chopped
2 tablespoons soy sauce	1 teaspoon salt
Dash of black pepper	1 teaspoon monosodium glutamate
3 or four cloves garlic	
2 teaspoons corn starch	½ cup Lou-Ana oil
1 tablespoon wine	2 teaspoons soy sauce
1 tablespoon sesame oil	

In ¼ cup oil, stir fry green peppers, 2 teaspoons soy sauce, Accent, salt for two minutes. Remove to plate. In the other ¼ cup oil, stir-fry beef, 2 tablespoons soy sauce, pepper, garlic, corn starch, wine and sesame oil, until meat is done. Add green pepper mixture, mix well, and serve with rice or fried noodles.

MRS. MARVIN STUCKEY

PICKLED CORN BEEF

3 pound piece of plain corn beef	4 stalks celery
1 large onion	1 teaspoon whole black pepper corns
3 teaspoons pickling spice	

Cover corn beef with cold water and bring to a brisk boil, then pour off water, cover again with cold water and add onions, celery, pepper and spices. Cook slowly until tender. Let cool completely in the water in which it was cooked. Chill thoroughly, slice and serve. This is a marvelous football menu compliment. Serve with rye bread and dry mustard preparation.

MRS. HENRY GEORGE McMAHON

CANADIAN HAMBURGER PIE
Serves 6

1 package (10 oz.)
pastry mix
½ cup grated sharp
Cheddar cheese
½ teaspoon paprika
Dash of cayenne
1½ pounds beef chuck,
ground
1 small onion, minced

1 can (10½ oz.) beef
bouillon or consommé
½ teaspoon salt
½ teaspoon pepper
¼ teaspoon each of
ground thyme and
marjoram
2 teaspoons
Worcestershire sauce

1½ cups dry bread cubes

Prepare pastry mix as directed on the label, adding cheese, paprika and cayenne before adding the liquid. Roll half of pastry on lightly floured board; fit into 9-inch pie pan. Cook beef and onion in skillet until meat loses its red color, breaking up meat with fork. Mix bread cubes and bouillon and let stand for a few minutes. Add beef mixture and remaining ingredients. Mix well and pour into pastry-lined pan. Roll remaining pastry and put over top, crimping edges. Bake in preheated moderate oven (375 degrees F.) for about 45 minutes.

MRS. WALTON F. HALPHEN

GALUBTSI (STUFFED CABBAGE ROLLS)

Large cabbage leaves
1 pound ground round
or chuck
1 onion, chopped

1 cup bread crumbs
4 tablespoons bacon fat
1 cup sour cream
Salt and pepper to taste

¼ cup water

Wilt cabbage leaves by covering them with boiling water. Let stand several minutes, then drain leaves. Mix ground meat with the onion and bread crumbs and season to taste. Place a spoonful of the mixture on each leaf, roll and tie with a string, making a bow in order to untie easily. Saute the cabbage rolls in bacon fat, turning to brown. Add ¼ cup water (more as needed), cover and steam until meat is done, about 20 minutes. Add sour cream, stirring carefully, and cook 5 minutes longer. Sprinkle with freshly ground black pepper. Serve piping hot with sauce over rolls.

MRS. LAUREN C. POST
San Diego, Calif.

This is a recipe from Mrs. Post's family in Vladivostok, Russia.

BEEF, SOUR CREAM AND NOODLE CASSEROLE
Serves 6

1 pound round steak, ground
1 tablespoon butter
1 teaspoon salt
1/8 teaspoon pepper
1/4 teaspoon garlic salt
1 can (8 oz.) tomato sauce
1 cup creamed cottage cheese
1 cup sour cream
1/2 cup chopped green onions
1 package noodles (403)
1 cup sharp cheese, grated

Cook meat in butter 5 minutes. Add seasonings and tomato sauce and simmer 5 minutes. Cook and drain noodles. Combine cottage cheese, sour cream, onions and noodles in bowl. Place 1/2 of noodle mixture into greased baking dish. Cover with meat. Top with remaining noodle mixture and sprinkle cheese over casserole. Bake in 350 degree oven for 20 minutes.

MRS. E. S. CROFT, III
Shreveport, La.

MEXICAN CORNBREAD CASSEROLE

2 pounds ground beef & pork
2¼ cups Rotel or hot tomatoes
4 ounce can of tomato purée and 1 pound grated sharp cheese
3 onions chopped fine

Salt and pepper to taste

Brown meat, add onions, Rotel, salt and pepper. Cook until all liquid is absorbed. Add tomato puree and set aside.

CORN BREAD MIXTURE

3 cups yellow cornmeal
2 cups yellow cream style corn
1½ teaspoon salt
1 teaspoon soda
4 eggs
2 cups buttermilk
1/3 cup Lou Ana oil

Mix all together and pour half the batter in an 11-inch iron skillet. Spread meat mixture next and then sprinkle with grated cheese. Pour rest of the batter on top, heat oven to 375 degrees and bake for 45 minutes.

MRS. HENRY GUERRIERO
Monroe, La.

SWEETBREADS

1 pair sweetbreads	1 teaspoon seasoned salt
½ stick butter	2 tablespoons minced
2 tablespoons flour	parsley
1 small green onion	1½ teaspoons basil (1
2 tablespoons tender	teaspoon fresh basil)
celery leaves	½ cup white wine

Sweetbreads, being very perishable, must be real fresh. Cover with very cold, salted water and let soak for about an hour. Drain and again cover with cold, salted water, bring to a boil, drain, cool and remove sinews. Saute onions and celery, chopped very fine, in 2 tablespoons butter. Make a roux with flour and remaining butter; add onion and celery mixture, herbs, salt and wine. Add sweetbreads, cover tightly, and let cook gently for 20 to 30 minutes. Garnish with parsley. Mushrooms may be added, if desired.

THE EDITORS

SWEETBREADS WITH MUSHROOMS

2 tablespoons butter	½ cup cream
1½ cups blanched	3/4 cup chicken stock
sweetbreads	¼ teaspoon salt
½ cup fresh mushrooms	¼ teaspoon paprika
2 tablespoons butter	1 egg yolk
2 tablespoons flour	¼ cup sherry

Cut sweetbreads and mushrooms into small pieces and sauté in 2 tablespoons butter. Make a cream sauce of butter, flour, cream, chicken stock, salt and paprika. Add beaten egg yolk and sherry, combine sauce and sweetbreads. Serve in patty shells or on toast.

MRS. E. S. GIRAULT

TO BLANCHE SWEETBREADS

Soak sweetbreads in cold water 1 hour, changing water once or twice. Drain and add 1 teaspoon salt, 1 tablespoon lemon or vinegar, 2 cloves, 2 pepper corns, sprig of parsley and ½ bay leaf. Simmer for 20 minutes. Cover with cold water and remove fibers. Separate into small sections.

Note: Do not buy flat sweetbreads. The only fine ones are rather heart shaped and are in small sections, not in one flat piece.

SMOKED TONGUE

1 large smoked tongue
   (3 to 5 pounds)
1 cup sherry
1 carrot (cut in
   sections)
1 onion—cut up
Accent
2 tablespoons brown sugar

1 orange—(cut in
   sections)
1 small stick cinnamon
2 cloves
1 bay leaf
1 rib of celery—
   (cut in sections)
Parsley

Place tongue in large pot and cover with cold water. Boil up three times and pour off water each time—adding cold water each time. After this is done add all of the ingredients and cover tongue with cold water and bring to a rolling boil for 30 minutes, then lower flame and let simmer for about 3 to 4 hours. Remove tongue and skin it and let it cool. Place in refrigerator to chill. Slice when needed.

MRS. WILLIAM A. GOTSCHALL

This recipe came from the Pa. Dutch country.

LESSIE'S CHILI

3 tablespoons bacon fat
3 tablespoons flour
2 large onions, chopped
1 cup celery, chopped
½ cup bell pepper,
   chopped
2 pods garlic
1 can tomato sauce
2 pounds ground chuck
2 bay leaves

2 cans (16 oz.)
   tomatoes
1 tablespoon ground
   cummin
½ teaspoon pepper
2 teaspoons salt
2 tablespoons chili powder
1 can red beans
   (optional)

Make a roux with bacon fat and flour, stirring constantly until dark brown. Saute onions, celery, bell pepper and garlic until onion is clear. Add tomato sauce, tomatoes and meat (broken and crumbled by hand) and cook a few minutes. Add bay leaves, cummin, pepper and salt and simmer for 1½ hours. Then add chili powder for last 30 minutes. Add red beans.

From the file of
MRS. DAVID GARRET, SR.
Monroe, La.

TONGUE WITH RAISIN SAUCE

1 fresh beef tongue,
   around 4 lbs.

SAUCE

1 cup vinegar
1 cup brown sugar

1 cup seeded raisins
½-1 lemon, sliced thinly

2 doz. whole cloves

Simmer tongue in water almost to cover for 3 to 4 hours. Remove skin when cool enough to handle. Place in baking pan with cover. Pour sauce over the tongue. Bake at 325 degrees to 350 degrees for about 40 minutes, basting several times.

MRS. R. T. MERRITT, JR.

CREOLE LIVER

1 pound beef liver,
   sliced ¼ inch thick
3 tablespoon shortening
¼ cup minced onion
Dash of Tabasco
1½ teaspoons salt

1/3 cup diced green
   pepper
2½ cups
   canned tomatoes
1/8 teaspoon
   chili powder

Melt shortening in skillet. Add onion and cook slowly for 5 minutes. Dredge liver in flour and brown with onion. Add green pepper, tomatoes and seasonings. Cover and simmer 45 minutes.

MRS. LEWIS HESS

HOT TAMALES

½ bunch parsley, chopped
4 or 5 pounds meat (pork)
2 or 3 onions
2 bell peppers, chopped
1 bunch green onions
1 tablespoon soda

3 garlic buds, chopped
red and black pepper
   to taste
salt to taste
1½ boxes yellow
   corn meal

Boil meat and seasonings in enough water to make 2 quarts of stock. When meat has boiled until tender, remove meat and seasonings and grind together. Into the 2 quarts of stock, gradually add 1½ boxes of yellow corn meal mixed with 1 tablespoon of soda. If mixture is sticky, add a small amount of Lou Ana oil. Put 1 tablespoon of the mush mixture on a piece of paper, flatten out with hand, and put 1 heaping teaspoon of the meat mixture in the center and roll up. Steam the rolls for 1½ hours.

MRS. J. H. WILLIAMS
Natchitoches, La.

LASAGNA

1 pound ground meat
  (pork sausage or
  Italian sausage)
1 tablespoon parsley flakes
1 tablespoon basil
1½ teaspoon salt
1 pound can (2 cups
  tomatoes)
2 6-oz. cans (1 1/3 cups)
  tomato paste
1 clove garlic minced

8 oz. lasagna
3 cups cream style
  cottage cheese
2 beaten eggs
2 teaspoons salt
½ teaspoon pepper
2 tablespoons parsley
  flakes
1 pound Mozzarella
  cheese
Parmesan cheese

Brown meat slowly, add next 6 ingredients. Simmer uncovered till sauce is thick (45 min.) stirring occasionally. Cook noodles in boiling water (with salt) till tender. Drain. Rinse in cold water. Combine cottage cheese with eggs, seasonings, and Parmesan cheese. Place noodles in pan, spread half of cheese mixture, and then meat mixture, then Mozzarella cheese, repeat. Cook for 30 min. at 375 degrees. Stand 15 minutes. 6-8 servings.

MRS. JOHN S. WHITE, JR.

RICH SPAGHETTI SAUCE

1/3 cup olive oil
4 large onions chopped
4 cloves garlic chopped
1 can tomato paste
1 cup water, then 2
  cups water

1 pound ground beef
Salt, cayenne &
  oregano to taste
1 teaspoon sugar
1 tablespoon
  Worcestershire sauce

Put olive oil in heavy pot, add onions and garlic and cook, stirring constantly until onions are pasty. Add I cup water and cook down. Remove garlic cloves. Season meat well with salt, cayenne and a dash of oregano, put in onion mix and brown very well. Add 1 can tomato paste and 2 cups water, add sugar and Worcestershire sauce. Bring to a boil, reduce heat to simmer and cook for at least an hour. Stir occasionally and add a small amount of water if necessary. This is a thick very rich sauce.

MRS. WALLACE GLADNEY

RIGATONI ALLA NEAPOLITANA

2½ cups chopped onions
1 tablespoon crushed
   garlic
½ cup Lou-Ana oil
3 6-ounce cans
   tomato paste
2 8-ounce cans
   tomato sauce
6 cups water
1 teaspoon sugar
3/4 tablespoon Italian
   seasoning

2 large bay leaves
Salt and pepper to taste
1 2-pound chuck or
   shoulder-round roast,
   or 2 pounds
   ground beef
3 medium eggplants
3 8-ounce packages
   Rigatoni (small ribbed
   noodles)
½ cup grated Romano
   cheese

Make sauce by sauteing onions in oil until soft. Add garlic and cook until light brown. Add tomato paste, stir constantly, and continue to cook until mixture gets dark red and oil begins to fry out—about 10 to 15 minutes. Add tomato sauce, mix well, and allow to simmer 10 to 15 minutes more, stirring occasionally. Add water, salt, pepper, sugar, Italian seasoning and bay leaves. Cover and cook over medium heat for about 3 hours. Sauce is cooked when it thickens and oil comes to the top.

If roast is used, cut into 4 large pieces, salt and pepper and fry in skillet with a small amount of oil. Drop meat immediately into sauce that has just begun to cook. If ground meat is used, fry in skillet with small amount of oil until brown. Drain off oil and add to sauce the last hour of cooking.

To prepare eggplant, slice and soak for 10 minutes in salted water. Drain well on paper towels. Fry eggplant in oil until brown on both sides. Place fried eggplant on cookie sheet that has been lined with paper towels. Place towels between each layer of eggplant and allow oil to drain off well. Blot each slice with more paper towels and pull each slice into 3 pieces. Place on more paper towels to drain off more oil. This is important to keep the casserole from being oily. After sauce is cooked, remove meat, if roast is used, and cut into small finger strips.

Boil Rigatoni in large kettle of boiling salted (to taste) water, about 15 minutes. Drain immediately in collander, transfer back to hot pot, add 1½ cups sauce and mix well.

Line a large casserole with a little of the sauce. Add

half the noodles, then a heavy layer of meat sauce. Next, a layer of egg plant, then half the cheese. Continue layers until casserole is full.

Cover the casserole and bake in a preheated 300 degree oven for 1 hour. When serving, spoon some of the remaining sauce over each serving and sprinkle with more grated cheese.

MRS. R. S. CRIFASI

ITALIAN MEAT BALLS AND SPAGHETTI
SAUCE

4 large onions, chopped fine	Can for can of water
4 pods garlic, chopped fine	1 teaspoon sugar per can
3 cans tomato sauce or 2 cans sauce and 1 can tomato paste	3 or 4 bay leaves
	1 tablespoon oregano
	Pinch of allspice
	Salt and pepper to taste
	Lou Ana oil

Brown onions and garlic in just enough oil, drain, and blot any remaining oil. Add tomato sauce (or a combination of sauce and paste), then a can of water for each can of tomatoes used. Add 1 teaspoon sugar for each can used, and seasonings and simmer to blend.

MEAT BALLS

4 pods garlic, chopped fine	2 pounds ground round
3 raw eggs	¼ pound ground pork
6 slices white bread with crust trimmed & soaked in water.	2 or 3 slices of bacon chopped
	½ to 1 cup Romano or Parmesan cheese

Squeeze water out of bread and work in all other ingredients with Italian cheese. Shape into balls and fry until brown on all sides. Drain and simmer in sauce for about an hour. Just before serving, add a little minced parsley. Serve on spaghetti, which will never be sticky if water is poured off after cooking and a little butter is added.

MRS. FRED BLANCHE, JR.

MEAT SAUCE BOLOGNESE

2 tablespoons olive oil
1 medium onion
  chopped fine
1 medium carrot
  chopped fine
1 small stalk celery
  chopped
3/4 pound ground beef
¼ pound ground
  lean pork

2 tablespoons butter
1 can tomato paste
1 No. 2 can Italian
  tomatoes
½ cup white wine
½ teaspoon thyme
½ teaspoon oregano
½ teaspoon salt
Pepper to taste &
  water as needed

Fry meat until it turns grey. Saute onion, carrot and celery until it softens. Add tomato paste and fry until dark red. Add tomatoes, seasonings, then meat and wine. Simmer slowly for about 1¼ hours, adding a little water from time to time. This sauce should be rather thick. Makes 2½ cups, and should be served over spaghetti or any other type of pasta.

MRS. J. CLIFTON HILL

Note: This recipe came from a personal friend who lives in Bologna, Italy.

BRUCCIALUNA AND SPAGHETTINI
Serves 4

1 cup seasoned
  bread crumbs
3/4 cup grated
  Romano cheese

2 tablespoons
  olive oil
4 veal or beef cutlets,
  sliced thin or cubed

1 clove garlic, minced

Make a stuffing with seasoned bread crumbs, grated cheese, minced garlic and olive oil. Spread sparingly on steaks, roll and hold together with string. Roll these lightly in flour and brown in olive oil using a heavy skillet.

TOMATO SAUCE

1 6-ounce can
  tomato paste
1 8-ounce can
  tomato sauce
Salt and pepper to taste

1 teaspoon Italian
  seasoning
1 clove garlic,
  minced
1 cup water

Mix all ingredients, bring to slow boil and add steaks. Simmer on very low heat for 2 hours, adding more water if needed and spooning tomato sauce over meat. Serve over hot spaghetti.

MRS. GARNER MOORE

MEAT SAUCE FOR SPAGHETTI
Serves 6

2 pounds lean ground beef
½ stick butter or oleo
2 teaspoons salt
1 large onion, cut fine
1 whole clove garlic,
  remove later
1 large can tomatoes,
  Italian
1 small can tomato sauce,
  Spanish
1 can beef consommé
1 bay leaf
1 tablespoon chili powder
6 peppercorns
Red pepper to taste
¼ teaspoon oregano
¼ teaspoon basil
¼ teaspoon savory or
  marjoram
1 small can mushrooms
1 tablespoon Kitchen
  Bouquet

Sauté meat in butter or oleo until pink is removed. Add chopped onion and garlic (remove garlic later) and saute until tender. Add tomatoes, tomato sauce, consomme, bayleaf, chili, garlic salt and pepper. Bring all to a boil, then simmer on low heat all afternoon with close fitting cover. If necessary, this can be cooked a shorter time. After about 3 hours, add oregano, basil, and marjoram, or savory, then add, 30 minutes before serving, the mushrooms and their juice. Just before removing from heat, add 1 tablespoon Kitchen Bouquet. Serve over spaghetti and pass Romano or Parmesan cheese, grated.

MRS. W. R. MC GAW

SPAGHETTI DISH
Serves 4-6

1 pound round beef,
  ground
½ pound salt pork,
  chopped in small
  pieces
1 quart can tomatoes
1 large can chopped
  mushrooms
1 large onion chopped
1 rib celery chopped
1 bay leaf
1 dash
  Worcestershire sauce
1 teaspoon salt
2 cups cooked spaghetti
Dash cayenne pepper

Chop salt pork into small pieces, fry in skillet till golden brown. Put the crisp pork into a pot containing the tomatoes. Cook celery, put in tomatoes, and then brown mushrooms and ground beef in same drippings. Add salt pork drippings, bay leaf, Worcestershire sauce, salt and pepper and simmer slowly (for ½ to 1 hour adding a little water and tomato juice if it thickens too much). Put cooked spaghetti in buttered pyrex dish— layer of spaghetti and then layer of sauce until dish is full and the sauce is on top. Cover with bread crumbs and then catsup and some sharp grated cheese. Cook in oven 350 degrees for 30 minutes until it is bubbly and brown on top.

MRS. M. J. RATHBONE, SR.

Fowl

PARTY CHICKEN

½ chicken breast per.
    person
Dried beef

1 cup sour cream
1 can cream of
    mushroom soup

Bacon slices

Have butcher debone chicken, if desired, and roll each piece, which is seasoned to taste with salt and pepper, around diced, dried beef. Wrap each piece with a slice of bacon and secure with toothpicks. Put in greased baking dish, pour the sour cream and cream of mushroom soup over all, and bake at 275 degrees for nearly 3 hours.

MRS. R. P. MATHIS

SEAFARER'S CHICKEN
Serves 4

4 large chicken breasts
1 beaten egg
1 teaspoon prepared
    mustard

1 tablespoon
    Worcestershire sauce
2 tablespoons butter
    or oleo

Seasoned bread crumbs

Have butcher debone chicken breasts. Save bones for Hawaiian chicken salad. Remove skin, rinse, pat dry and sprinkle with salt, pepper and MSG. To beaten egg, add mustard and Worcestershire sauce. Dip chicken into egg mixture and then into seasoned bread crumbs. Place in Pyrex dish with butter or oleo and bake at 400 degrees for 15 minutes, then turn over and bake another 10 minutes.

HAWAIIAN CHICKEN SALAD—(LAGNIAPPE)
Serves 2

Chicken bones from
    Seafarer's Chicken
1 hard boiled egg
¼ cup ripe olives

¼ cup toasted almonds
½ cup chopped celery
1 tablespoon green
    onion tops

1½ tablespoon capers

(When as many as 12 chicken breasts are deboned, there is enough meat clinging to the bones that these can be used in making this "Lagniappe" dish for two.)

Boil bones until tender in salted water with red pepper sauce, celery tops and ½ onion. Cool. Remove chicken from bones. Add remaining ingredients. Season with red pepper sauce, mayonnaise and lemon juice.

Serve in avocado halves, over tomato slices, or on lettuce leaves surrounded with several kinds of fresh fruit.

(Note: One large chicken breast per person may also be used for this salad and the other ingredients increased accordingly)

Mrs. Asher Whitley

CHICKEN MOUSSE
Serves 8

2 envelopes gelatine
2 cups chicken broth
3 tablespoons lemon juice
1 teaspoon dry mustard
1 cup celery
2½ teaspoons curry powder
1 teaspoon onion salt
2 cups sour cream
3 cups chicken

¼ cup diced almonds

Sprinkle gelatine over ½ cup cold water. Let stand 5 minutes. To the hot chicken broth add lemon juice, mustard, curry, onion salt. Mix with gelatine. Cool 5 minutes. Stir in sour cream, mix well. Refrigerate about 40 minutes· Fold in chicken, celery, almonds. Use 1½ qt. mold.

Mrs. Donald McAndrew

OVEN-FRIED PARMESAN CHICKEN
Serves 12

3/4 cup butter or margarine
3 broiler-fryer chickens cut into serving pieces
3 teaspoons salt
¼ teaspoon pepper
½ teaspoon paprika
1½ to 2 cups bread crumbs
3/4 cup Parmesan cheese
1 cup buttermilk
1½ teaspoon monosodium glutamate

Line two 15x10x1 inch shallow baking pans with aluminum foil. Divide butter between pans; put in 425 degree oven for about five minutes, or until butter is melted. Combine bread crumbs, Parmesan cheese with seasonings. Mix well. Put in shallow pan or pie plate. Dip chicken pieces in buttermilk; roll in the crumb mixture; place skin side down in the melted butter, placing half the chicken pieces in each of the two pans. Bake at 425 degrees for 30 minutes. Turn chicken, bake 20 minutes longer or until done.

Mrs. Henry P. Allendorph
Oscar, La.

CHICKEN ASPIC I

2 envelopes unflavored
  gelatine
1/3 cup water
2¼ cup chicken broth (or
  make from bouillon
  cubes)
3/4 cup mayonnaise
3 hard boiled eggs

1 tablespoon
  chopped onion
½ cup chopped celery
1 tablespoon chopped
  sweet pickle
1 tablespoon chopped
  dill pickle
½ teaspoon mustard

Salt & Tabasco to taste

Sprinkle gelatine on cold water. Stir in hot chicken broth until gelatine dissolves. Turn 1¼ cups of mixture into a greased mold. Garnish with hard cooked eggs, asparagus, pimento or artichoke hearts and chill until set. Mix other ingredients into remaining gelatine and blend in blender. Pour over set gelatine and return to refrigerator until entire aspic is set. This is also delicious with tuna fish, ham, crabmeat, or salmon. With seafood, use some lemon juice, dry mustard and more Tabasco.

Mrs. George T. Tate
Alexandria, La.

CHICKEN ASPIC II
(Will serve 50 people at tea or coffee)

1 five or six pound hen
¼ cup mayonnaise
1 package gelatine
1 cup finely chopped
  celery

1 can tomato soup
½ cup chopped stuffed
  olives
Parsley and pimiento
  to decorate

Boil hen as for chicken salad with 1 onion, 2 celery stalks, 1 small green pepper and 1 lemon cut in pieces.

Remove chicken when tender and boil stock down to 2 cups. Strain and cool.

Beat mayonnaise into cooled stock. Chop the white meat of hen and grind dark meat, skin and scraps.

Dissolve gelatine in small amount of cold water—add a little more gelatine if weather is hot. Add dissolved gelatine to heated tomato soup. Combine with chicken and celery and olives. Add the stock and mayonnaise mixture. Season to taste with salt and red pepper or seasoning you desire.

Chop very fine parsley and pimiento—just enough

to decorate the bottom of the mold. (Be sure the parsley is dried with a cloth)

Rinse mold with cold water. Sprinkle parsley and pimiento in bottom of mold for decoration.

Pour in aspic and chill thoroughly. Your mold is more successful if you unmold on your serving tray and let stand for 30 minutes to an hour to regain its composure.

MRS. M. E. SAUCIER
Lafayette, La.

This recipe has been served at many Carnival receptions in Lafayette.

POULET A L'OIGNON ET A L'ORANGE
Serves 6-8

2 2½-pound fryers
2 medium oranges
1 envelope onion soup mix

1 6-ounce can frozen
   orange juice
1 cup water

Preheat oven to 400 degrees. Cut chicken for frying, and slice unpeeled oranges and place both in a large roasting pan. Blend onion soup with thawed orange juice and water and spoon some of this over the chicken and oranges. Bake about 1½ hours, or until tender and glazed, basting with remaining onion mixture and turning occasionally. Serve with pan juice.

MRS. M. F. MAGRUDER

CHICKEN SAUTERNE

2 fryers (3 or more
   pounds each)
3/4 cup butter
1½ packages frozen onions
2 cups sauterne

½ package frozen
   bell peppers
2 cups mushrooms,
   stems & pieces
   with juice

Quarter fryers, salt, pepper and brown in melted butter. Transfer chicken to tightly covered pan. Brown onions and peppers, chopped up, in remaining butter. Add mushrooms and juice and pour this mixture over the browned chicken. Add sauterne and bake in a 350 degree oven until chicken is tender, basting occasionally. Best when cooked the day before and it freezes well.

MRS. HENRY GEORGE MCMAHON

CHICKEN WITH BANANAS
Serves 5

3 pound chicken	½ cup white wine
2 tablespoons butter	Pinch of ginger
4 tablespoons Lou-Ana	5 bananas
cooking oil	Salt and pepper

1½ tablespoons Rum

Cut the chicken into pieces. Heat the butter and oil in a deep, heavy skillet and when hot, brown the chicken over moderate heat. Turn the chicken so that it will be well browned on all sides. Season with salt and pepper and add the rum. Touch with a lighted match and stir until the flame subsides. Add the white wine and a pinch of ginger and cook covered over low heat for 1 hour. Peel the bananas and poach them in simmering water for about 2 minutes. Drain. Cut in rounds and keep warm. Put the chicken with its sauce on a heated platter and surround with bananas.

MRS. DEAN MOSELY

CHICKEN IMPERIAL I

2 2½ lb. chickens, cut up	¼ cup chopped parsley
	1 clove garlic crushed
3/4 cup grated Parmesan or Romano cheese	2 teaspoon salt
	1/8 teaspoon pepper
	1 cup melted butter

2 cups bread crumbs

Mix crumbs with cheese, parsley, and seasonings. Dip each piece of chicken in melted butter then into crumb mixture, coating well. Arrange in an open shallow pan. Pour remaining butter over and bake 1 hour until fork tender at 350 degrees. Do not turn chicken but baste frequently.

MRS. EGERIA BARNETT

CHICKEN IMPERIAL II

1 loaf French bread	2/3 cup parsley, chopped
1 fryer cut up	1 cup Romano cheese grated
1 stick butter or oleo	

1 pod garlic, mashed

Trim crust off bread, saving crusts for dry bread crumbs. Close loaf tightly in a plastic bag and put in freezer over night. Remove and grate on medium grater. Into these crumbs place salt and pepper to taste, the parsley and the cheese. Melt butter and add garlic thru a press. Dip chicken pieces in the garlic butter then coat well with crumbs. Arrange in baking pan in only one layer. Bake 1 hour in 350 degree oven. Now, for my suggestions: I use only meaty pieces like a box of breasts, a box of thighs and one of drumsticks. I also remove skin from chicken pieces. Freezing the bread is also my idea, and you can use frozen hamburger buns or hot dog buns instead of the French bread, and these do not have to have the crust trimmed. The idea is to have moist crumbs, so do not use parsley flakes. Freezes beautifully. I keep a jar of such crumbs in the freezer all the time.

THE EDITORS

BROILED CHICKEN LIVERS

3/4 pound chicken livers
4 tablespoons butter or oleo
½ teaspoon salt
¼ teaspoon whole savory
2 teaspoon lemon juice
Few drops Tabasco sauce

Wash livers; dry well and put in a shallow baking pan. Melt butter, add other ingredients and pour over livers. Preheat broiler and place a piece of aluminum foil on broiler rack. Put livers on top of foil and broil for approximately two minutes on each side.

MRS. WALLACE PEARSON
Lafayette, La.

CHICKEN PROVENCAL
Serves 4

1 stick oleo
1 frying chicken (cut up)
1 can mushroom soup
1 can mushrooms
4 oz. can slivered almonds
1 can onion soup
½ cup sherry

Melt oleo in oblong pyrex dish. Place chicken in dish and brown in 350 degree or 400 degree oven **about** 30 minutes. Combine soups, sherry together to make sauce and add to browned chicken. Cook in slow oven (250-300 degrees.) for **about** an hour. Add mushrooms and almonds last 10 minutes of baking. Very good.

MRS. A. L. POSTLETHWAITE

LEMON CHICKEN

1 cut up fryer
Salt & pepper to taste
½ stick of butter

1/3 cup lemon juice
2 cloves of garlic
1/8 teaspoon oregano

Salt & pepper chicken and place pieces in oblong pyrex casserole. cut butter into small slices and place over chicken (skin side up). Bake in 350 degree oven for 45 minutes, then pour lemon juice, garlic, (which has been put through press) and oregano, which have been mixed together, over the chicken and bake another 20 minutes. Baste the chicken once or twice during baking.

THE EDITORS

CHICKEN CRUNCH
Serves 8

1 2/3 pound fryer,
    disjointed
1 cup flour
1 teaspoon salt

1 teaspoon freshly
    ground black pepper
2 cups Lou-Ana
    cooking oil

Crisp fry chicken in oil. Let cool and cut meat from the bones. In a large bowl add to cut up chicken the following:

1 can mushroom soup,
    undiluted
1 4½-oz. can pitted
    black olives cut in
    half (about 24)
1 4-oz. can green chili
    peppers cut in
    small pieces
1 5-oz. coarsely crushed
    potato chips
1 dash nutmeg

1 package Hollandaise
    sauce mix (dry)
¼ teaspoon red pepper
1 tablespoon peppered
    vinegar sauce
1 pinch saffron shreds
1 cup chicken stock
    or broth
2 ounces dry white wine
Worcestershire sauce
Salt to taste

1 tablespoon dry or fresh parsley

Place all ingredients in a two quart casserole and bake in 375 degree preheated oven for about 45 minutes, or until bubbly hot. Serve over rice, noodles, or creamed potatoes. Slivered almonds or can of mushrooms may be added. Freezes well. Dish was originally made to use leftover fried chicken. Cut up turkey may also be used, or any other left over meats.

MRS. ELWOOD ANDERSON

CHICKEN A LA KING

2 tablespoons butter	¼ cup butter
½ green or red pepper	3 egg yolks
(chopped fine)	1 teaspoon onion juice
2 tablespoons flour	4 tablespoons Sherry
2 cups cream	Salt to taste
3 cups cooked chicken	½ teaspoon paprika

Melt butter-saute in this green or red pepper. Add flour and cook, stirring, until flour is smooth but not brown. Add cream, simmer and cook until sauce is thick. Add chicken. Cream butter and add yolks of eggs, one at a time, beating steadily. Stir this into chicken mixture until egg thickens. Season with Sherry, salt to taste and paprika. Serve in pattie shells or on toast.

MRS. FRANK LOWE

SCALLOPED CHICKEN

1 large hen (reserve broth)	2 cups chopped celery
	1 box spaghetti
4 hard cooked eggs (chopped)	½ pound crackers butter

Boil hen with onion, celery, salt and pepper until tender. Remove from bone and cut up. Cook spaghetti. Mix cut chicken, eggs, celery, cracker crumbs and spaghetti with chicken broth, making it very juicy. Sprinkle top with crumbs, dot with butter and bake in slow oven. Mushrooms may be added, if desired.

MRS. JACK ABRAUGH
Rayville, La.

PAELLA

2 frying chickens cut up	3 green peppers chopped
2 cups rice	1 box frozen peas
2 tablespoons Lou Ana oil	1 can tomatoes or
3 onions chopped	tomato sauce
Salt and pepper to taste	4 cups water

Fry chicken until brown. Add rice and stir. Add onion and pepper and stir, add peas, then water, cover and cook until chicken is almost done—add rice and seasoning and cook until rice is dry.

ELENA HULINGS

CHICKEN AND RICE WITH BROCCOLI

1 fryer (or 12 big slices cooked left-over chicken	2 cans cream of chicken soup
3 packed-down cups cooked rice	½ cup chicken broth, or use ½ cup hot water and 1 chicken bouillon cube
2 packages frozen broccoli spears	Grated Parmesan cheese
Bread crumbs	

Boil fryer in small amount of water with salt and black pepper. When done, cool and slice. Cook broccoli according to package instructions and drain. In long Pyrex dish, put rice mixed with 1 can of soup. Put chicken slices next, then a layer of broccoli. Mix other can of soup and broth. Pour over all. Sprinkle well with cheese, then with bread crumbs or crumbled crackers. Bake uncovered at 250 degrees for 30 or 40 minutes until light brown and bubbly.

MRS. S. L. WRIGHT
Crowley, La.

FRIED CHICKEN

Soak chicken for ½ hour or longer in:

½ teaspoon soda	1 cup buttermilk

Drip dry, Drop in sack of well seasoned flour, which has a little garlic salt. Fry in usual manner

MRS. CHARLES E. BEADLES

CHICKEN AND WILD RICE CASSEROLE

2 3-pound chickens	½ cup chopped celery
1 cup water	1 pound fresh mushrooms
1 cup sherry	¼ cup margarine
1½ teaspoons salt	2 boxes wild rice
½ teaspoon curry	1 cup sour cream
1 sliced onion	1 can mushroom soup

Cook first 7 ingredients in a large covered pot. Strain broth and place it and the chicken in the refrigerator at once. When cool, debone and cut chicken into bite size pieces. Wash mushrooms and pat dry. Saute in oleo until golden (reserve enough to circle top of casserole) Measure broth and use for cooking rice as directed on the box. Combine chicken, rice and mushrooms in a 3 to 4 quart casserole. Blend sour cream and undiluted mushroom soup and toss all ingredients together. Arrange mushrooms on top. Refrigerate. Bake at 350 degrees for one hour.

MRS. ANDREW P. GAY
Plaquemine, La.

GREEN NOODLE CASSEROLE

2 fryers	1/4 pound oleo
1 cup celery, chopped	2 cans mushroom soup
1 cup green pepper,	1 small package Velveeta
chopped	cheese
1 cup onion, chopped	1 can mushrooms

2 packages green noodles

Cook fryers until tender and debone, saving stock. Saute celery, pepper and onion in oleo until wilted. Add mushroom soup, cheese, mushrooms and cut up chicken. Cook noodles in stock until tender. Add to vegetables and chicken. Place in casserole and sprinkle with seasoned bread crumbs. Bake in 300 degree oven until bubbly.

MRS. MULLER HOCHENEDEL

FRICASSÉE DE POULET

1 4-pound hen cut	1 large onion chopped
in pieces	4 cups water
Salt & black pepper to taste	* Bouquet garni
1 teaspoon red pepper	¼ pound fresh
2 tablespoons Lou-Ana oil	mushrooms, or 1 can
2 tablespoons flour	mushrooms, drained

Make a roux of the flour and oil. When brown, add chicken and onion and cook until brown. Add water and bouquet garni, then cook one hour over moderate heat. 15 minutes before serving, add the mushrooms. If fresh mushrooms are used, cook until tender. Remove bouquet garni before serving on hot platter garnished with parsley.

* Bouquet garni consists of 3 or 4 sprigs parsley, a sprig of thyme and 1 bay leaf. Tie into a piece of cheese cloth, surrounding the thyme with parsley. This may be used also with meats.

MRS. CHARLES HUSTMYRE

CHICKEN PAPRIKA I

2 to 3 pound fryer	2 teaspoons salt
1 cup Lou-Ana oil	1 tablespoon paprika
½ cup sifted flour	¼ teaspoon black pepper

Cut chicken for frying, wash thoroughly and pat dry with toweling. Place pieces, cut side down, on a shallow baking pan. Make a paste by creaming together the shortening, flour, salt, paprika and pepper until well blended. Spread generously over top surface of each piece of chicken. Bake in a 325 degree oven for one hour, or until golden brown. A good, crunchy chicken dish, easy to prepare, needs no watching.

MRS. HUNTLEY B. FAIRCHILD
Manchac Plantation

CHICKEN PAPRIKA II

3½ pound fryer	6 tablespoons butter
1/3 cup flour	or oleo
1 teaspoon salt	1½ tablespoon paprika
¼ teaspoon pepper	1 teaspoon sugar
4 large onions	1 can consommé
1 cup cream	

Cut chicken in quarters and coat with a mixture of flour, salt and pepper. Chop onions coarsely and cook in butter until limp, then stir in paprika and sugar. Add chicken to paprika mixture and fry over low heat for about 10 minutes turning occasionally.

Pour in consommé, cover tightly and cook gently for about 20 min. Add the cream and continue cooking 10 minutes longer (this time uncovered) or until chicken is tender and sauce is thick. Serve sauce over the chicken. Good with hot noodles.

MRS. ANTHONY J. DOHERTY

CHICKEN CURRY I

1 cup diced celery	1 cup milk
1 cup diced onion	2 cups cooked chicken
1 stick butter or oleo	½ to 1 teaspoon curry
½ cup flour	1 can water chestnuts,
1 cup chicken broth	sliced

Boil chicken in water seasoned with a small onion, a stalk of celery, salt, pepper and lemon juice. Remove chicken from bone, reserve broth. Make paste of butter and flour, put in skillet, add milk, chicken broth, onion and celery. Cook until slightly thickened, add chicken, and curry powder to taste. Serve on hot boiled rice, with the following condiments on the side: Chopped almonds, ·chopped hard boiled eggs, chopped bacon, crushed pineapple, shreaded coconut, and chutney. You never use all the chicken broth, so put it in the freezer and use to make shrimp curry like above recipe, except start with butter, peeled and deveined shrimp, etc. A recipe for chutney follows:

CHUTNEY

1 can (20 oz.) apples	¼ cup vinegar
or pears sliced	½ cup raisins
½ cup molasses	1 teaspoon curry powder
1 teaspoon ginger	

Bring to boil, let simmer 10 minutes, and serve hot or cold with all chicken dishes.

MRS. LUCILLE DUTTON

CHICKEN CURRY II

2 hens	Condiments:
1 onion (chopped)	
1 cup celery (diced)	Bacon crumbles
1 stick butter	Green onions (cut fine)
1 quart broth (strained)	hard boiled eggs (riced)
¼ to ½ jar curry powder	Peanuts (chopped or
3 tablespoons cornstarch	ground)
Salt	Cocoanut (browned in
Red pepper	oven)
2 egg yolks	Chutney
1 pint breakfast cream	Watermelon rind preserves
cooked rice	(optional)

Boil hens with celery tops, 2 tablespoons salt and few dashes red pepper. When done remove meat from bones and cut in bite size pieces. Saute onions and celery in butter. When clear add cut up chicken, strained broth and curry powder. Thicken with cornstarch and cook about 20 minutes. Beat egg yolks into cream and add to mixture just before serving. Serve over rice with the condiments.

MRS. WILLIAM H. WRIGHT, JR.

HONOLULU CURRY
Serves 6

6 tablespoons butter
1 small onion, grated
1 clove garlic
6 tablespoons flour
1 teaspoon ginger
1½ teaspoons salt

1 tablespoon curry powder
3 cups coconut milk
1 chicken bouillon cube
3 cups diced, cooked chicken

Melt butter, add onion and garlic and simmer 5 minutes. Remove garlic. Add flour and cook 3 minutes, add ginger, salt, curry powder and bouillon cube. Add coconut milk, and stir over low heat until thick. Add chicken. If you desire, you may use 2 or 3 pounds of cooked, shelled and deveined shrimp instead of chicken. Serve with rice, chutney, flaked cocoanut (slightly toasted), chopped, salted peanuts, sliced scallions and raisins.

MRS. ALMA STROUBE CUMMINGS
Miami, Florida

CHICKEN SAUCE PIQUANTE I

2 packages chicken breasts
1 package chicken thighs
1 package chicken legs
2 medium onions chopped
4 shallots chopped
1 medium green pepper chopped
2 cups celery chopped
5 pods garlic chopped

1 can tomato sauce
1 or 2 bay leaves
½ lemon
1 large can mushrooms
Parsley
Flour, salt, red and black pepper, file, coriander and marjoram
1 cup Lou Ana Cooking Oil

Put about a cup and a half of flour in a paper bag, add other seasonings with complete abandon, shake a skillet full of chicken pieces at a time, then fast fry in hot shortening. While chicken is frying, chop all vegetables, and put them and the remaining seasoned flour in the skillet after chicken is finished and saute till limp. As chicken is fried, drain on paper towels, and then put chicken, vegetables, tomato sauce, bay leaves, lemon and ¼ cup chopped parsley into a large pot. Cover with water, cover and simmer until chicken starts to leave the bone (about an hour). Stir frequently to prevent sticking. Remove chicken, let cool, de-bone and de-skin. Put the chicken back into the sauce, correct seasoning, add more parsley and mushrooms about a half hour before serving on hot boiled rice. This can be stored in the freezer indefinitely, but remember to thaw thoroughly before reheating, so the chicken will not string. If thickening is needed, use arrow root or wondra flour.

Same recipe can be used with squirrel or turtle meat.

MRS. LUCILLE DUTTON

CHICKEN SAUCE PIQUANTE II

1½ cup Lou Ana oil	2 quarts water
2½ cups flour	1 5 to 6 pound chicken
½ cup onion, chopped	cut up
½ cup bell pepper,	Dash cinnamon & nutmeg
chopped	(optional)
2 cloves garlic, minced	2 bay leaves
1 can tomato paste	1 can mushrooms
1 can Rotel tomatoes	1 cup chopped onion tops
Salt and pepper to taste	1 cup chopped parsley

Put oil in large, heavy pot over medium heat. Add flour to make a roux and cook, stirring constantly until golden brown. Add onions, bell pepper and garlic. Add tomato paste and cook 1 minute. Add Rotel, water, cinnamon, nutmeg and bayleaf. Stir to mix. Let simmer 1 hour over medium heat, stirring occasionally to keep from sticking. Add hen and mushrooms and correct seasoning to taste. Cover and simmer for 1½ hour, or until hen is tender. Add onion tops and parsley. Serve over hot rice with green salad and garlic bread. This dish is better when sauce is allowed to simmer at least 2 hours before adding chicken.

MRS. HAROLD J. BROUSSARD
Abbeville, La.

CHICKEN LOAF I

1 whole boiled fryer	¼ cup chopped pimiento
2 cups seasoned bread	½ cup sliced ripe olives
crumbs	4 whole raw eggs
3 cups chicken broth	1 can heated cream-of-
1 cup cooked rice	mushroom soup
Slivered almonds	

Bone chicken and cut in bite size pieces. Mix with all other ingredients except mushroom soup and almonds. Pack in flat casserole, sprinkle with slivered almonds and pour can of heated soup over entire top. Bake 1 hour at 300 degrees.

MRS. T. LUSTER JAMES

CHICKEN LOAF II

6½ pound chicken
1 cup celery chopped
¼ teaspoon onion juice
2 small pieces parsley
2 teaspoons
    Worcestershire sauce
1 small can English peas
    (save liquid—optional)

1 large can chopped
    mushrooms (save
    liquid)
2 beaten egg yolks
1½ cups cream sauce
    (Make with chicken
    stock and fat—add
    milk if too rich)

Salt & pepper to taste

Cook chicken, then chop. Add remainder of ingredients. Fold into mixture two lightly beaten egg whites. Grease and flour lightly a loaf pan, pour mixture into loaf pan. Place loaf pan in skillet (or pan) of water and heat on burner before placing loaf pan (in water) in 350 degree oven. Bake about 2 hours.

MUSHROOM SAUCE FOR CHICKEN LOAF

Place ½ cup of flour in a frying pan and place in oven with chicken loaf. Stir occasionally until brown— just off white color. Heat chicken fat and add flour, liquid saved from peas and mushrooms, broth of chicken, and milk if not thin enough. Just before serving, add I can mushrooms and pour sauce over chicken loaf. Sauce may be used as gravy over rice.

MRS. MARY NOTTINGHAM

FRICASSEE OF CHICKEN POINTE COUPEE

3 or 4 pound chicken
2 tablespoons butter
2 tablespoons flour
10 small onions
½ pound mushrooms or 1
    medium size can

2 cups warm water
1 bay leaf, chopped
    parsley, thyme,
    lemon juice, salt,
    pepper and cayenne
    to taste

1 egg yolk

Cut chicken for frying and soak for an hour in warm water, with a little vinegar added, to make tender. Make a roux with the butter and flour, then add warm water, stirring constantly. Add seasonings and herbs, then pieces of chicken. Let cook gently for about one hour. Add mushrooms a half hour before serving. For the "liaison", take 3 tablespoons of the gravy, beat it well with the yolk of an egg, then add juice of ½ lemon. Mix well and pour over chicken after placing it in a serving dish. Croutons fried in butter make a nice garnish.

MRS. GRAHAM BIENVENU
with the permission of the
family of Natalie Scott

CHICKEN SPAGHETTI

1 boiled chicken, 3 or 4 pounds	1 bell pepper chopped
1 pound spaghetti, cooked nearly done	1 pint breakfast cream
1 large can tomatoes	½ pound New York State Cheese
2 onions chopped	2 tablespoons chili powder
	Pinch soda

Boil chicken in small amount of water with an onion, a piece of garlic and a rib of celery until tender. Add salt and pepper and water if needed to make a full cup of broth, and include in the sauce.

Remove skin and bones and cut chicken in bite-size pieces. Boil spaghetti according to directions on package taking care not to overcook. Saute onions and pepper until just tender. Add tomatoes and chili powder and cook until thick. Now stir in a pinch of soda, then the cream and cheese and remove from heat at once. Butter a large casserole and place alternate layers of spaghetti and chicken, adding sauce to each layer and ending with spaghetti on top layer. Preheat oven to 350 degrees and bake 15 minutes.

MRS. LAZARD BLUM

JAMBALAYA

4 chicken livers (ground)	½ cup chopped onion
4 chicken gizzards (ground)	½ cup chopped green onion
½ cup bacon fat or Lou Ana oil	2 tablespoons chopped parsley
	Salt to taste and pepper

4 cups cooked rice

Soften onions and green onions in bacon fat. Add ground livers and gizzards. When cooked season and add parsley, then stir in cooked rice. Do not add water, this should be rather dry. Serve hot with chicken and gravy.

THE EDITORS

BRUNSWICK STEW I

1 large hen
½ teaspoon red pepper
Onion and carrot
2 tablespoon flour
Lou Ana oil or chicken fat
2 onions
Bunch green onions
Rind of lemon
Four hard-boiled eggs
   chopped fine

Large can tomatoes
Can of white cream corn
Small can of white
   shoepeg corn
Bay leaf
1 tablespoon
   Worcestershire sauce
Parsley
Tabasco
Mushrooms

Pressure cook a large hen in 2 cups water, red pepper, large onion and carrot until tender—about 20 minutes.

Take meat off bone and cut into medium pieces. Save stock to use in stew (discard onion and carrot).

Brown slightly in pot, 2 tablespoons flour with Lou Ana oil (chicken fat may be substituted). Add 2 dried chopped onions, green onions, lemon rind, and simmer with some of the stock until tender. Press tomatoes through sieve into roux and onions. Cook one hour and add stock as needed. Add corn, bay leaf, and simmer gently. Lastly, add chopped chicken, Worcestershire sauce, chopped parsley, Tabasco, mushrooms and hard-boiled eggs. Put 1 or 2 tablespoons sherry in each serving.

MRS. ROLAND C. KIZER

BRUNSWICK STEW II

1 hen (5 pounds)
1 large can peeled
   tomatoes
1 large can yellow cream
   style corn
2 large cans mushrooms
   (buttons or stems
   and pieces)

½ cup chopped parsley
1 bunch green onions
5 large white onions
4 hard boiled eggs
1 cup flour
Salt, pepper, Tabasco,
   Worcestershire sauce
   to taste

The day before making the stew, boil the hen in enough water to cover and let cook until completely done. Strain stock into bowl; put chicken in another bowl, let cool and put both in refrigerator and let stay overnight.

Next day, remove enough grease from top of stock to make dark brown roux with the flour (approximately 4 large kitchen spoons of grease). Add most of stock

to roux (leave some aside in case needed later), but
do not add the extra grease.

Put canned tomatoes in skillet and let simmer for
about an hour; stir and mash with a spoon.

Sauté white onions (chopped) in a little of the
chicken grease until they are tender.

Combine roux mixture, tomatoes and cooked
onions. Cut chicken into medium sized hunks with kitchen
scissors. Add chicken (no bones), mushrooms and juice,
green onion tops, and all seasonings to this; let simmer
for about 20 minutes. Now add corn, finely chopped
hard boiled eggs, and parsley. Let all of this cook
slowly for about 30 minutes, stirring frequently as corn
has a tendency to stick to bottom of pot. If too thick,
add more stock.

Ready to be eaten. Serve in soup bowls with salad
(avocado and grapefruit sections on lettuce with French
dressing) and garlic bread.

Freezes beautifully.

From the file of
MRS. MAUD C. WAX

BAKED CHICKEN AND MUSHROOMS

1 large fryer
1 large can mushrooms,
   drained
1 teaspoon prepared mustard
1 tablespoon sugar

1 tablespoon Worcester-
   shire sauce
1 clove garlic minced
1 teaspoon pureed onion
½ cup red wine

MAKE SAUCE OF:

1 can steak sauce
½ stick butter

1 tablespoon
kitchen bouquet

or

1 stick butter
   melted with

1 tablespoon
   kitchen bouquet

½ cup flour to make roux

Cut up chicken, season to taste, and place in large
flat pan. Cook your choice of sauces in sauce pan until
thickened, then pour over chicken, along with remaining
ingredients. Bake in 300 degree oven for about an hour,
or until tender, basting frequently.

MRS. RALPH BURGE

CHICKEN A LA ST. MARTIN
(To be served with Jambalaya)
Serves 6-8

2 large fryers
2 large onions sliced
½ bell pepper sliced
   (optional)

3/4 cup bacon fat or
   Lou Ana oil
Salt
Red pepper

Heat fat in iron pot until blue smoking. Add chicken which has been rubbed inside and out with salt and red pepper. After it has been turned on all sides and seared, reduce heat and brown slowly, turning until dark brown. all over. Remove from pot, add sliced onion and brown. Place chicken back in the pot. Add demitasse cup of water, cover tightly and cook until the chicken is very tender, adding water as needed. Skim fat from dark gravy adding enough water to make at least one cup. This is served over jambalaya.

THE EDITORS

CREOLE BAKED FRYERS

2 large fryers cut in
   serving pieces
1 cup chopped onion
1 cup chopped celery
1 cup chopped
   green pepper

1 can chicken gravy
¼ teaspoon Tabasco
1 clove garlic
1 can mushrooms
1 cup red wine
1 cup olive oil

Salt and pepper to taste

Rub chicken with salt and pepper. Place in roasting pan with as little space between pieces as possible. Cover with coarsely chopped onions, celery and pepper, and pour olive oil over all. Bake covered in 375 degree oven for one hour. Uncover and lift chicken to the top. Add the wine and mushrooms. Continue baking uncovered till brown. Stir in one can chicken gravy, if to be served with rice. If not, smooth 2 teaspoons cornstarch in ½ cup water and cook until thickened.

MRS. DANIEL HENDERSON

BARBECUED HEN

Put in open Dutch oven 5 or 6 pound hen. Brown in hot oven at 500 degrees about 15 minutes. Remove from oven when brown. Salt and pepper. Make mixture of ½ cup vinegar, 3 or 4 tablespoons Worcestershire sauce. Add water to make mixture 1 cup. Pour most of mixture over hen. Put hen in oven with top on Dutch oven. Bake in slow oven, basting often. When nearly done, drop in liver and gizzard. Let cook until liquid makes dark sticky substance and hen is ready to fall off bone. Take hen out. Make gravy on top of stove with flour and water, mashing liver and gizzard into gravy. Serve with rice.

MRS. LOCK PARET
Lake Charles, La.

OVEN BARBECUED CHICKEN

3 tablespoons tomato catsup	1 fryer or 2 or 3 chicken breasts halved
2 tablespoons Worcestershire sauce	1 lemon sliced
	1 teaspoon mustard
3 tablespoons brown sugar	Paprika, chili powder and
4 tablespoons water	red pepper to taste

Combine the sauce ingredients, adding a little garlic or onion, if desired, and simmer until flavors blend. Cut chicken as for frying, and salt and pepper to taste. Line Dutch oven or roaster with heavy foil. Dip chicken pieces in sauce, place on foil and put remaining sauce over the chicken. Close the aluminum foil. Cover and cook at 500 degrees for 15 minutes. Reduce heat to 350 degrees and cook about 1 hour and a quarter, or until chicken is very tender. May be prepared in advance and frozen. Heat when ready to serve.

MRS. W. E. BINGHAM

SMOKED TURKEY

Turkey	1 part of each:
Curing Salt (buy from store in 5-lb. package. Will do 6 to 8 turkeys)	Coca Cola Vinegar Wine

Rub turkey with curing salt. Then refrigerate for 5 days in a plastic bag. Then wash inside and out (be sure to clean out all salt.) Build your barbecue fire (you have to use barbecue pit with cover), use dampened hickory saw dust, and keep adding this wet saw dust to the fire from time to time to keep smoke going. REMEMBER you are not barbecuing; you are smoking the turkey. Smoke for 36 hours, turning every now and then. Baste every hour with Coca Cola, vinegar and wine (1 part each).

THE EDITORS

HERBED STEWED CHICKEN
Serves 4-6

1 fryer cut up
3 tablespoons flour
1 large onion, chopped
2-3 pods garlic, chopped
2 tablespoons parsley,
    chopped
1 teaspoon thyme leaves

1 bay leaf, crushed
Dash of
Worcestershire sauce
2 cups water
2 beef bouillon cubes
Salt and pepper to taste
Rose wine

Season chicken highly and brown in oil and butter. Remove chicken and replace enough oil and butter to cover bottom of pot. In this, brown flour, onion, garlic. Add parsley, thyme, bay leaf and Worcestershire sauce. Turn down heat and add water in which bouillon cubes have been dissolved. Correct seasoning and add browned chicken. If liquid does not cover chicken, add enough water or rose wine to cover. Cover pot and simmer over low heat until chicken is tender. Serve with rice.

MRS. BRYCE MORELAND
Abbeville, La.

CHICKEN ORIENTAL

1 broiler-fryer cut up
¼ cup butter or
    margarine
1 4-ounce can mushrooms
1 14 ounce can
    pineapple chunks
2 tablespoons sugar
1 tablespoon soy sauce

2 tablespoons vinegar
2 green peppers
1 medium onion
1 5-ounce can water
    chestnuts
1½ tablespoons
    corn starch
3 cups hot cooked rice

Brown chicken pieces on all sides in butter in skillet. Drain mushrooms and pineapple chunks; combine and measure liquid and add enough water to measured liquid to make 2 cups. Add to chicken in skillet and bring to boil; cover, reduce heat and simmer for 1 hour. Stir in sugar, soy sauce and vinegar. Add mushrooms and pineapple chunks. Cut green peppers in strips, slice onions, drain and slice water chestnuts and add to skillet. Cook 15 minutes longer. Blend cornstarch with a small amount of water; stir into hot mixture. Cook stirring until slightly thickened. Serve over the hot rice. Makes 4 servings.

MRS. MELVIN D. ROBINSON

MISSOURI OVEN-BAKED CHICKEN
Serves 4

1 frying chicken (2½ to 3 pounds)
1 quart buttermilk
¼ pound unsalted butter, melted
¼ cup flour
Dash of Tabasco sauce
1 teaspoon Worcestershire sauce
2 bay leaves
1 teaspoon sweet basil leaves

Cut fryer into serving pieces, place in a shallow pan, cover in buttermilk and let stand for one hour. Remove chicken from milk, salt and pepper to taste. Dredge with flour, dip chicken thoroughly, on both sides, in melted butter to which Tabasco and Worcestershire sauces have been added. Put bay leaves on sides of pan*. Place chicken on a cookie sheet in 375 degree oven for approximately 1 hour. Delicious!

* Sprinkle sweet basil leaves over top of chicken before putting in oven.

MRS. ESTELL GORDON CURRIE

RAMEKIN CHICKEN PIE

1 3 to 4 pound hen
½ onion, chopped
2 stalks celery, chopped
4 hard boiled eggs
2 tablespoons flour
2 tablespoons butter
6 sliced carrots
1 tablespoon parsley, chopped
1 quart of broth from chicken
Salt and red pepper to taste
Pastry strips

2 bunches green onions

Cook chicken with onions and celery about 2½ hours, or until tender. Cut in rather large pieces. Cook carrots and green onions in chicken broth until tender. Stir flour into melted butter and add broth until smooth. Then add chicken, parsley and the rest of the broth with vegetables added. Broth should not be more than 1 quart. Pour into ramekins and put strips of pie pastry across the top of each one. Bake in 400 degree oven until pastry is light brown. This can be made and refrigerated and baked when needed.

From the file of
MRS. GEORGE HILL
Homestead Plantation
Submitted by Mrs. John Hill

BREASTS OF CHICKEN KATHERINE
Serves 6

Breasts of 3 plump
    2½ pound chickens
¼ pound butter
2 tablespoons grated
    onion
2 cups heavy cream

1 pound sliced
    mushrooms
¼ cup good brandy
    (about 3/4 cup
    white wine can be
    substituted)

Bone chicken breasts. Lightly brown them in butter. Remove and keep warm. To butter add onion and mushrooms and saute about 5 minutes. Reduce heat and gradually add cream and brandy. (I add arrowroot to some of the cream to thicken sauce after adding brandy). After adding cream, cook about 5 minutes to thicken sauce. Arrange chicken on thin slices of ham on a bed of wild rice and pour sauce over chicken—reserve some sauce to serve separately.

MRS. KATHERINE H. LONG

CHICKEN BREASTS À LA DOROTHY

10 half chicken
    breasts boned
2 cups commercial
    sour cream
1 tablespoon
    Worcestershire sauce

½ teaspoon hot pepper
    sauce
1 clove garlic pressed
2 teaspoons salt
1¼ teaspoons paprika
Bread crumbs

Wipe chicken on both sides with a damp cloth, carefully removing any bits of bone, and place in shallow dish. Mix sour cream and seasonings and pour over chicken. Turn each piece so as to coat thoroughly. Cover closely and place in refrigerator over night. In the morning, drop chicken one piece at a time, into a shallow dish of bread crumbs, shaking more crumbs on top. Shape each piece with fingers and place one layer deep in baking pan. When all pieces are dipped, cover pan closely and return to refrigerator for 1½ hours. Uncover and bake in 325 degree oven for 1 hour and 15 minutes. Lift out with pancake turner and garnish with parsley or water cress.

MRS. LASLEY J. DOWNES
Rayville, La.

CHICKEN CHOWDER
Serves 8

1 6-pound stewing chicken cut up	1 cup cream
7 medium size onions	Bay leaf
5 large potatoes	Salt
3 thin slices of salt pork	Pepper corns
1½ quarts milk	¼ teaspoon poultry seasoning

Put chicken and quartered onion in pot with a little more than one pint of cold water. Cover, bring to boil, lower heat and simmer. After ½ hour, add ½ teaspoon salt and continue cooking for an hour or until chicken is tender. Meantime peel potatoes and dice size of sugar cubes. Par boil 5 minutes. Cut salt pork about half size of potatoes, put in iron skillet. Add remaining onions, chopped fine. Sauté until transparent.

When chicken is tender, remove it and let stock simmer 15 minutes. Remove meat from bones, cut into large cubes. You should have approximately 1½ cups broth. Strain, add potatoes, onions, salt pork scraps. Season to taste with salt and pepper. Add 6 cups milk and 1 cup cream. Heat.

May be prepared ahead.

MRS. LOUIS WELCH

GREEN NOODLE & TURKEY CASSEROLE

5 cans cream of mushroom soup	1 can pimiento, drained and chopped
2½ soup cans milk	12 ounce package green noodles, cooked
1 pound grated sharp cheddar cheese	2 quarts of chicken or turkey plus 2 cups
1 cup slivered almonds	

Mix soup, milk and cheese in sauce pan and heat until cheese melts. Stir in pimientos, salt and pepper.

Pour a little sauce in large baking dish and spread half of cooked noodles, turkey sauce, repeat. Sprinkle almonds on top. Bake at 375 degrees for 1 hour. Rinse noodles well so they'll steam out.

MRS. CHARLES KENNON

BAKED TURKEY WITH OYSTER DRESSING

Rub the turkey inside and out with salt, pepper and margarine. Stuff with dressing. Place in regular roasting pan, put foil over the top to be removed ½ hour before turkey is done, and bake in moderate oven 20 minutes to the pound.

OYSTER DRESSING FOR 20-POUND TURKEY

4 medium onions, chopped	2 4-ounce cans button
4 green onions, chopped	mushrooms
1 cup celery, chopped	3½ pounds veal,
8 cloves garlic, minced	ground up
3 sprigs parsley, minced	½ pound pork sausage
2 cups stale French bread	5 dozen oysters
soaked in oyster liquid	4 giblets
1 cup green olives, chopped	1 bay leaf
1 egg	Pinch paprika and thyme

In one cooking spoon Lou Ana oil, cook onions, ground veal and pork, salt, pepper and paprika. Add giblets (to be removed later), a pinch of thyme, 1 bay leaf and the bread soaked in oyster liquid, after the meat loses color. Add the oysters and cook until edges curl. Add mushrooms and olives, cook 1 minute, and lastly, add 1 raw egg, mix thoroughly, and turn off the heat. Make dressing the day before, since it is to be put into the turkey cold.

From the file of
MRS. MARGUERITE ANDREE
New Orleans, La.

Game

ROAST DUCK

2 ducks, mallards or
    pintails
1 onion
2 ribs celery
¼ cup orange juice

Salt, pepper, monosodium
    glutamate to taste
3 tablespoons orange
    marmalade
½ cup red burgundy wine

¼ cup butter

Wash carefully 2 nice ducks. Dry thoroughly inside and out and season highly with salt, pepper and monosodium glutamate. Stuff inside with half an onion and a rib of celery. Set ducks on rack in roaster pan with ½ cup water in bottom. Cover and let bake in 350 degree oven for about an hour. Remove cover and baste with portion of sauce you have prepared. Sauce: Melt butter and orange marmalade. Add wine and orange juice. Use this sauce to baste ducks every 15-20 minutes until nicely browned and a crisp crust is formed on breast (about another hour).

MRS. ROBERT KENNON, JR.

DUCK AND DUMPLINGS

2 wild ducks
2 ribs celery chopped
1 large onion chopped

¼ stick butter
Salt and pepper
Water

Salt and pepper ducks inside and out, putting onion and celery in, and cover with water. Cook until ducks are tender, adding more water as needed. Remove ducks from broth, add butter and salt to taste. Make dumplings:

1 cup flour

1 teaspoon salt

½ cup milk

Mix all ingredients and roll very thin on floured board. Cut in 1 inch wide strips about 2 inches long. Drop in boiling broth, a few at a time. Return ducks to pot, cover and let set for 10 minutes.

MRS. ROBERT C. KEMP

PIGEONS NORMANDS

Procurez-vous 3 beaux pigeons; faites-les dorés dans une cocotte avec 3 cuillers rasés de beurre et 1 d'huile; sales, poivrez légèrement.

Pendant ce temps, épluchez et épépinez 5 pommes douces, reinttes ou autres, coupez-les en tranches et faites-les revenir dans 5 cuillers de beurre. Une fois dorés, sortez les pigeons de la cocotte, mettez-les pommes émincées et revenus au beuree au fond; reposez délicatement les pigeons sur ce lit parfumé et remettez le tout au four.

Entourez les pigeons de 3 pommes épluchées, épépinées en grosses tranches. Laissez cuire 35 a 40 minutes a four chaud ou sur le feu.

Au moment de servir, arrosez avec 250 grs de crème fraiche et un filet de Calvados; remeuz sur feu dous, la crème ne doit pas bouillir.

Servez les pigeons avec de petits croissants de pate feuilletée.

PIGEON NORMANDY (SQUAB)

Take 3 full-size pigeons and brown in heavy pan with 3 tablespoons (level) of butter and 1 of Lou Ana oil; salt and pepper lightly.

Meanwhile peel and slice thickly 5 fresh apples. Heat through in 5 tablespoons of butter. Place apples (sliced and sautéed lightly in butter) in bottom of heavy roaster or baking dish and lightly place pigeons on top of apples. Place in oven and cook 35 to 40 minutes.

When ready to serve cover with 1 cup fresh cream and dash of brandy, heated over low fire. Do not permit cream to boil.

Serve with light croissants (crescent rolls).

DANIELE FAGAN WRIGHT
Hammond, La.
Formerly LeHavre and Paris

Try this with Cornish hen or chicken—The Editors

DOVES I

| Doves | ½ cup red wine |
| 1 medium onion | Salt and pepper |

Butter

Salt and pepper doves inside and out, then brown in butter. Add onion, water and wine. Cook in an iron pot, preferably, until done. Wonderful with grits, biscuits and fig preserves.

MRS. J. W. ANDREE

DOVES II

Salt and pepper birds inside and out using both black and red pepper.

Put sliver of garlic and small pat of butter in each bird.

Place birds in dutch oven, back side up, with about ½ inch of water. Cover and cook in oven at 325 degrees for 1 hour, adding water if necessary. Combine 1 cup sherry, 2 tablespoons Kitchen Bouquet, 1 tablespoon Worcestershire sauce. Pour over birds and cook uncovered about 1 hour more, basting frequently until birds are brown and tender.

MRS. FRANK JONES

QUAIL AND CABBAGE

1 quail per serving	Salt and pepper to taste
1 cabbage, cleaned	Flour
and cut	Lou Ana oil

Pick the feathers from the quail. Do not skin. Cut in half, salt, pepper, flour and brown in oil. Remove from pot and add 1 tablespoon flour and brown. Add water, put cut up cabbage in, with quail on top. Cover and cook about 2 hours, or until quail are tender. Add salt and red pepper to taste. Serve with corn bread.

MRS. SCHORTEN MONGET

ROASTED DOVE

Olive oil	Curry powder
Dry Mustard	Pepper
Celery salt	2 tablespoons
Garlic salt	Worcestershire sauce
Salt	Juice of 1 orange
Juice of 1 lemon	

Roll doves in enough olive oil to get them well greased. Sprinkle curry powder, dry mustard, celery salt, garlic, salt, salt & pepper over doves. Put in covered Dutch oven with a little water and cook 1½ hours in 250 degree oven. Add Worcestershire Sauce, orange and lemon juice. Cook 10 or 15 minutes longer or until tender.

MRS. NANCY LACEY
Monroe, La.

DUCKS

5 cleaned ducks	Salt
1¼ apple	Pepper
5 pieces of celery	1¼ onion
1 can beef consommé	1 tablespoon flour

½ can cooking sherry

Clean inside of ducks well. Use lots of black pepper inside, and a little salt inside and out. Place in each duck the following: ¼ apple, a piece of celery, and ¼ onion. Place in a roasting pan, breast side down, pour over ducks one can of beef consomme; fill the consomme can half full with cooking sherry and pour over the ducks. Brown back side up under broiler, basting frequently, then turn breast side up and baste and brown. Place the ducks breast side down in the pan and put the roaster top over, set the oven at 350 degrees and cook breast side down for 1 hour. Then turn breast side up, let pan remain covered, cook for half hour. Take the ducks out and thicken the gravy with heaping tablespoon of flour. Put the ducks back in breast side down, covered, and cook for 30 minutes.

THE EDITORS

BAKED DUCK WITH ORANGE-CURRANT SAUCE

Clean ducks thoroughly. Put salt into duck cavity. Also put ¼ orange, apple and turnip into cavity. Place ducks in pan and cover with strips of bacon. Surround with celery, onions and little water. Bake 3 hours. Start in hot oven and turn down to moderate.

Sauce for duck to be served at table.

ORANGE CURRANT SAUCE

6 tablespoons currant jelly	3 tablespoons sugar

Grated rind of 1 orange

Combine the above and beat 3 minutes with rotary beater. Add:

2 tablespoons port wine	2 tablespoons lemon juice
2 tablespoons orange juice	¼ teaspoon salt

Dash red pepper

Stir well. Serve room temperature.

MRS. H. F. BRADFORD

DUCKS WITH CANTONESE SAUCE

2 ducks. Sprinkle with salt and red pepper in and out. Sprig of parsley and ½ lemon in each duck. Cover breasts with bacon. Roast 350 degrees for about 3 hours, or until tender. Baste ducks with butter and sauce at least once while roasting.

1 teaspoon curry powder	1 teaspoon grated
1 cup apricot preserves	orange peel
1 tablespoon lemon	2 tablespoons soy sauce
½ cup beer or sherry wine	1/8 cup dry mustard

In double broiler, put dry mustard and beer. Season with MSG. Add to above mixture. Keep warm. Slice duck over hot rice and cover with sauce.

Mrs. J. J. Fletcher
Lonoke, Arkansas

WILD DUCK
Serves 4

2 wild ducks	Bacon fat or Lou Ana oil
1 small onion	Water
2 stalks celery	Red pepper and salt

Rub inside and outside with red pepper and salt. Stuff with one-half onion and one small celery stalk. Drop into ¼ inch hot bacon fat or Lou-Ana oil and brown on all sides. Takes about 20 minutes to a half hour on hot fire. When duck is very brown, add one after-dinner coffee cup of water. Cover tightly and steam on very low fire until meat can be separated from breast bone. Takes about 3 or 4 hours. As water cooks out of pot, add another small coffee cup of water. Use iron pot, if available.

The Editors

SMOTHERED QUAIL

6 quail	¼ cup Lou Ana oil
1 medium onion	Salt and pepper to taste
2 cups water	Flour

Salt and pepper quail and dredge in flour. Brown in oil, add water and chopped onion. Stir well, cover tightly in skillet and simmer until quail is tender. You may also cook squirrel and doves this way and both are excellent.

Mrs. Robert C. Kemp

STUFFED WOODCOCK

1 woodcock per serving	1 clove garlic, minced
½ cup cooked cornbread	1 tablespoon
½ cup cooked rice	parsley, minced
1 bag herb stuffing	Salt and pepper to taste
1 onion chopped	Margarine

Pick, do not skin, woodcock. Make dressing of remaining ingredients, except oleo. Salt and pepper birds, stuff each one, flour and bake at 250 degrees, basting with oleo often. Cook until tender and brown. Add small amount of water, as needed.

MRS. SCHORTEN MONGET

PHEASANT
Serves 8

4 pheasants	2/3 cup milk
2/3 cup Claret wine	Salt and pepper
2/3 cup coffee cream	Flour

Unjoint and season pheasants with salt and pepper. Roll in flour and fry. Mix liquids, put in roaster and place in 350 degree oven. When simmering begins, place fowl in roaster and turn oven down to 325 degrees. Let simmer in oven for 1 hour and 20 minutes. Baste often. Lastly, remove pheasants to baking sheet and drain. Put back in oven just before serving for 20 minutes at 450 degrees until crust is formed. One young turkey or 4 broiler chickens may be prepared this same way. Reduce cooking time for chicken. Serve with gravy left in pan.

THE EDITORS

ROAST VENISON

Venison roast	Salt
Beef kidney fat	Pepper

Pierce holes in the roast, enlarge with finger and stuff strips of beef kidney fat into the holes with salt and pepper. Bake in a 325 degree oven for 25 or 30 minutes to the pound. Beef kidney fat has no taste, will keep the venison from being dry, and the butcher will give it to you if you ask for it. It is not on the counter.

MRS. ROBERT C. KEMP

BAKED VENISON

2 round or sirloin steaks
½ cup vinegar
2 cups water
¼ cup Lou Ana oil
1 chopped onion
4 green onions chopped
1 bell pepper chopped
2 ribs celery chopped

½ cup wine
1 small jar stuffed olives
1 small can ripe olives
2 bay leaves
1 teaspoon
    Worcestershire sauce
Salt, black pepper and
    red pepper to taste

1 can mushrooms

Trim membrane layer and cut venison steaks into small pieces. Soak for about 15 minutes in solution of vinegar and water. Wash, drain, and pat dry with paper towels. Salt, pepper and flour meat and brown in oil in Dutch oven. Remove meat and add onion, bell pepper and celery to drippings and saute. Put meat back in pot and add 1 cup water, wine, mushrooms with juice, olives, Worcestershire sauce, bay leaves and seasonings. Finely cut parsley or fresh sweet basil may also be added. Cover pot and bake in 350 degree oven until tender— About 1½ to 2 hours. Serve over rice.

MRS. ODIS F. HAYMON

VENISON EPICUREAN

A steak from leg or chop
    from loin about 1½
    inches thick
Butter, size of a walnut

Salt and pepper to taste
1 wine glass of sherry or
    port wine
1 tablespoon currant jelly

Put butter, salt and pepper into chafing dish. When butter is melted, put in steak or chop. Cook on one side a few minutes, then turn over. Add wine and jelly. Simmer gently about 7 minutes if liked rare, 12 minutes if required well done.

MRS. ROY FIELD

VENISON HUNT STEAK
Serves 12

6 pounds small venison
    steaks
1 cup flour
1 cup vinegar

1 quart water
Salt
Pepper
Lou Ana oil

Pound steaks until assured of tenderness. Place in vinegar water and soak for 5-10 minutes. Lift from vinegar water and salt and pepper. Dredge with flour and fry quickly in hot Lou Ana oil about 1 inch deep. Do not try to fry dark brown; quick cooking is the secret. Serve with hot grits cooked in milk for 1 hour. This with hot biscuits, homemade preserves or jelly and scrambled eggs makes a delicious "Hunt Breakfast."

THE EDITORS

STUFFED VENISON STEAK

1 large venison steak	2 eggs
¼ pound fresh mushrooms, cut	1 teaspoon salt
	1 teaspoon poultry seasoning
½ pound lean pork, cut to bite size	3 tablespoons Lou Ana oil
1 large onion, chopped	3 tablespoons butter
1 cup celery, diced	1 cup sherry or Madeira wine
1 cup bread crumbs	

Cut steak 1½ inches thick. Salt, pepper and flour well on both sides. Make dressing of the next 8 ingredients. Place dressing in the center of the steak, roll and tie ends with heavy cord. Put steak in hot skillet with butter and oil, brown, then remove to roasting pan. Add 1 tablespoon flour to butter and oil remaining in skillet and brown slowly, stirring constantly. Add 2 cups water and continue stirring until smooth. Pour gravy over steak and bake at 350 degrees for about 1 hour and 20 minutes, basting regularly. Add more boiling water to make 2 cups gravy, add sherry and serve piping hot. Flank steak with whole, brown potatoes and brandied peaches. Garnish with parsley or water cress.

THE EDITORS

A good Madeira wine sauce should be served with this.

DEER SAUSAGE

5 pounds boned venison	1 clove garlic
5 pounds pork sausage	Salt and pepper to taste

Grind venison that has been boned and trimmed. Mix with sausage and seasoning, then run through the grinder again, which mixes the ingredients thoroughly. Shape in patties, or put in casings and smoke. Patties can be wrapped and frozen until ready to fry. Venison lacks fat which the sausage supplies.

MRS. AMY MCNUT
Gallagher's Ranch
Helotes, Texas

ROAST POSSUM

First catch the possum. Dress it and soak in salted water 6-12 hours, depending on size and age of possum. Pour off water· Then parboil in salted water ½-3/4 hour. Prepare a dressing, the same as for turkey, being sure to include oysters. Stuff possum, sew ·up and place in baking pan with just a little water. Place in oven 15-20 minutes. Pour off liquor and keep. Lay around possum partially boiled sweet potatoes. Place slices of bacon across possum and potatoes. Pour liquor over both and let bake 1 hour or more, basting frequently. We have copied this recipe exactly as it was given to us.

THE EDITORS

Seafood

AVOCADO SAUCE FOR SHRIMP

4 eggs	1 teaspoon white pepper
1 pint Lou Ana oil	6 whole ripe avocados
1 tablespoon dry mustard	2 bunches green onions
1 tablespoon	1½ pods garlic, or
Tabasco sauce	1 teaspoon garlic
½ cup wine vinegar or	powder
juice of 4 lemons	½ can (13 oz.) anchovies
½ cup Worcestershire	1 teaspoon saffron
sauce	½ gallon mayonnaise

1 tablespoon salt

Blend egg and mustard together, add oil and mix thoroughly. Add Tabasco, vinegar, Worcester, salt and pepper. Remove stones and peel avocados. Cut onion tops from onions and peel garlic. Grind all together with anchovies into a smooth paste. Add to above, blending gently but thoroughly. Add mayonnaise and saffron. Mix well. Pour into containers and chill at least 2 hours. Makes 4 quarts.

MRS. JOHN MCKOWEN, JR.

SARDINES FARCIES
(stuffed sardines)

For approximately 2 pounds big and fresh sardines. Cut open and clean well, removing bones. Make stuffing with:

8 ounces of blettes—type of	Parsley
Swiss chard—washed,	7 ounces grated
dried and finely cut	Parmesan cheese
1 clove of garlic	3 eggs
1 or 2 shallots	Nutmeg

Mix all above ingredients. A bit of breadcrumbs soaked in milk can be added to mixture (optional). Spread mixture in each sardine and pan fry till golden after each sardine has been rolled in sifted flour. Serve with lemon slices.

H. S. H. PRINCESS GRACE
DE MONACO

BAKED FISH

Fresh or salt water fish may be used. Salt and pepper red fish filets and marinate them for 30 minutes in half Lou Ana oil and half wine vinegar. While fish is marinating, place in a broiler pan a layer of onion rings and a layer of bell pepper rings. Then add the fish and another layer of onion and bell pepper rings. Cover with aluminum foil and bake in a 400 degree oven about 40 minutes, or until done. Remove foil, drain off liquid, sprinkle with wine vinegar and dot with butter. Run under broiler until brown. Delicious!

MRS. SADIE PERRIN
Grand Isle, La.

FISH VERA CRUZ STYLE

1 red snapper or trout	½ cup chopped sweet
½ cup lemon juice	pepper
½ cup butter or oleo	½ cup chopped carrots
1 cup cubed tomatoes	3 cloves garlic
1 cup onions chopped	6 hot peppers cut in half

Filet fish, salt and pepper it well, and place skin side down on oiled baking dish. Preheat oven to 450 degrees. Melt butter and garlic and simmer for five minutes, add lemon juice. Spoon half of the lemon butter over the fish, and place the hot peppers (cut side down) over the fish. Cook in oven for 20 minutes, or until fish is flaky. Add the chopped ingredients and cook 10 minutes more. Place fish on a large platter and pour the remaining hot lemon butter over it. Remove the hot peppers to a side dish.

MRS. KNIGHT A. LAVENDER

GRILLED RED SNAPPER STEAKS
Serves 6-8

3 pounds red snapper,	¼ cup lemon juice
filleted, or red fish or	¼ teaspoon cumin
speckled trout	½ teaspoon oregano
½ cup Lou Ana oil	½ teaspoon salt

Cut steaks about 1 inch thick and marinate in sauce 10 or 15 minutes. Grill on slow charcoal fire 6 to 8 minutes or until fork easily penetrates fish. Surplus sauce can be used as a baste.

THE EDITORS

If desired, small, square "boats" can be made out of foil by turning up edges for individual fish steaks. This is good for cook-out.

MOLDED RED SNAPPER

1 whole red snapper (3 to 5 pounds)	Celery
	Garlic
2 sliced lemons	Onion
Salt	Bay leaf
Pepper	1 package of crab boil

Wrap whole fish in cheese cloth and tie at both ends. Boil in large container until fish is tender—adding all ingredients listed above. When fish is done let it remain in container for about one hour. Remove fish from water and skin it and break meat into small sections and let cool. Chill in refrigerator for several hours (preferably overnight).

SAUCE:

To a good sized bowl of home made mayonnaise add finely chopped parsley, riced hard boiled eggs and capers. When fish is cold flake the meat and in a mold put a layer of fish and a layer of the sauce along with slivered almonds—all in layers until all meat is used. Then on the top "ice" it with mayonnaise, more almonds and hard boiled egg rings. Decorate with parsley, ripe olives or any other pretty garnish.

MRS. WILLIAM A. GOTSCHALL

BAKED RED SNAPPER PIQUANTE
Serves 6-8

Sauce

One 14-ounce can mushrooms (stems & pieces)	1 cup chopped celery
	3 large onions chopped
	1 bunch green onions
1 can tomatoes (16-ounces-peeled)	¼ bunch parsley chopped
	1 can tomato sauce

Brown tomato sauce and tomatoes separately in olive oil or bacon fat.

Brown celery, onions in bacon fat and when golden brown add green onions and parsley and mushrooms and cook until green onions are tender. Mix with browned tomatoes. Add 2 pounds of peeled shrimp and simmer 10 minutes. Sauce is ready to serve on fish.

12 to 15 pound Red Snapper

This is the secret of the dish. Cook the fish in a covered baking pan in the oven **only** long enough for a fork to go through the fish. Over cooking ruins it. Rub salt and pepper on fish and put one inch of water in the pan before baking. Be sure to brown red pepper in the hot fat for the sauce. Never use raw red pepper. Sauce served over the fish **after** it is baked.

MRS. E. S. GIRAULT
Monroe, La.

STUFFED TROUT FILET

1 large trout filet per serving	1 can seasoned tomatoes
1 can seasoned bread crumbs	1½ bay leaves
2 cups fresh, cooked shrimp	1 onion, chopped
Imported olive oil	2 cloves garlic, cut fine
1 can crab meat	2 ribs celery, chopped fine
	2 tablespoons parsley, minced

Salt, pepper & lemon juice

Salt and pepper fish. Make dressing: saute ½ bay leaf, cut fine, in olive oil, onion, celery, parsley, salt, pepper and lemon juice until wilted, but use only half of the seasosing. Add water to bread crumbs to soften, add crab meat and shrimp cut fine. Put into seasoning mixture and cook ten minutes. Put on each filet, roll up and secure with toothpicks. Flour the filets well, put in pan with olive oil and cook about 25 minutes at 300 degrees, basting often. In a sauce pan, put tomatoes, the rest of the seasoning and a whole bay leaf to be removed before serving. Add a little more salt and pepper and a cup of water. Cook about 5 minutes, then pour over fish and cook about 30 minutes, basting often. Serve on platter with garnish of parsley and lemon wedges.

MRS. SCHORTEN MONGET

CHARCOALED FILET OF FISH

Place a thin layer of sliced lemons on aluminum foil in shallow pan. Lay filets of fresh or salt water fish on the bed of lemon slices. Melt 1 stick of butter, add 1 teaspoon salt and 1 teaspoon freshly ground pepper, pour over fish. Cover with layer of foil and bake over charcoal 1 to 1½ hours depending on thickness of filets. Baste at 15 minute intervals with trapped butter mixture. When serving pour remaining juice over fish.

THE EDITORS

TROUT IN FOIL

1 speckled trout filet per person	3 bay leaves
Imported olive oil	Juice of 1 lemon
1 onion, quartered	Dash of Worcestershire sauce
2 garlic cloves, split	Salt and pepper to taste
2 celery ribs	Dash of Tabasco

Pour olive oil on foil paper, salt and pepper fish and place on foil. Put seasonings on top of fish, cover all with a little olive oil, and fold paper tightly closed. Put in pan and bake about 30 or 40 minutes. Open foil and brown under the broiler. Remove seasonings and serve on platter with lemon wedges.

MRS. SCHORTEN MONGET

BOILED SHRIMP

After washing and draining 5 pounds shrimp, put them into enough boiling water to cover (approximately 4 quarts) into which has been added the following seasoning:

1 teaspoon celery seed	¼ cup salt
1 tablespoon mustard seed	Peeling of 1 lemon
2 teaspoons whole all spice	1 clove garlic
	1 medium onion, sliced
1 teaspoon whole cloves	2 stalks celery
1 tablespoon pepper corns	with leaves

Let water come to a boil again and cook for 10-12 minutes (depending on size of shrimp). Let shrimp cool in same water.

THE EDITORS

BAKED SHRIMP

2 pounds cleaned raw shrimp	¼ teaspoon salt
¼ pound melted butter	¼ cup soft bread crumbs
¼ cup lemon juice	¼ cup dry sherry
¼ cup chopped chives	¼ cup slivered blanched almonds

Arrange shrimp in a single layer in shallow baking dish. Combine butter, lemon juice, chives and salt. Sprinkle over shrimp. Top with bread crumbs; sprinkle sherry over all.

Bake at 400 degrees F. for 20 minutes. Sprinkle almonds over shrimp during last 5 minutes of baking.

MRS. LEWIS HESS

CHARCOAL BROILED SHRIMP

No one will miss steaks, even You serve enough of these from your barbecue grill (can be done in the oven). You must have jumbo shrimp or prawns (larger than jumbo).

2 pounds raw jumbo shrimp (shells on)	1 clove garlic
1/3 cup cooking oil	2 bay leaves
1/3 cup sherry	2 teaspoons Worcestershire sauce
1/3 cup soy sauce	Dash Tabasco

Wash shrimp thoroughly—drain. With sharp knife cut down back and remove the black vein. Leave shells on. Mix oil, sherry, garlic, soy sauce, Worcestershire, bay leaves and Tabasco in shallow pan or dish. Marinate shrimp in this mixture for 3 or 4 hours, turning every 30 minutes. Drain; save marinade. Then arrange in a wire broiler with closely spaced grids. Cook over a bed of coals for about 8 or 10 minutes—Baste often with marinade and turn the wire broiler after each basting.

Serve shrimp in their shells. Each guest shucks his own. A bowl of melted butter, lemon and soy sauce is provided for dunking. This may be used as a main dish with salad and bread and dessert—or for an outdoor cookout as "hors d' oeuvrs."

MRS. ETHERT HAGAN

GRILLED SHRIMP WITH LEMON BUTTER SAUCE
Serves 6

6 dozen large shrimp	2 tablespoons minced onion
6 tablespoons butter	
6 tablespoons lemon juice	Freshly ground black pepper
1 tablespoon brown sugar	

1 teaspoon dry mustard

Place 12 shrimp on each skewer and cook until pink (about 7 minutes on each side), baste and serve over Rice Viennese with drawn butter as a gravy or sauce.

THE EDITORS

SHRIMP ON SKEWERS
Serves 6

Sauce for 2 pounds of shrimp	½ teaspoon paprika
1/3 cup salad oil	1/3 cup lemon juice (Fresh or frozen)
3 or 4 garlic cloves	1½ teaspoon salt

Combine salad oil, lemon juice, garlic and seasonings. Pour over shrimp and refrigerate over night. Place shrimp on skewers, alternating with onion and green pepper (quarter big onions and cut in half small ones; quarter green pepper). Use 3 shrimp, piece of pepper, piece of onion, etc. Broil them 3 inches from heat about 13 minutes, or until done, using sauce frequently. During last 2 or 3 minutes add tomatoes to end of skewers. Serve with lemon wedge.

MRS. HEIDEL BROWN

SHRIMP CREOLE

2 tablespoons Lou Ana oil	Pinch of sage leaf
2 tablespoons flour	½ teaspoon chervil
2 onions	¼ teaspoon Rosemary leaves
1 bell pepper	
2 cans tomato sauce	¼ teaspoon sweet basil
2 cloves garlic	1 bay leaf
½ teaspoon red pepper	2 pounds raw shrimp
Salt to taste	Few slices of lemon
¼ teaspoon powdered thyme or crushed thyme leaves	2 teaspoons Worcestershire sauce
	2 teaspoons parsley
1/3 teaspoon celery seeds	¼ cup shallot tops

In an iron pot, with a lid, make a roux with the oil and flour. When brown add chopped onions and bell pepper. Saute, stirring constantly, until onions are slightly brown. Then add tomato sauce and all seasonings. Cook very slowly, for you will not add water unless necessary. (Shrimp, to be added last, are 40% water). When tomato mixture is perfectly blended, in about 45 minutes, add shrimp and lemon. Cover and continue cooking for 30 minutes. Add Worcestershire sauce and cook 15 minutes more. Add finely chopped parsley and shallots the last 5 or 10 minutes before serving. These not only add color but are much tastier than fully cooked.

MRS. VERNON E. LACOUR
Plaquemine, La.

CREAMED SHRIMP WITH SHERRY ON TOAST

1 can frozen	2 tablespoons sherry
Shrimp Soup—thawed	1/8 teaspoon red pepper
1 pound cooked well	1 cup heavy cream
seasoned shrimp	Salt to taste after
1 can water chestnuts	completion

Smooth while beating slowly the thawed soup. Add shrimp and water chestnuts, smooth slowly in the cream and red pepper. Cook gently, stirring carefully for about 5 minutes. Then stir in the sherry. Taste and add salt and more sherry if desired.

TOAST

Trim, butter and cut into triangles 6 slices of fresh thin bread. Put on rack or cookie sheet in 250 degree oven for about 12 minutes or until very crisp all the way through.

Cover toast with creamed shrimp and garnish with parsley. Serve immediately.

MRS. ROBERT BARRY

SHANGHI SHRIMP

2 tablespoons cornstarch	¼ teaspoon monosodium
1 pound pineapple chunks	glutamate
2 tablespoons honey	1 teaspoon fresh
3 tablespoons soy sauce	ginger, finely chopped
1 tablespoon cream sherry	2 pounds shrimp, peeled
½ teaspoon Tabasco	and deveined
sauce	2 6-ounce cans of large
1 tablespoon vinegar	mushroom crowns

1 teaspoon salt

Combine cornstarch with the juice from can of pineapple chunks and stir to dissolve. Add remaining ingredients except shrimp and mushroom crowns. Simmer over low heat until thick. Add peeled and deveined fresh shrimp and the large mushroom crowns. Cook over very low heat until shrimp are almost, but not entirely, done. Then add the pineapple chunks and continue cooking until shrimp are done.

GLENNA K. UHLER
Plaquemine, La.

SHRIMP PILAF

2 cups rice	1 large onion
3 cups water	(or 2 small)
2 teaspoons salt	½ green pepper minced
Pepper to taste	2 pounds shrimp, cleaned

Lou Ana salad oil

Parch rice in salad oil until slightly browned. Add seasoning—cook until onions are withered Add boiling water and shrimp, stir well, cover, lower heat and steam until rice is cooked.

MRS. CONVILLE HOBGOOD, SR.
St. Francisville, La.

SHRIMP DE JOHNE

3 pounds shrimp	½ pound butter
Crab Boil	2 cloves garlic, crushed
Salt	White pepper
1½ cups seasoned	1 tablespoon minced
bread crumbs	parsley

1 tablespoon lemon juice

Boil shrimp in water and crab boil for 5 to 7 minutes. Peel and devein. Rub iron skillet with garlic, melt butter and add crushed garlic. Add shrimp and seasonings and cook a few minutes. Serve on platter of toast points with lemon slices to garnish.

MRS. JOHN S. FOX
Monroe, La.

SHRIMP WITH CHEESE-ONION SAUCE

1 pound cooked shrimp	½ teaspoon dry
4 tablespoons butter	mustard
½ cup grated onion	½ clove garlic (crushed)
½ cup grated cheese	1 teaspoon salt
(or more)	Sherry to taste

Melt butter in skillet with grated onion. Stir in cheese and other seasoning and let simmer for few minutes. Add shrimp and sherry. Pour in casserole and bake until brown on top. This is a delicious entree or luncheon dish·

EDITORS

SHRIMP CASSEROLE I
Serves 6-8

Clean 2 pounds of raw shrimp. Brown 1/3 cup fine chopped onions in 2 tablespoons butter with 1 or 2 minced garlic cloves. Put into a casserole the onion, garlic, shrimp, 1 cup raw rice, 1 large can tomatoes, 2 cups chicken bouillon or canned consomme. Add 1 bay leaf, 2 tablespoons chopped parsley, ½ teaspoon cloves, ½ teaspoon marjoram, 1 teaspoon chili powder, dash of cayenne, 1 teaspoon salt and ¼ teaspoon black pepper. Cover tightly and bake 1½ hours in 350 degree oven.

MRS. ROY A. WALLACE

SHRIMP CASSEROLE II

2 pounds shrimp	3 cans mushrooms
½ cup chopped onion	(medium)
½ cup chopped celery	3 cans mushroom soup
½ cup chopped green	Curry powder to taste
pepper	½ teaspoon ginger

2 cups cooked rice

Peel and saute the shrimp in **butter** with the onions, celery, green pepper, and mushrooms. Add the mushroom soup, curry powder, and ginger. Shrimp mixture and rice can be prepared early. Reheat shrimp mixture and mix part of it with the rice in a casserole. Add the remainder over the top. Place in oven long enough to heat the rice. (No salt is required with this recipe)

MRS. HOWARD DE LAUREAL
New Orleans, La.

SHRIMP CASSEROLE III

½ stick butter or oleo	½ green pepper
1 small onion	

Let this cook slowly until onion and pepper are tender, then add:

2 tablespoons flour and stir.

Slowly add:

2 cups of milk, salt and pepper to taste. Cook until thick, add ¼ pound grated sharp cheese. Add 1 pound shrimp, sauted in butter until barely cooked. Bake in greased casserole, topped with bread crumbs, for 20-25 minutes at 350 degrees.

MRS. EDWARD L. SIMON
Baton Rouge, La.

SHRIMP CURRY

½ cup minced onion
5 tablespoons butter.
5 tablespoons flour
2 teaspoons curry
  powder
1 teaspoon dry mustard

¼ teaspoon salt
1 teaspoon pepper
1 cup chicken stock
2 teaspoons catsup
2 cups milk
3 cups cooked shrimp

Melt butter and stir in flour. Add onions and let soften. Add milk stirring in carefully and then other ingredients. Serve over cooked rice. Use for condiments:

Pecans
Cocoanuts
Green onions

Shredded boiled egg
Crumbled bacon
Chutney

MRS. FRANK CONTOIS
Lake Charles, La.

SEAFOOD CURRY

¼ cup butter or
  chicken fat
Chicken stock (a cup
  or two)
2 cans frozen
  shrimp soup
1½ cups cooked shrimp
1½ cups cooked and
  chopped lobster tails
  (or lump crabmeat or
  crayfish)
2 tablespoons lemon juice
1 cup chopped onion
½ teaspoon pepper

1 cup chopped celery
1 large firm apple,
  chopped
¼ cup raisins plumped
  in hot water
4 tablespoons chopped
  chutney
1 tablespoon minced
  crystallized ginger
  (or powdered ginger)
4 teaspoons curry
  powder
1 clove garlic (or bud)
½ teaspoon salt

Saute onions, celery and apple that has had the lemon juice poured over it in fat. Cook gently about ten minutes. Add defrosted shrimp soup and bud of garlic, blend and mash garlic slightly, cooking very gently (never cover completely until it is completed and cool.) Make a paste of curry powder and soft butter or fat, add and blend. Add salt, pepper, raisins, chutney, the remainder of the lemon juice, and the ginger. Add enough chicken stock to form a nice consistency. Set aside for at least an hour. Then adjust seasonings.

Makes 8 portions or more served over fluffy rice. Accompannying condiments may be any or all of the following:

Chopped chutney
Toasted slivered almonds
Chopped green onion tops
Chopped crisp bacon
Grated fresh coconut

MRS. I. H. RUBENSTEIN

INDIAN SHRIMP CURRY

1 chicken boullion cube
5 tablespoons butter
  or oleo
½ cup minced onion
6 tablespoons flour
2½ teaspoons curry
  powder
1¼ teaspoon salt

1½ teaspoon sugar
¼ teaspoon powdered
  ginger
2 cups milk
4 cups cleaned, cooked
  shrimp (3 pounds
  raw)
1 teaspoon lemon juice

Dissolve boullion cube in 1 cup boiling water. Melt butter in top of double boiler over direct heat. Add onion and simmer until tender. Stir in flour, curry, sugar, salt and ginger. Gradually stir in milk and boullion. Cook over boiling water, stirring until thickened. Add shrimp and lemon juice and heat. Serve with hot, fluffy rice.

MRS. W. R. MCGAW

CRAB MEAT RAMEKINS

1 pound crab meat
2 tablespoons butter
1/3 pint cream
1 tablespoon capers or
  sour pickles
1 tablespoon chopped
  parsley

1 tablespoon chopped
  bell pepper
Salt, white pepper and a
  dash of cayenne
2 hard boiled eggs
  chopped
2 tablespoons sherry

1 medium can mushrooms

Chop mushooms, pepper, eggs, parsley capers, and add to the crab meat in a sauce pan. Pour in melted butter and then the cream. Season well, let it come to a boiling point, then remove from the stove. Add the sherry. Put in ramekins or shells, sprinkle with buttered bread crumbs and put in moderate oven for 15 minutes.

Submitted by
MRS. GRAHAM BIENVENU
With permission of the family of
Natalie Scott

SHRIMP A LA NEWBURG

6 pounds shrimp—
   cut in pieces
2 cans mushrooms, sliced
1 onion, chopped fine

½ cup butter
2½ tablespoons lemon
   juice
1 tablespoon salt

Dash of cayenne

Cook shrimp, mushrooms and onion in butter for 3 minutes, adding lemon juice, salt and dash of cayenne.

SAUCE FOR THE ABOVE

6 cups milk
6 tablespoons flour
¼ cup butter
1 can (small) pimiento
   sliced

12 tablespoons cooking
   sherry
Buttered bread or
   cracker crumbs
5 egg yolks

Melt butter in top of a double broiler. Stir in the flour. Gradually add scalded milk, stirring constantly. Cook until thickened. Add sherry. Last the beaten egg yolks. Remove from heat, add shrimp mixture. Put in baking dish or individual shells. Cover with buttered crumbs. Run in 350 degree oven about 30 minutes. Serves 10 to 12 shells.

MRS. HENRY P. ALLENDORPH
Oscar, La.

SHRIMP AND CRAB POULETTE
Serves 8

1 cup butter
4 shallots, finely chopped
3 pounds medium shrimp,
   cooked, peeled and
   deveined
½ cup white wine
3/4 cup flour

2 cups milk
2 cups heavy cream
1 teaspoon lemon juice
3 egg yolks
2 cups lump crab meat
Salt and freshly ground
   pepper to taste

Melt ¼ cup butter in sauce pan, add shallots and cook over medium heat for 4 or 5 minutes. Add white wine and bring mixture to a boil. Remove from heat. In separate sauce pan, melt remaining butter, add the flour and stir with wire whisk until well blended. Gradually add milk and cream, stirring constantly and cook, stirring, until sauce is thick and smooth. Season with lemon juice, salt and pepper. Lightly beat egg yolks with a little of the sauce and add, stirring, the remainder of the sauce. Add the wine-onion mixture to the white sauce and blend. Add shrimp and crab meat and simmer 5 minutes. Serve in pastry shells.

MRS. TROYE SVENDSON

SEAFOOD SHELLS
Serves twelve

3 cans frozen shrimp soup
3 cans frozen mushroom
  soup
1 can frozen potato soup
2 teaspoons seasoned salt
1 2-pound box frozen
  shrimp

2 packages lobster meat
2 cans lump crab meat
1 cup wine (sherry or
  sauterne)
1 carton whipping cream
Salt and pepper to taste
Bread crumbs

Blend the soups and salt in mixing bowl. Add the cooked and dressed shrimp, and remaining ingredients. Put in artificial shells, cover with buttered bread crumbs and bake until hot. Serve at once. If you wish to use fresh shrimp, boil 3 pounds in salted water with onion, celery and sliced lemon. Boil about 10 minutes and when cool, dress and use instead of frozen shrimp.

MRS. ROLAND B. HOWELL

CREAMED CRABMEAT AND MUSHROOMS IN SHELLS

1 pound lump crabmeat
1 cup celery, finely
  chopped
1 can sliced mushrooms
5 tablespoons butter
5 tablespoons flour
2½ cups milk
Salt, pepper, celery salt
1 teaspoon curry powder

1 tablespoon
  Worcestershire sauce
1 tablespoon
  lemon juice
1 tablespoon pimiento,
  chopped
3/4 cup sharp cheese,
  grated
Buttered bread crumbs

Sauté celery and mushrooms in 3 tablespoons butter. Make a sauce with the 5 tablespoons butter, flour, milk and seasonings. Add crabmeat and sauted vegetables to the white sauce. Add lemon juice and pimiento, taste, and season more if needed. Add cheese. Put in shells, cover with buttered crumbs and brown in 450 degree oven about 20 minutes.

MRS. EUGENE FLOURNOY
Monroe, La.

CRABMEAT BLANCHE

4 tablespoons butter	1 teaspoon finely chopped
2 tablespoons flour	parsley
1 cup milk	1 pound lump crab meat
2 tablespoons finely	1 can water chestnuts
chopped onions	Parmesan cheese

½ cup good white wine

Make cream sauce by melting butter, stirring in flour, then add milk, stirring constantly until it thickens. Add wine, onions and parsley, then add crab meat and sliced water chestnuts. Season with salt, cayenne, paprika, and Worcestershire sauce to taste. This cooks only the time it takes to put it together. Put in baking shells, top with cheese and buttered crumbs. Bake long enough to warm through.

MRS. WALLACE GLADNEY

SEAFOOD CONTINENTAL
Serves 6

2 cans cream of celery	4 cups drained, cooked
soup	seafood (a combina-
1/3 to ½ cup milk	tion of crab, lobster,
2 tablespoons dry	shrimp or white fish)
white wine or.	2 tablespoons minced
cooking sherry	parsley
1 cup shredded, mild	¼ cup seasoned
process cheese	bread crumbs

Blend soup, milk and wine. Mix with seafood, cheese and parsley. Spoon seafood mixture into shallow baking pan 10x6x2 inches, or into individual oven-proof dishes. Top with bread crumbs, dot with butter and bake at 400 degrees for 20 to 30 minutes.

MRS. CHARLES KYLE

CRAB OR SHRIMP NEWBURG

½ stick butter	Salt
6 tablespoons flour	Pepper
½ onion chopped	Tabasco sauce
1 clove garlic chopped	1 pound white crab meat
3 cups milk	3 hard boiled eggs
4 tablespoons sherry	4 oz. can mushrooms
Worcestershire sauce	stems and pieces

Chopped parsley

Melt butter. Saute onion and garlic. Add flour and mix to form paste. Gradually add milk, stirring constantly. Cook until sauce thickens. Then add sherry, Worcestershire sauce, salt and pepper to taste and a little Tabasco sauce. In another dish put crabmeat, hard boiled eggs, chopped mushrooms, and some chopped parsley. Add all of this to white sauce. Cook for a short while over low heat, stirring constantly. Serve on toast or in pastry shells. May also be used in chafing dish as a dip.

MRS. JOHN W. MAYFIELD, JR.

CRAB AND SHRIMP CASSEROLE
Serves 6-8

1 pound King Crab
½ pound shrimp
2 cups milk
3 tablespoons butter
   or margarine
3 tablespoons flour
1 cup grated cheese

4 oz. can stems and
   pieces mushrooms
1 tablespoon sherry
   (or more)
Onion salt, Worcestershire
   sauce, white pepper
   to taste

Cornflake crumbs

Make white sauce of butter, flour and milk. Add seasonings. Add shrimp and crab coarsely cut. Add cheese, mushrooms and sherry. Put in 2 quart casserole. Top with crumbs. Bake at 350 degrees until bubbly. (20 to 30 minutes).

MRS. DONALD McANDREW

DEVILED CRABS

6-9 fresh crabs or 1 pound
   crab meat
2 slices bread
1 large onion
2 tablespoons celery
Crushed red pepper to taste

2 tablespoons onion tops
2 teaspoons parsley
1 pod garlic, crushed
3 tablespoons bacon fat
¼ cup milk
Coffee cup of cream

Soften seasoning in hot bacon fat. Wet bread in milk. Add to crabmeat with seasoning. Fry in skillet for a short time. Do not let dry. Add coffee cup of cream as it begins to cook. Season well. Fill shells or casserole and sprinkle with homemade bread crumbs. Brown in oven. This is an old family recipe.

THE EDITORS

BREAD CRUMBS

1 cup fresh bread crumbs   ½ stick butter

SEAFOOD CASSEROLE

1½ pounds shrimp	3 cloves garlic
boiled & cleaned	½ cup celery
1 pound crabmeat	2 cups cooked rice
1 bell pepper	2 cans mushroom soup
1 onion	Tabasco to taste
½ cup onion tops	3 tablespoons
½ cup parsley	Worcestershire sauce

Chop all seasonings **fine**. Combine all ingredients, place in a greased casserole and bake at low temperature about 45 minutes. Decorate top of the baked casserole with red or jalapenos peppers. (Some pepper can be added to the other ingredients before baking if highly seasoned food can be eaten by all.

Mrs. Robert Lee, III
Jennings, La.

BAR B QUE CRABS

12-16 hard shelled crabs	8 or 10 dashes Tabasco
2 sticks butter	1 teaspoon garlic salt or
1½ tablespoons salt	seasoned salt

½ teaspoon paprika

With a sharp knife, remove top shell and clean crabs. Leave meat in bottom shell. Cut legs at first joint, leaving remainder of legs. Make sauce and simmer a few minutes. Place crabs shell side down on barbecue grill. Baste every 10 minutes with sauce. Cook 30-45 minutes. Turn over last few minutes to brown.

Mrs. Heidel Brown

QUICHE AU CRAB

1/8 inch pastry shell	1 tablespoon grated
partially baked	onion
6½ ounce can crabmeat	3 oz. grated Gruyere
2 large eggs	cheese
1 cup cream	4 oz. grated Swiss Cheese
3/4 teaspoon salt	1 tablespoon flour
1 tablespoon dry Vermouth	Pinch nutmeg

1/8 teaspoon pepper

Partially bake pastry shell for 10 minutes at 400 degrees. Cool, while draining crab and flaking it. Beat together eggs, cream, and seasoning, adding crab, wine, flour, and chesses. Pour into pastry shell and bake 35 minutes at 375 until firm. Remove and cut into 5 or 6 portions and serve with watercress salad or other green salad and spiced apple rings and pickled watermelon rind. This is perfect for an elegant luncheon or summer Sunday Supper. The quiche may also be allowed to cool and served in small portions as hors d'oeuvres.

From the files of
BARRON AND BARONESS
VON BRENNIG
Through their grandson and his
wife Mrs. Charles Coudart
Brennig, Jr.

CRAB MEAT CASSEROLE I

1 package herbed
  rice cooked
1 stick of butter

1 medium onion chopped
3 ribs celery chopped
1 pound lump crab meat

SAUCE TO BE SERVED SEPARATELY:

Juice of 1 lemon
1 stick of butter

1 tablespoon
  Worcestershire sauce

Saute celery and onion in a stick of butter and mix with cooked rice. Add crab meat. Bake in 350 degree oven for a half hour. Melt butter, add lemon juice and Worcestershire sauce, blend well, and serve over individual servings of crab meat casserole.

MRS. TOM W. DUTTON
New Orleans, La.

CRAB MEAT CASSEROLE II
Serves 6

1 cup cooked crab meat
3 cups thick white sauce
1 teaspoon celery salt
Buttered cracker crumbs
    1 green pepper chopped

2 cups grated cheese (½ pound)
¼ ounce can mushrooms (stems & pieces)

Remove spines from crab meat. Heat white sauce and cheese in double boiler and stir until smooth. Add celery salt, green pepper, mushrooms and crab meat. Pour into casserole, cover with cracker crumbs and bake in 350 degree oven about 30 minutes. If preferred, use ¼ cup chopped pimiento instead of green pepper.

WHITE SAUCE

2 tablespoons butter
2 tablespoons flour
    1/8 teaspoon pepper

1 cup milk
¼ teaspoon salt

MRS. JOHN McKOWEN, JR.

STUFFED CRABS I

2 tablespoons bacon
　grease
1 onion
1 bell pepper
1 clove garlic
Parsley
1 stick celery
1 pound fresh crab meat

3 hard boiled eggs
1 can mushroom stems
　and pieces
2 slices bread soaked in
　milk and drained
1 can pimientoes
Seasoned bread crumbs
White sauce (recipe below)

Chop fine and saute in bacon grease, onion, bell pepper, garlic, parsley, and celery. Put crabmeat, eggs, mushrooms, soaked bread, pimientoes in a bowl. Add sauteed vegetables and mix well. Then add enough white sauce to make a fairly compact mixture. Season with Worcestershire sauce, Tabasco sauce. Put in shells. Cover with crushed cracker crumbs. Put a wedge of butter on top and cook until brown. Serve with tartar sauce.

WHITE SAUCE

1 heaping tablespoons
　flour

1 tablespoon butter
Salt and pepper to taste

1 cup milk

Melt butter. Add flour, salt and pepper. Mix until smooth. Add milk gradually, stirring constantly. Cook over low fire until thick, continuing to stir constantly.

TARTAR SAUCE

½ onion
2 stalks celery

1 sour pickle
Parsley

Mayonnaise

Grate onion, chop celery, pickle, and parsley real fine. Mix with mayonnaise. Add lemon juice to taste.

MRS. JOHN W. MAYFIELD, JR.

STUFFED CRABS II

1 pound can of lump
　crab meat
4 tablespoons butter
2 tablespoons flour
1 tablespoon minced
　parsley

2 tablespoons lemon
　juice
1 teaspoon mustard
½ teaspoon horseradish
1 teaspoon salt
1 cup milk

2 hardboiled eggs, chopped

Make a white sauce with the butter, flour and milk. Add other ingredients and carefully fold in crab meat.

Put bread crumbs on top, dot with butter and bake 10 minutes in 400-450 degree oven.

MRS. FRED O. TAYLOR

MARYLAND CRAB CAKE

1 pound regular crab meat	1 pound claw crab meat

To each pound of crab meat, add:

2 eggs, well beaten	½ teaspoon pepper
2 tablespoons mayonnaise	Hot pepper to taste
1 teaspoon prepared mustard	2 slices of bread, crust removed, and soaked
1 teaspoon salt	in milk

Combine egg and seasonings, beating well. Add crumbled bread to crab meat. Then add egg mixture. Shape into cakes and fry. Or put a pat of butter or margarine on top of each cake and brown each side of cake under broiler.

MRS. R. T. MERRITT, SR.
Baltimore, Maryland

CRABMEAT IN INDIVIDUAL SHELLS OR CASSEROLE

1 pound lump crabmeat	1½ tablespoon chopped green onion "Half.and
1 stick butter	Half" (cream, milk)
2 slices toasted bread	1 tablespoon parsley,
1½ tablespoons chopped bellpepper (red bellpepper is best)	finely minced
	1½ tablespoons minced celery

2 soft cooked eggs

Saute the vegetables in butter until clear in pan. Fold in lump crab meat and try not to break up the lumps. Add the two soft boiled eggs and toasted bread broken up into small pieces.

Add enough cream (Half and Half) until the mixture is only well moist. Season with salt needed and red pepper.

Put mixture in individual shells or in a casserole and cover with fine bread crumbs. Heat in the oven at about 300 degrees until heated hot and serve immediately.

You may fix this in the morning and heat just before serving. In this case wait until ready to heat to sprinkle top with bread crumbs.

MRS. C. C. WOOD

SUPERB CRAB MEAT MOLD

2 envelopes plain gelatin
½ cup water
1 package cream cheese
  (8 ounces)
1 can cream of mushroom
  soup
1 pound fresh crab meat
1 cup mayonnaise
1 medium sized onion—
  grated
1 tablespoon
  Worcestershire sauce
½ teaspoon salt
Red pepper to taste
1 cup chopped celery
1 small green pepper—
  chopped
½ cup chopped olives
1/3 cup pimiento
Juice of one lemon

Soften gelatin in water and put soup in double boiler. When soup begins to warm, add gelatin and heat enough to dissolve gelatin. Remove from fire and cool. Add mayonnaise and cream cheese which is at room temperature. Mix in other ingredients. Pour in fish mold which has been greased. Decorate eyes and tail with olives and strip of green pepper and pimiento. Sprinkle with paprika.

MRS. WILLIAM B. BATES

CRABMEAT LOUIS

1 pound crabmeat
½ cup mayonnaise
¼ cup chili sauce
1 tablespoon lemon juice
3 tablespoons
  chopped shallots
Dash Worcestershire
2 tablespoons sweet
  pickles
3 tablespoons bell pepper
¼ teaspoon celery salt
Pepper to taste
1 tablespoon horseradish
¼ teaspoon salt

Chop shallots, pickles and celery very fine. Mix all ingredients and serve over the crabmeat, or boiled shrimp. Serve in avocado, in tomato, or on lettuce. Garnish with sliced, or quartered hard boiled eggs

MRS. R. B. RICHARDSON

CRAYFISH ELEGANTE

1 pound crayfish tails
1½ sticks butter or oleo
1 small bunch green onions
½ cup chopped parsley
1 pint half and half
3 tablespoons sherry
Salt and red pepper
  to taste

3 level tablespoons flour

In skillet sauté crayfish tails in ½ stick butter or oleo for 10 minutes. In another skillet sauté green onions and parsley in 1 stick of butter or oleo. Blend in flour and gradually add half and half stirring constantly to make a thick sauce. Add sherry, then crayfish tails being careful not to include fat in bottom of skillet. Season with salt and red pepper to taste. Serve in pattie shells. Will freeze well. Note: Before cooking crayfish tails, lay on paper towels and wipe gently to remove some of the fat.

MRS. LYTTLETON T. HARRIS

DEVILED OYSTERS I

3 pints oysters
4 medium onions
8 pieces celery
    (1 cup)
10 slices bread toasted and
    rolled into crumbs
    (2 cups)
1½ sticks butter or oleo
3 tablespoons lemon juice

4 tablespoons
    Worcestershire sauce
4 eggs beaten
White sauce made with 2
    tablespoons each
    butter and flour and
    1 cup milk
2 teaspoons salt
½ teaspoon red pepper

Grind onions, celery and oysters, using coarse cutter. Fry onions until nearly brown in half the butter. Add celery and fry a little longer. In separate sauce pan, melt remaining butter, put in oysters and simmer for 2 or 3 minutes. In another sauce pan, make the white sauce. When moderately thick, add beaten eggs. Mix all together and add seasonings. Save out 3/4 cup of buttered bread crumbs for the tops of 24 shells. Fill shells, sprinkle with crumbs and bake 10 or 15 minutes in a 400 degree oven. Garnish with tiny wedges of lemon and small sprigs parsley.

MRS. EUGENE FLOURNOY
Monroe, La.

DEVILED OYSTERS II

50 oysters
1 cup bread crumbs
3 eggs (well beaten)

Salt and pepper
Dash of red pepper
1 onion (chopped)

½ stick butter

Put oysters in bowl and chop fine. Put in skillet with red pepper and salt and let simmer. Chop onion very fine and brown in butter. Add bread crumbs with well beaten eggs to oysters and onion and let simmer until some of juice gets out. Put in shells, cover with bread crumbs, dot with butter and bake.

MRS. FRANK M. WOMACK

DEVILED OYSTERS III
Serves 6-8

6 dozen oysters cut to
medium size
1 cup bread crumbs
½ pint cream
1 tablespoon flour

1 cup chopped celery
2 bunches green onions,
chopped
2 cups chopped parsley
1 stick butter

Melt butter, add celery and green onions, saute well; add flour, let dissolve, add cream. In separate pot, heat drained oysters and add them to cream sauce. Let cook about 10 minutes, then add bread crumbs and parsley. Thin with milk, if necessary. Fill shells or casserole, sprinkle with bread crumbs and heat in oven.

MRS. DANIEL FOURRIER

BAKED OYSTERS

1 3/4 sticks butter
6 or 8 dozen large oysters
1 cup chopped green
onions, including tops
1 cup celery chopped
5 tablespoons milk

1½ tablespoon
Worcestershire sauce
½ cup parsley chopped
1 tablespoon seasoned salt
3½ cup Italian style
bread crumbs

Saute onion, celery and parsley in ½ stick butter. Add seasoning. Melt 1 stick butter and stir in bread crumbs. Add to onion mixture and correct seasoning. Divide into three equal portions. Cover the bottom of a well greased shallow baking dish with 1/3 of the mixture. Cover this with a layer of closely packed oysters. Repeat, ending with crumb mixture as final layer. Sprinkle top with milk and dot with remaining butter. Bake in a 400 degree oven for 35 to 40 minutes. Serve hot.

MRS. CARLETON BATES

OYSTERS DUNCAN

6 dozen large oysters
2 sticks butter
1 small bottle
Worcestershire sauce
½ clove garlic, mashed
3 shallots, chopped

2 dashes Tabasco
3/4 cup celery,
chopped fine
Salt and pepper to taste
2 tablespoons lemon juice
Buttered cracker crumbs

Make a sauce of all ingredients, except cracker crumbs and oysters, and let simmer for 10 to 15 minutes. Drain oysters and place in shell dishes. Cover with sauce. Sprinkle cracker crumbs on top, and run in a 350 degree to 400 degree oven for about 10 or 15 minutes, or until oyster edges curl. You may run this under the broiler for about 1 minute to brown the cracker crumbs.

MRS. JOHN HUTCHINSON, JR.

CREAMED OYSTERS

1 pint oysters
1 stick butter
8 green onions, chopped
3 stalks celery, chopped
1 small white onion,
   chopped
1 tablespoon parsley,
   chopped

1 small bell pepper,
   chopped
3 pods garlic, crushed
2 tablespoons flour
1 teaspoon
   Worcestershire sauce
1 small can mushrooms,
   drained

Salt and pepper to taste

Drain 1 pint of oysters, saving the liquid. Cook oysters in ½ stick of butter until they curl. Set aside. Cook onions, celery, bell pepper, and garlic in ½ stick of butter, add 2 tablespoons flour, the Worcestershire sauce and salt and pepper to taste. Add liquid and oysters to the above mixture and 1 small can of mushrooms, drained. Serve in ramekins sprinkled over with bread crumbs, or, in chafing dish with toast points.

MRS. BEN DOWNING

MRS. ALLEN'S OYSTER PIE
Serves 8

4 dozen oysters
1 large tablespoon flour
1 large tablespoon
   shortening
2 medium dried onions
3 pods garlic

1 stalk celery
2 green onions
3 pieces parsley
4 eggs
1 stick butter
1 cup milk

Make pie pastry and line deep baking dish. Save enough for a top. Melt flour and lard until smooth in skillet, add dried onions and garlic. (cut very fine). Brown lightly. Add oysters and juice to above and let simmer. Cut fine, celery, green onions, parsley and add to oyster mixture. Pour in pastry lined pan. Hard boil the eggs and slice over the above. Cut up butter and dot around, add milk. Put pastry top on and bake 1 hour in oven 350 degrees.

From the file of
MRS. ESTELLE LEWIS CORBETT

OYSTERS ETHEL
Serves 4

1 quart oysters	1 small bottle Durkee's
1 pint milk	dressing
1 cup chopped celery	1 teaspoon dry mustard
Browned bread crumbs	2 tablespoons butter
Salt and pepper to taste	2 eggs

Place oysters in sauce pan and heat in their own liquid until edges curl. Drain, reserving liquid. Add milk, celery and onion to the liquid and cook until tender. Add chopped oysters, dressing, eggs, butter and enough bread crumbs to thicken. Season to taste with salt and pepper. Bake 45 minutes at 350 degrees.

MRS. ETHEL MARS
Knoxville, Tenn.

FROG LEGS

Frog legs	1 egg
Seafood seasoning	2 tablespoons milk
Salt	1 cup flour

1 cup bread crumbs

Sprinkle frog legs thoroughly with seafood seasoning and salt and let stand for a short while. Mix egg and milk and beat slightly. Mix flour and bread crumbs in paper bag. Dip seasoned frog legs first in egg mixture, then shake in paper bag. Fry in heavy skillet in Lou Ana oil (to cover legs halfway) approximately 10 minutes on one side and less on the other. Drain and serve piping hot.

MARGARET FREEMAN
Garden City, La.

TUNA TETRAZZINI
Serves 6

½ 8-oz. package spaghettini	1 8-oz. package process
3 tablespoons bottled	American cheese,
garlic spread	grated
¼ cup all purpose flour	½ teaspoon seasoned salt
1 cup milk	Pepper
¼ cup sherry	2 cans chunk tuna, drained
2 4-oz. cans button	2 tablespoons Parmesan
mushrooms	cheese, grated

Cook spaghettini as directed. Drain. In double boiler melt garlic spread. Stir in flour. Add milk, gradually, sherry, and ½ cup mushroom juice. Cook until thickened, while stirring. To the sauce add American cheese, seasoned salt, pepper. Stir until cheese is melted. Add the spaghettini, tuna, and mushrooms. Pour into 1½ quart shallow baking dish. Sprinkle with Parmesan. Bake 20 minutes at 350 degrees, or until brown.

MRS. CHARLES E. BEADLES

TUNA CASSEROLE

1 can tuna fish flakes	1 small can water chestnuts
1 can cream mushroom	(chopped)
soup	1 5-oz. can chow mein
1 cup chopped celery	noodles
3 green onions chopped	½ cup cashew nuts

Prepare all chopped ingredients the day before, if you like. Mix tuna, mushroom soup, chopped ingredients and noodles. Top with cashew nuts. Bake in covered casserole dish ½ hour in a 350 degree oven. This should be **mixed** and cooked just before serving, so that noodles will not become soggy.

MRS. WILLIAM HEARD WRIGHT

REMOULADE SAUCE

1½ cups green onions with tops	2 tablespoons grated fresh ginger
2 cups celery chopped	4-5 tablespoons Worcestershire sauce
1 medium dry onion, chopped	3 bay leaves, whole
1 small bell pepper, chopped	3 tablespoons fresh, sweet basil
1½ cups parsley, minced	2 tablespoons roquette, chopped
1 lemon rind minced fine	Cayenne pepper,
3 large cloves garlic, pressed	Tabasco, freshly ground white and
3¼ cups olive oil	black peppercorns
2 cups cider or wine vinegar	to taste
¼ cup lemon juice	Salt and seasoned
1 teaspoon dry mustard	salt to taste

½ cup horseradish

All chopped ingredients should be chopped very, very fine. While tedious, this is the secret of success. Pack chopped items down to measure. Mix all ingredients, correct seasoning, and let stand for several hours before using. Should be piquant and zesty, but not distastefully hot. This amount will marinate 5 to 7 pounds of cooked and cleaned shrimp. Delicious on lump crab meat as Hor D'ouvre or shrimp remoulade on lettuce. Keeps well in the refrigerator and may be also used to season mayonnaise or other oil dressings.

MRS. CARLTON BATES

ALBERTHA'S SAUCE FOR BROILED FISH

1½ sticks butter
1 can tomato paste
2 tomato paste cans
    filled with water
2 tablespoons soy sauce
1 tablespoon
    Worcestershire sauce
Tabasco, several dashes

¼ cup lemon juice or
    more to taste
Onion salt
Celery salt
Garlic salt or 1 clove
    pressed garlic
1 tablespoon
    parsley flakes

Simmer 10 minutes. Do not let mixture boil. Stir often. Good on any broiled fish.

MRS. JOHN W. BARTON

Vegetables

WHITE SAUCE (THIN)

1 tablespoon butter	½ teaspoon salt
1 tablespoon flour	1 cup milk

Melt butter over low heat; add flour and salt and stir until well blended. Stir in milk gradually. Cook stirring constantly, until thick and smooth. This is a thin sauce. For a medium sauce, double the amounts of butter and flour. For a thick sauce, triple the amounts of butter and flour.

THE EDITORS

SAUCE FOR BROCCOLI

3 egg yolks	Pinch paprika
½ teaspoon mustard	¼ cup vinegar
1 teaspoon sugar	1/3 cup Lou Ana oil

Cook over low heat, stirring constantly, until it thickens. Serve hot on broccoli or green asparagus. Should sauce separate, add few drops of hot water.

MRS. PHILIP R. FARNSWORTH

NEVER FAIL HOLLANDAISE SAUCE

2 tablespoons flour	3 tablespoons lemon juice
2 tablespoons butter	1 cup boiling water
2 egg yolks	Salt, red pepper, paprika

Melt butter and flour in double boiler. Add salt, pepper, paprika, and boiling water, and lemon juice. Just before serving add beaten egg yolks. Return to boiler and heat.

MRS. ASHTON FENET
Lake Charles, La.

LAMB STUFFED ARTICHOKES

4 whole fresh artichokes	2 beaten eggs
1 pound ground lamb	½ teaspoon salt
3/4 cup chopped onion	¼ teaspoon pepper
2 tablespoons Lou-Ana oil	¼ teaspoon ground
½ cup bread crumbs	nutmeg
¼ cup chopped parsley	1 clove garlic, minced

Wash artichokes and cut off stem close to base. Cook in boiling salted water for 25 to 30 minutes or until leaf can be pulled out readily. Drain upside down. Cut off tips of leaves with kitchen shears. Remove center leaves and chokes.

Lightly brown lamb and onion and garlic in oil. Add crumbs, parsley, egg, salt, pepper and nutmeg. Mix well. Spread leaves slightly. Fill centers and in between leaves with mixture. Place in baking dish. Pour hot water around artichokes to the depth of 1 inch. Bake in moderate oven 350 degrees for 30 or 40 minutes or until heated through.

SERVE WITH SAUTERNE SAUCE:

In small saucepan combine ¼ cup sauterne, 1 tablespoon minced onion, let stand 10 minutes. Add 3/4 cup mayonnaise, 2 tablespoons chopped parsley, 1 tablespoon lemon juice. Cook and stir until mixture is heated through. Do not boil.

MRS. R. O. RUSH

STUFFED ARTICHOKES

6 artichokes	1 teaspoon thyme
3 cups bread crumbs	1 tablespoon chopped
1½ cups Parmesan or	parsley
Romano cheese	2 cloves garlic crushed
1 teaspoon sweet basil	½ teaspoon black pepper
1 teaspoon Beau Monde	½ teaspoon salt
seasoning	1 cup Lou Ana or olive oil

Cut stems off artichokes. Open leaves and wash. Rub lemon around sides of artichokes. Mix dry ingredients, place between leaves and pour oil around the leaves. Put in deep pot with 3 inches of water. Add 1/3 teaspoon salt. Be sure that water does not boil over artichokes. Boil 30 minutes, or until they are tender.

MRS. RICHARD MAESTRI

JERUSALEM OR GROUND ARTICHOKES
Simple, but excellent to serve with wild duck

Peel artichokes. Put in a saucepan with enough milk to cover. Season with salt and simmer until tender. Drain off excess milk. In hot pan put a liberal piece of butter and a bit of salt if needed. Shake pan to coat vegetables.

MRS. WALTER H. CLAIBORNE
Bella Vista Plantation

HOLLANDAISE SAUCE

2 egg yolks
½ teaspoon salt
2 specks Cayenne pepper

½ cup melted butter—
no substitute
1 tablespoon lemon juice

With a rotary beater, or electric beater at high speed, beat egg yolks until thick and lemon colored. Add salt and pepper. Then add 3 tablespoons of the melted butter, a little at a time, beating constantly. Beat in rest of butter alternately with the lemon juice. If made ahead, chill until serving. Then stir until softened over lukewarm, not hot, water.

This may be kept indefinitely in refrigerator.

MRS. E. S. DAVID

ARTICHOKE HEARTS CASSEROLE
Serves 10-12

3 cans artichoke hearts
1 box seasoned bread
crumbs (15 oz.)
1½ cups olive oil
Worcestershire sauce

2 cups liquid from
artichokes
Salt and red pepper
3 ounce can Parmesan
cheese

Drain artichokes and cut each into four pieces. Save liquid. Mix all ingredients in casserole and season with salt, red pepper and Worcestershire sauce. Bake in 350 degree oven until bubbly hot, approximately 45 minutes.

MRS. ELWOOD ANDERSON

ASPARAGUS-ARTICHOKE CASSEROLE
Serves 6

1 (14 ounce) can green
asparagus
1 (14 ounce) can
artichokes
2 (4 ounce) cans mushrooms
Salt and pepper to taste
½ cup artichoke juice

¼ pound cheese
(sharp), grated
2 cups milk
4 tablespoons butter
(heaping)
4 tablespoons flour
(heaping)

Be sure to save artichoke juice when opening can. Place asparagus, artichokes and mushrooms (all drained) into layers in casserole dish. Make a heavy cream sauce using milk, artichoke juice, butter and flour. Add salt and pepper and part of the grated cheese to cream sauce. Pour over vegetables. Top with rest of cheese and bake at 350 degrees for about 25 minutes. Serves 6. Artichokes may be cut in halves if too large.

MRS. CARRIE J. ELLIS, JR.
Rayville, La.

GREEN ASPARAGUS CASSEROLE

2 cans green asparagus (cut in half)
½ cup ripe olives, slivered
6 hard cooked eggs, sliced
1 cup thick cream sauce
1 cup grated, sharp Chaddar cheese (well packed)
1 tablespoon Worcestershire sauce
Salt, red pepper and Paprika to taste

Grease casserole well with butter. Place half of the asparagus, eggs and olives in casserole. Pour over half of the sauce to which has been added the cheese, seasoning and some liquid from the asparagus. Repeat this procedure. Top with seasoned bread crumbs, dot with butter and bake at 350 degrees until hot and bubbly. Can be made in advance and baked just before serving.

MRS. GORDON M. RONALDSON

HOT SPICED BEETS

8 medium sized beets, sliced
½ small onion, sliced
1/3 cup water
2 tablespoons butter
6 tablespoons vinegar
6 whole cloves
2 tablespoons sugar
¼ inch stick cinnamon

Place alternate layers of beets and onions in covered dish. Mix remaining ingredients and pour over beets. Cover. Place over low heat for about 15 minutes just before serving. Very delicious with a vegetable meal.

MRS. ESTELL GORDON CURRIE

CANDIED BEETS

1 can small whole beets
1 tablespoon melted butter
½ cup sugar
1 tablespoon flour
¼ cup vinegar

Make sauce with butter, flour, vinegar and sugar— when thick add can of beets well drained—add salt, pepper and cinnamon to taste and cook until glazed.

MRS. MULLER HOCHENEDEL

BAKED AVOCADO

½ large avocado per person	Worcestershire sauce
Shrimp, crabmeat or chicken	Garlic to taste
	Red pepper to taste
1 can mushroom soup	Butter or oleo
	Bread crumbs

Leave shell on avocado and slice a piece of each bottom off so it will stay upright. Scoop out a small amount of the pear. Fill hollow with shrimp, crabmeat or chicken mixed with a can of mushroom soup. Season highly with Worcestershire, garlic, salt, red pepper and salt to taste. Cover with bread crumbs, dot with butter or oleo and put under broiler for 20 or 25 minutes. Not too close to flame.

MRS. FELIX SPILLER

BAKED AVOCADO HALVES
Serves 6

3 ripe avocados	2 tablespoons flour
1 small can green asparagus cut into 1 inch pieces	1 cup milk
	1 tablespoon pimiento, chopped
2 tablespoons butter	2 slices bacon

Cut avocados in half and remove seeds. Make a cream sauce with the butter, flour and milk. Season with salt and pepper to taste. Add pimiento and cut asparagus to sauce and fill cavaties of avocados with the mixture. Cut bacon into small pieces and place on top of filled avocados. Bake in 350 degree oven for 10 minutes, then place under broiler to crisp bacon.

MRS. WALTER PARLANGE, JR.
Parlange Plantation

RANCH BEANS

6 slices bacon	½ cup green pepper chopped fine
1 large onion, chopped fine	½ cup tomato sauce
1 large clove garlic, crushed	2 tablespoons molasses
Dash of pepper	2 1-pound cans pork and beans

Cook bacon until crisp; drain on paper towel; crumble. Pour off all but ¼ cup drippings. Saute onion, garlic and green pepper in drippings about 5 minutes, or until tender. Add tomato sauce, pepper, molasses, pork

and beans and crumbled bacon and mix well. Pour into
1½ quart casserole and bake in 350 degree oven for
thirty minutes.

MRS. FRANK BOGARD
Ruston, La.

BEAN CASSEROLE
Serves 8

1 clove garlic minced
1 medium onion—chopped
3 tablespoons bacon
   drippings
2 cups pork and beans
2½ cups kidney beans
2½ cups green lima beans

½ cup catsup
3 tablespoons vinegar
   (apple cider)
2 tablespoons dark
   brown sugar
1 teaspoon dry mustard
1 teaspoon salt

½ teaspoon pepper

Sauté garlic and onion in bacon drippings. Add all
other ingredients and bake in 350 degree oven about an
hour.

MRS. HARALSON BARROW
St. Francisville, La.

BROCCOLI AND CHEESE SAUCE

1 bunch fresh broccoli
1½ teaspoon salt

1/3 cup buttermilk
1/3 cup Parmesan Cheese

Cook broccoli 20 minutes or until tender. Drain and
combine buttermilk and cheese in saucepan. Cook 5
minutes. Pour over cooked broccoli and serve.

THE EDITORS

CABBAGE IN MILK

3 cups raw finely
   shredded cabbage
3/4 cup boiling milk
¼ cup cream

½ teaspoon salt
½ teaspoon paprika
1 tablespoon butter
1 tablespoon flour

Pepper to taste

Drop finely shredded cabbage gradually in boiling
milk and boil for 2 minutes. Stir in cream, salt, and
paprika and pepper. In separate pan, melt the butter,
stir in the flour and blend until smooth. Add a little
liquid from the cabbage. Add this sauce to the cabbage.
Cook, while stirring, over a quick fire for 3 minutes.

MRS. HUBERT N. WAX

BROCCOLI PUDDING
Serves 8

1 cup medium cream sauce   1½ quarts chopped
1 cup mayonnaise   broccoli
    1 tablespoon lemon juice

Mix together. Pour in 2 quart casserole and sprinkle a little nutmeg on top. Bake 325 degrees in hot water until set.

(Spinach can be prepared the same way).

THE EDITORS

BARBECUE BAKED BEANS
Serves 14

1 large can lima beans   Small chunk of ham or
1 large can New Orleans   salt port or both
   red kidney beans   3 large onions chopped

SAUCE

¼ cup brown sugar   1 tablespoon
1 tablespoon dry mustard   Worcestershire sauce
  (optional)   1 tablespoon molasses
Red pepper to taste   ¼ teaspoon salt
1½ cups ketchup   3 tablespoons vinegar
    1 clove garlic crushed

Let sauce come to a boil. In bean pot or casserole, layer beans, onions, salt meat and ham, and sauce until top of pot is reached. Bake 3 hours at 300 degrees.

MRS. CHARLES KYLE

CABBAGE ROLLS
Makes 20 large rolls

2 pounds ground lean beef   2 small cans tomato sauce
2 cups raw rice   1½ cups green onions,
4 teaspoons salt (level)   chopped
2 teaspoons red pepper   1 cup chopped parsley
    2 cloves garlic, chopped

Mix together. Moisten well with Lou Ana oil and tomato sauce. Roll into cabbage leaves that have been wilted by steam. Pressure cook at 15 pounds for 15 minutes.

MRS. ATWELL E. CHAMPION

SWEET AND SOUR RED CABBAGE

1 medium red cabbage	Juice of 2 lemons
2 apples	1 clove or a little
4 or 5 heaping table-	cinnamon
spoons sugar	1 teaspoon flour

Boil cabbage which has been cut in thin strips in about a cup of water until nearly done. Peel apples and remove core, slice and put on top of cabbage. Add spice, sugar and lemon juice. Continue cooking until liquid has cooked down. Mix flour with a little water and pour over cabbage and cook for another minute. Adjust to your own taste, as sweet or as sour as you like. If you prefer the taste of vinegar substitute it for the lemon juice.

MRS. ERICH STERNBERG

BELL PEPPERS STUFFED WITH SHRIMP

4 large bell peppers	2 tablespoons Lou Ana oil
½ to 1 cup minced onion	2 tablespoons flour
1 pound shrimp peeled	Salt, cayenne &
3 slices stale bread	Worcestershire sauce
soaked in water	to taste

Wash, halve and core peppers. Saute shrimp until pink in butter. Make a small light roux with the oil and flour. Add onions to roux and cook until onions are tender. Add shrimp and bread (with the water that clings to it), then add seasonings to taste—it takes a good bit of seasoning because of the bread. Mix thoroughly, stuff the dressing into the pepper halves and top with bread crumbs. Place in baking dish with ½ inch of hot water surrounding the peppers. Bake at 375 degrees for 45 minutes to an hour.

MRS. WALLACE GLADNEY

FRIED CAULIFLOWER

1 large cauliflower	Cracker crumbs
1 egg and milk	Salt and pepper to taste

Break cauliflower into bite size flowerettes and parboil 5 minutes in salted water. Beat egg and milk together. Make cracker crumbs with fresh crackers. Dip flowerettes in beaten egg, roll in cracker crumbs, seasoned with salt and pepper, and fry in deep fat.

MRS. W. J. SPANO

BAVARIAN RED CABBAGE

1 1/3 pound red cabbage (green cabbage may be used)
3 tablespoons butter or bacon drippings
1 large onion, minced
1 cup hot water
1 large tart apple peeled and sliced
1/3 cup vinegar
2 tablespoons brown sugar
5 whole cloves

Shred the cabbage. Melt the butter in pan in which cabbage is to be cooked. Add onion and cook slowly until soft and yellow. Add cabbage, apple, water, vinegar, sugar, cloves and salt. Toss together. Cover and cook just until cabbage is wilted. Uncover and cook 20 minutes, stirring occasionally.

MRS. HENRY P. ALLENDORPH
Oscar, La.

CARROT CASSEROLE

1 small bunch carrots
1 small to medium onion (chopped fine)
1 cup milk
1 small bell pepper (chopped fine)
2 tablespoons butter
2 level tablespoons flour
Salt and pepper to taste

Scrape and cut carrots into slices (not over ½ inch) and cook in boiling water until done. Make a white sauce with the butter, flour and milk. Place a layer of carrots in pyrex casserole and cover with a layer of onion, bell pepper and a portion of the cream sauce. Repeat. Sprinkle with bread crumbs, dot with butter and bake at 350 degrees 20 minutes.

MRS. HAMILTON CRAWFORD

BRAISED CELERY AMANDINE

4 small—or two large— bunches of celery
1 10½-oz can condensed chicken broth
2 tablespoons melted butter
Paprika
1 tablespoon blanched slivered almonds

Use lower part of celery stalks. Scrape off fiber and cut into 5-inch lengths. Split these 5-inch lengths in half. Put in skillet and pour on chicken broth (undiluted). Cover and cook 25 minutes or until tender. Arrange in serving dish. Pour melted butter over them, sprinkle with paprika and slivered almonds.

MRS. R. B. RICHARDSON

CORN PUDDING
Old Virginia Recipe
Serves 6

2 eggs
2 cans cream style corn
¼ cup flour
1 teaspoon salt

½ teaspoon black pepper
2 tablespoons butter
   (melted)
1 can evaporated milk

Beat eggs, flour, salt and pepper. Add corn, milk, butter and blend well. Pour into buttered casserole and place into shallow baking dish with water. Bake at 300 degrees for 1 hour and 15 minutes.

MRS. J. B. HEROMAN, JR.

CORN AND TAMALE CASSEROLE

2 No. 2 cans whole
   kernel corn

1 large can Tamales
½ can hot tomatoes

Salt to taste

Cut tamales in one inch pieces, add salt, pepper and corn. Mix well and pour in well greased casserole. Bake at 350 degrees for 1 hour.

MRS. HENRY GEORGE MC MAHON

MOCQUE CHOUX (Mock-Shoo)

15 or 20 ears fresh,
   tender corn (freshly
   gathered)
1 large or 2 medium
   onions chopped
1 clove garlic mashed
1 teaspoon hot red pepper

2 tablespoons chopped
   parsley
1 large bell pepper
   chopped
2 hot green peppers
½ cup Lou Ana oil, or a
   little more

Salt to taste

Cut corn off the cob, slicing the kernels twice, after which scrape the cobs to get all the corn juice. Heat oil in a heavy deep pot, add chopped onion and saute until tender, but not brown. Add corn, bell pepper, garlic and hot peppers, then salt to taste. Stir mixture over medium heat for about a half hour, stirring constantly. If corn does not have enough moisture to make consistency of soft mush, add milk or water. Just before serving, add parsley.

MRS. RHEA WATTS
Solitude Plantation
St. Francisville, La.

CORN PUDDING

¼ cup butter
¼ cup flour
2 teaspoons sugar
(heaping)
3 eggs

1 teaspoon salt
1 3/4 cups milk
3 cups fresh or frozen
creamed corn

Melt butter in pan, stir in flour, salt and sugar. Cook until bubbly, add milk and cook until thick. Stir in corn and eggs which have been beaten frothy. Pour in well buttered casserole and bake in pan of hot water at 350 degrees for about 45 minutes.

MRS. JAMES M. LOWRY

FRESH CORN OFF THE COB

6 ears of mature but
tender corn
1 tablespoon sugar
1/3 stick butter

2 tablespoons of bacon
grease
1 teaspoon salt

In a bowl cut off the tip of corn and then scrape. When complete take your hand and squeeze corn in bowl to make creamy. If necessary add a small amount of water. Heat bacon grease until hot, add corn and stir constantly over medium heat until it changes color and bubbles up once. Remove from heat add seasonings and place top on sauce pan until ready to serve. If any is left over heat with small amount of milk.

MRS. W. J. OLIVER, JR.

RANCH CORN

2 cans cream style yellow
corn
2 cans white hominy
1 can tamales
Cracker meal

2 tablespoons chili
powder
Crushed red pepper or
cayenne

Mix corn with chili powder and red pepper and hominy. In a buttered baking dish pour ½ of mixture. Cut tamales into bite size pieces and arrange on top of mixture. Cover tamales with rest of mixture, dust top with cracker meal and black pepper. Bake at 350 degrees for 30 to 35 minutes. This is particularly good as a Barbecue accompaniment.

MRS. FONVILLE WINANS

MEXICAN CORN

½ stick oleo
1 medium onion
1 can hot tomatoes

1 can cream style corn
1½ tablespoon dried
  onion soup

2 cans Niblet corn

Sauté onion in oleo until tender. Add can of hot tomatoes and cook down. Add 2 cans Niblet corn and cream corn. Add dried onion soup. Cook at 375 degrees for about 1 hour. Let set before serving.

MISS ARABELLE WOODSIDE

BAKED EGGPLANT

2 large eggplants
½ loaf French bread (wet)
2 eggs
1 pound clean, deveined
  shrimp
1 tablespoon thyme
½ stick butter

Salt, pepper & hot
  pepper to taste
1 pound lump crab meat
1 hard onion & 3 green
  onions
1 cup celery chopped fine
2 tablespoons parsley

3 tablespoons Lou Ana oil

Boil eggplants, cool, peel and place in collander to drain. Add onions, parsley, thyme, celery and squeezed out bread. Add eggplants and mix well. Add shrimp, crab meat and eggs. Fry in oil with ½ stick of butter. Put in large baking dish, sprinkle with bread crumbs and bake about 20 minutes.

MRS. RICHARD MAESTRI

EGGPLANT TOP HATS

2 medium eggplants
½ cup chopped onions
½ cup shredded Swiss
  cheese

1 egg
1 tablespoon cream
½ teaspoon salt
½ cup flour

Slice eggplants into 8 slices and peel. Put in bowl of salted water under a weight and let stand 15 minutes. Drain and parboil until barely tender. Make batter of egg, cream, salt and flour. Dip each slice of egg plant in batter then brown in butter. Place on heat-proof platter, cover with chopped onions and cheese. Run under broiler until cheese is melted. Serve immediately.

MRS. AMY MC NUT
Gallagher's Rranch
Helotes, Texas

CORN FRITTERS

1 3/4 cups flour	2 eggs
3 teaspoons baking powder	½ cup milk
½ teaspoon salt	1½ cups cream style corn

1 tablespoon melted shortening

Sift together dry ingredients. Add rest of ingredients, beating well. Do not have too watery. Drop into hot deep Lou Ana oil (about 1 inch deep). Brown. Turn over once and brown other side.

MRS. RUDOLPH E. KRAUSE
Lake Charles, La.

CORN CASSEROLE
Serves 6

1 can cream corn	½ stick oleo or butter
1 small can whole kernel corn	6 hot tamales
1 bunch green onions	½ teaspoon Worcestershire sauce

Salt and pepper to taste

Saute onions (chopped) in oleo and break up tamales in small pieces. Add remaining ingredients and bake at 350 degrees for 30 minutes.

MRS. ROBERT GUIDRY

GREEN EGGPLANT WITH SHRIMP

1 medium green eggplant	2 green onions (chopped fine)
¼ stick butter	
½ pound medium shrimp	Salt and pepper to taste
2 tablespoons butter	2 slices white bread

Cut eggplant into two halves. Scoop out thoroughly and boil in small amount of water seasoned with salt. Chop whole green onions and soften in ¼ stick butter. Peel and devein shrimp. When eggplant is tender add onions and shrimp. Correct seasoning. Put stuffing into eggplant shells which have been saved. Prepare breadcrumbs:

Coarsely crumble the two slices of white bread and sauté in heavy skillet with 2 tablespoons butter until thoroughly coated. Place on top of eggplant and bake in oven 350 degrees until brown and bubbly. (The homemade breadcrumbs are essential to this recipe).

MRS. E. S. GIRAULT
Monroe, La.

BAKED CUSHAW

1 medium cushaw	2 sticks butter
2 cups sugar	1/3 cup cream
2 eggs, beaten	1 teaspoon vanilla

Cinnamon to taste

Wash cushaw, cut in half and remove seeds. Cut in squares, place in large pot and boil until tender. Remove peeling. Mix cushaw with other ingredients. Put in baking dish, sprinkle with cinnamon and sugar. Bake in 350 degree oven until brown.

MRS. BERLIN E. PERKINS, JR.

BAKED CUSHAW IN SHELL
Serves 8

1 small cushaw	Juice of 1 orange
1½ cups sugar	Several slices orange rind
1 cup water	2 tablespoons butter

Take only the globe of the cushaw and cut into pieces (about 2 inches wide and 3 inches long) to cover bottom of oblong pyrex baking dish. Remove seeds, leaving string of the cushaw intact. Place pieces with shell up and meat part down. Dissolve sugar in water, add orange juice and rind and pour over cushaw. Bake in 350 degree oven about 1 hour and 15 minutes. If syrup is not thick enough to your liking, remove cushaw carefully with a spatula and cook syrup a few minutes longer. Then add 2 tablespoons of butter, stir, and spoon syrup over cushaw to serve.

MRS. L. W. WINDSOR
Rayne, La.

SPANISH GREEN BEANS

2 slices bacon, chopped	Salt and pepper to taste
¼ cup onion, chopped	1 tablespoon flour
2 tablespoons green pepper, chopped	2 cups canned tomatoes, drained

1 cup green beans, drained

Fry the bacon, onion and pepper in skillet until bacon is crisp and onions and pepper are brown. Add flour, stir and add drained tomatoes and beans, season to taste, and place in casserole. Bake at 350 degrees for 30 minutes.

MRS. ALDRICH STROUBE

RATATOUILLE NICOISE
(4 servings)

Mince:

1 onion	2 cloves of garlic
1 pound squash (long	a leaf of basil
and thin)	a leaf of laurel
2 eggplants	a bit of thyme
6 fresh tomatoes	Salt and pepper
2 peppers—1 red, 1 yellow	Oil

Pour oil (olive) in pan not too hot and stew all vegetables together. Simmer till well cooked. Serve hot or cold.

H. S. H. PRINCESS GRACE
DE MONACO

STRING BEAN CASSEROLE

2 cans whole string beans	1 can French fried onion
Juice from 1 can beans	rings
1 can condensed	3½ ounce package slivered
mushroom soup	almonds
¼ cup sherry	

Arrange drained string beans evenly in 10 x 10-inch casserole. Stir the juice from 1 can, wine and almonds into the mushroom soup and pour over the beans. Arrange onion rings on top and place in a pre-heated 350 degree oven for about 20 minutes, or until onions are golden and crisp.

BARBARA TOLER
Cinclare Plantation

FRIED EGGPLANT I

Use the number of eggplants needed. (one medium peeled eggplant serves 2 or 3). Slice about ½ inch across. Sprinkle with salt on both sides. Put in bowl and cover with ice cubes for one or two hours.

Wash off salt and wipe with paper towel. Cover each piece with egg white—one egg white is sufficient for several slices.

Season flour with salt and pepper and put in brown paper bag. Shake one or two pieces of eggplant at a time in flour.

Heat heavy frying pan with just enough olive oil

to cover the bottom. Place three or four pieces at a time in pan and fry on medium heat until brown on both sides. Drain on paper toweling and eat while hot.

Children love having a little sugar sprinkled over each piece and some adults do too.

* * * *

You may fry okra the same way but do not soak in salt and ice. About 1 cup of akra, cut in 1 inch pieces may be fried at a time.

MRS. C. C. WOOD

FRIED EGGPLANT II

1 eggplant	1 tablespoon water
Salt and pepper	Bread crumbs
1 egg	Lou Ana cooking oil

Peel eggplant and cut in very thin slices. Sprinkle each slice with salt and pepper. Pile evenly on plate, cover with another plate with weight on top. Let stand 1 hour to remove juices. Beat egg lightly and add boiling water. Dip each slice in this mixture, then in bread crumbs, and fry in hot oil on one side and then the other. Drain on paper and serve very hot.

THE EDITORS

GREEN BEANS ORIENTAL
Serves 8-10

3 packages (9 ounce) frozen French-style green beans	2 teaspoons soy sauce
	1 teaspoon salt
	1/2 teaspoon black pepper
1 medium onion, sliced	1 teaspoon monosodium
1/2 cup butter or margarine	glutamate
1/3 cup flour	1 can (8 ounce) sliced
2 cups milk	mushrooms, drained
3/4 cup shredded sharp cheddar cheese	1 can (5 ounce) water chestnuts, drained and sliced
1/8 teaspoon Tabasco	

1/3 cup sliced almonds

Cook beans in salted water until just barely tender. Drain and set aside. Saute onion in butter until soft. Add flour and blend. Slowly add milk and cheese. Cook until smooth and thick, stirring constantly. Add seasonings. Stir in cooked beans, mushrooms and water chestnuts. Spoon into 2 quart casserole. Sprinkle almonds over top. Bake, uncovered, at 375 degrees for about 30 minutes, or until bubbly.

MRS. MARTIN P. BRODERICK, JR.

GREEN BEANS SUPREME
(Serves 8)

2 cans French style
   green beans, drained
1/3 cup chopped onion
1 tablespoon parsley flakes
2 tablespoons flour

2 tablespoons butter
1 teaspoon salt
¼ teaspoon pepper
1 teaspoon lemon peel
1 cup sour cream

Melt butter. Add parsley and onions and then blend in flour. Add salt and pepper, lemon peel and sour cream. Mix into beans. Put in casserole and top with bread crumbs. Dot with butter. Put in 350 degree oven until brown and bubbly.

MRS. WILLIAM Y. LOBDELL

GREEN BEANS PENNSYLVANIA DUTCH STYLE

3 strips bacon
1 small onion sliced
2 teaspoons corn starch
¼ teaspoon salt
¼ teaspoon dry mustard

1 one-pound can
   green beans
1 tablespoon brown sugar
1 tablespoon vinegar
1 hard boiled egg, sliced

Fry bacon in skillet until crisp, pour off all but 1 tablespoon fat, add onions and brown, then stir in cornstarch, salt and mustard. Drain beans and reserve ½ cup of liquid. Add liquid to skillet and stir until it boils. Add brown sugar and vinegar, then add beans and heat thoroughly. Turn into serving dish and garnish with egg and crumbled bacon.

MRS. JOHN W. PERRIN
Ruston, La.

SMOTHERED OKRA I

2 pounds okra
3 tablespoons bacon fat
   (or more if needed)
1 tablespoon flour
1 medium onion, chopped
½ bell pepper

2 medium stalks celery
5 fresh tomatoes or 1
   large can
1/8 teaspoon basil
1/8 teaspoon thyme
Salt, pepper, Cayenne

Wash okra, cut and fry in 2 tablespoons bacon fat until dry. In another skillet, make a medium dark roux with 1 tablespoon bacon fat and 1 tablespoon flour. Add chopped onion, bell pepper and celery and simmer until wilted. Add tomatoes and simmer for 5 minutes. Add okra, season well, turn fire down low and cook for 1 hour, stirring frequently.

MRS. RICHARD MORNHINVEG

SMOTHERED OKRA II

This is really just a different method of cooking okra; it can be used for large quantities of okra to put in the freezer, or for a small amount for family use.

Put a small amount of bacon fat in the bottom of a turkey roaster—a large amount of fat for a large amount of okra. Chop okra, onions, bell pepper and garlic in pan and season to taste with salt and pepper. (Canned or fresh tomatoes can also be added).

Place roaster in oven, 350 degrees to 375 degrees, uncovered, and cook about 2 hours, stirring several times. Heat may be raised to 400 degrees in the last half hour to brown. You do not have to watch and stir the okra by this method to keep it from burning, as you do when cooking on top of the stove.

MRS. VIOLA SIMON
Jennings, La.

CREOLE CROWDER PEAS AND PEANUTS

4 cups crowder peas shelled	2 teaspoons seasoned salt
1 cup raw peanuts shelled	1 teaspoon salt
Ham hock or ¼ pound salt pork	1 bay leaf
3/4 cup onion chopped	2 tablespoons olive oil
6 cups water	1 tablespoon Worcestershire sauce
1 can chicken broth	1½ teaspoons monosodium glutamate
Dash of cayenne (optional)	

Cover ham with water and bring to a slow boil for about 20 minutes. (If bacon or salt pork is used, cut in small pieces, render, discard grease, and proceed as with ham). Add peanuts, salt, bay leaf, pepper, bring to a boil and cook until peanuts are about half cooked. Add chicken broth, olive oil, Worcestershire sauce, monosodium glutamate, onions and crowder peas. Correct seasoning and cook until peas and peanuts are tender. Let stand a few hours to blend seasonings. Serve with rice and your favorite pickle relish.

MRS. CARLETON BATES

GREEN BEANS WITH DILL

2 cans whole green beans	3 level tablespoons
1¼ teaspoons dill seed	bacon fat

Mix and simmer for about 30 minutes. Let beans cool in juice. Strain juice from beans and reserve it for the sauce. Wash dill seed from beans.

SAUCE

6 scant tablespoons flour	3 tablespoons grated onion
6 tablespoons butter	½ teaspoon cracked
1 cup of bean juice	pepper
1½ cups milk	2½ teaspoons Accent
Dash of Tabasco	2½ teaspoons monosodium
Salt and pepper to taste	glutamate

Melt butter and add flour to make a paste. Heat bean juice and milk to scalding temperature. Add gradually to butter and flour, stirring constantly so that sauce will be smooth. Add remaining ingredients to boiling sauce. Place hot beans in a hot baking dish and pour sauce over beans. It is better to have the beans hot and the sauce boiling to avoid risk of the sauce becoming watery. Top with buttered cracker crumbs or slivered almonds and bake at 350 degrees until bubbly.

MRS. BEN BOGARD
Ruston, La.

CA-LA-LOO
(Mustard greens with Corn Meal Dumplings)

1 bunch fresh mustard	½ teaspoon salt
greens or	¼ pound slab bacon
1 Package frozen mustard	2½ cups water
greens	

Put cleaned and chopped greens in pot with ½ cup water and salt and boil until tender. Cut bacon in small pieces and cook in 2 cups of water until very tender. This reduces water to about ½ cup. Add to greens.

DUMPLINGS

1 cup of yellow corn meal	1 tablespoon bacon fat
½ cup boiling water	½ Teaspoon salt

Mix all ingredients and add boiling water, stirring until it makes a thick dough. Form into small balls and drop into boiling pot liquor and cook 5-7 minutes. To cook longer will make the dumplings too hard.

THE EDITORS

PEAS LORRAINE
Serves 5 or 6

3 tablespoons butter
½ cup water
2 pounds English peas
  (need 2 cups)
2 tablespoons onion,
  chopped
1 tablespoon parsley

1 teaspoon sugar
½ teaspoon salt
½ teaspoon pepper
¼ teaspoon nutmeg
  (optional)
4 or 5 outside leaves
  of lettuce

½ cup breakfast cream

Heat butter and water. Add peas, parsley, sugar and seasoning. Cover and cook until tender. Add finally the shredded lettuce. Cook several minutes more. Add cream and serve.

MRS. JAMES W. MCLAURIN

ENGLISH PEAS CASSEROLE

2 cans of your favorite
  English peas #2 can
½ bell pepper
3 sticks of celery (chopped)
3/4 stick butter

2 chopped pimientoes
1 cup water chestnuts
1 can of cream of
  mushroom soup
1 tablespoon milk

Sauté onion, pepper, celery in butter add soup and melt, add peas, pimientos and water chestnuts that have been sliced, stir well pour into baking dish. When ready to serve sprinkle fresh cracker crumbs lightly over top and bake at 350 degrees for 30 minutes. This may be prepared the day before and then cooked when needed.

MRS. W. J. OLIVER, JR.

CREAMED ONIONS

12 small, white onions
6 tablespoons butter
8 level tablespoons flour
2 cups milk

½ pound Cheddar cheese
salt, pepper, Cayenne to
  taste
Paprika

Boil onions in salted water until fork tender. Melt butter over low heat, add flour and stir well until blended. Remove from heat, gradually stir in milk and return to heat. Cook, stirring constantly until thick and smooth. Add grated cheese and season with salt, pepper and Cayenne. When ready to serve, sprinkle with paprika.

MRS. RICHARD MORNHINVEG

HUNGARIAN NOODLE PUDDING
Serves 10

1 package medium noodles	2 whole eggs
1 carton creamed cottage cheese	½ cup grated yellow cheese
1 carton sour cream	Salt and pepper to taste

Boil noodles in salted water to which a few drops of olive oil have been added. Drain well and mix with rest of ingredients. Pour in well greased casserole and bake at 350 degrees until bubbly. Delightful with fowl or meat dishes.

MRS. RALPH PERLMAN

GRITS AND CHEESE CASSEROLE

8 cups water	2 tablespoons Worcestershire sauce
1 teaspoon salt	
2 cups quick cooking grits	2 cloves garlic minced
1 roll garlic cheese	Dash of Tabasco sauce
2 sticks butter	Pepper to taste
2 tablespoons sherry	2 eggs

Bring water and salt to boil, add grits slowly stirring often. Cook for 2½ minutes. While still hot, stir in other ingredients—let cool. Preheat oven to 400 degrees. Beat egg and stir in grits. Bake 1 hour. Serve hot. Good with meat or chicken.

MRS. YVONNE OBEUCHAIN
Dallas, Texas

MIRLITON STUFFED WITH SHRIMP

3 mirlitons	1 sprig parsley minced
1 tablespoon butter	1 sprig thyme minced
1 well chopped onion	1 bay leaf minced
1 clove garlic minced	3/4 cup bread crumbs
1 chopped tomato	1 dozen boiled shrimp

Cut mirlitons in half and boil in salted water until tender. Scoop out tender insides, mash and leave shells in nice condition to stuff. Put butter into frying pan, heat and add onion and garlic. Add tomato, parsley, thyme and bayleaf. Season with salt and pepper to taste. Next, take the mashed mirliton and mix with 3/4 cup bread crumbs (soaked and squeezed out). Season well and fry for 5 minutes. Add shrimp to pulp. Combine these mixtures and fill mirliton shells. Sprinkle grated crumbs over the tops, dot with butter and bake in oven until a nice brown.

MARY ELLISON
Monroe, La.

POTATO BALLS
Makes 15

2 cups mashed potatoes
¼ cup grated Parmesan
    cheese

2 tablespoons melted
    butter
Salt and pepper to taste

2 eggs

Combine and shape into rounds the size of golf balls. Dust in flour. Dip into beaten eggs. Coat with seasoned bread crumbs. Brown in ½ inch olive oil in skillet. These may be made early, refrigerated and fried later.

MRS. JOHN W. BARTON

PANTJE FISH
(German Fried Potatoes)

2 cups left over fish boned
    (either broiled or
    steamed)
1/3 stick butter or oleo

6 boiled and sliced
    potatoes
½ teaspoon prepared
    mustard

Pinch of salt

Melt butter in skillet, add potatoes and fry until light brown. Add fish and mustard. Continue frying until fish is hot. Add another piece of butter just before serving.

MRS. ERICH STERNBERG

1-2-1 METHOD OF COOKING RICE

1 cup rice

2 cups water

1 teaspoon salt

Combine rice, water and salt in a 3 quart saucepan that has a tight fitting lid. Bring to a boil, stirring once or twice as water comes to a boil. Lower heat to simmer. Cover pan and cook 18 minutes without removing lid or stirring.

For extra flavor, add a tablespoon butter

For extra whiteness, add a tablespoon vinegar.

CHERIE GRIFFITH
Grand Chenier, La.

JAMBALAYA

1½ cups cooked rice
1 large onion (chopped)
1 bell pepper (chopped)
1 stalk celery (chopped)
2 pods garlic (crushed)
1 tablespoon butter
  or oleo
½ can beef consomme

heaping tablespoon
  capers
½ pound each of beef and
  pork (ground)
1 small can mushrooms
1/3 cup Lou Ana oil
1 tablespoon butter
  (heaping)

Salt and pepper to taste

Sauté onion, bell pepper, celery and garlic in oil. Add beef and pork and simmer. Stir in rice, mushrooms, capers, butter and consomme. Pour mixture into baking dish which has been dampened on inside only. Bake in 350 degree oven for 20 to 25 minutes. Dish is ready but should not be browned.

MRS. B. BIENVENUE
Opelousas, La.

CREOLE RICE CAKES

1 pound cooked rice
Cinnamon sugar
Flour

Brown sugar
Pinch of salt
Deep fat for frying

Sprinkle cinnamon sugar, brown sugar and a pinch of salt into the cooked rice. Roll into balls and roll through flour till coated. Fry until brown in deep fat.

MRS. WALTER C. PARLANGE
Parlange Plantation
Mix, La.

RICE AND SHRIMP FIESTA
Serves 6

2 tablespoons Lou Ana oil
2 tablespoons flour
1 cup chopped green
  onions
1/4 teaspoon garlic juice
½ cup chopped green
  pepper
1 (14½ ounce) can
  stewed tomatoes

1 teaspoon pepper
1 teaspoon monosodium
  glutamate
¼ cup minced parsley
2 cups cleaned shrimp
1 can cream of mushroom
  soup
3 cups cooked rice (cook
  1 cup raw rice)

1 teaspoon salt

Heat oil, add flour and stir until golden brown. Add onion, garlic juice, bell pepper, tomatoes, salt, pepper, and monosodium glutamate. Cook until onions are tender. Add shrimp, parsley, and mushroom soup and cook about 6 minutes more. Remove from heat, add rice, and fold in gently. Serve on platter garnished with whole fantail boiled shrimp, parsley and lemon wedges.

CHERIE GRIFFITH
Grand Chenier, La.

Note: In 1966 Miss Griffith won first prize with this recipe at the International Rice Festival in Crowley, La. The following year she won first prize in the Louisiana Egg Cookery Contest, using eggs in the place of shrimp. She also won first place in the Rice Cookery 4-H Demonstration contest at Short Course in Baton Rouge in 1969.

GREEN RICE

2 cups uncooked rice
2 cups grated cheese
½ teaspoon salt
1 box chopped spinach
½ cup melted oleo
1 medium onion (chopped)
2 cups milk
2 eggs (beaten well)

Steam rice until done, combine with other ingredients. Pour into two well greased casseroles and bake for 45 minutes at 350 degrees.

MRS. ORDA MCKENZIE
Natchitoches, La.

RICE DRESSING I

½ cup Lou-Ana oil
10 chicken livers, chopped
   or 6 livers and 6
   gizzards
1 large onion, chopped
1 bell pepper, chopped
2 stalks celery, chopped
¼ cup minced parsley
6 packed cups cooked rice
3 green onions and tops,
   chopped
2 teaspoons salt
¼ teaspoon red pepper
½ teaspoon powdered
   thyme
1 bay leaf or ½
   teaspoon oregano
2 cups water

In oil cook onions, pepper and celery on low flame, stirring until onions are clear, not brown. Add livers, salt, water, red pepper, thyme and bay leaf. Simmer 30 minutes. Remove bay leaf. Mix with rice after removing from fire. Add green onions and parsley. Cover and let stand 10 minutes.

MRS. S. L. WRIGHT
Crowley, La.

RICE DRESSING II

3 cups cooked rice
Giblets from chicken or
  turkey chopped
3 eggs well beaten

1 cup chopped celery
1 cup chopped onion
  (some green onions
  if available)

Salt & pepper to taste

Mix all ingredients well. Put small amount of gravy or meat drippings in heavy skillet. Cook dressing just until egg is done. Stir while cooking—takes only a few minutes. Serve with brown gravy.

MRS. ALEX SOMPAYRAC
Natchitoches, La.

RICE VIENNESE

1 cup Uncle Ben's
  Converted rice
2½ cups chicken broth
¼ stick butter

½ small onion
Saffron (size of pea)
Large can mushrooms
  (stems and pieces)

Salt to taste

Chop onion very fine and soften in melted butter. Bring broth to boil and all other ingredients. Use enough saffron to make rice a pale yellow color. Cover and cook for about 25 minutes over low heat.

MRS. GEORGE SIMON

FRIED RICE

4 cups day old boiled rice
1½ cups cooked beef,
  lamb, pork, shrimp or
  chicken cut up
2 tablespoons
  Worcestershire sauce
Seasoned salt to taste
Sweet basil, dried or
  fresh, to taste
1 stick of butter
  (or chicken fat)
1 tablespoon cornstarch
Mushrooms, if desired

1 tablespoon fresh
  ginger grated
½ cup green onions
  with tops
½ cup celery chopped
1 teaspoon monosodium
  glutamate
½ cup consommé,
  chicken or beef
2 tablespoons safflower
  oil
1 can water chestnuts
  sliced

2 teaspoons soy sauce

Sauté finely chopped onions and celery in oil until just tender. Add chopped meat or fish (If raw meat is used, cut in small pieces and sauté in oil before adding to onions and celery). Add all seasonings. Dissolve cornstarch in consommé and add this to the mixture. Let simmer until gravy is nearly absorbed, stirring occasionally. Add mushrooms and water chestnuts and correct seasoning to taste. Separate rice grains and stir into browned butter until each grain is well coated. Add to meat mixture and serve.

THE EDITORS

OPELOUSAS RICE DRESSING

1½ pounds ground chuck
1 large onion
½ large bell pepper
1/8 teaspoon
   garlic powder
1 large egg
1½ cups rice

1 cup seasoned bread
   crumbs
¼ cup onion tops, chopped
¼ cup parsley, chopped
¼-½ teaspoon red pepper
¼-½ teaspoon black
   pepper
1 teaspoon salt

Brown meat in approximately ½ cup Lou Ana cooking oil. Add salt and pepper to meat. Wilt onion, bell pepper. Sprinkle garlic powder and mix well with meat mixture. Steam rice. When cooked, add to meat mixture. Mix thoroughly. Add onion tops and parsley. Mix. Serve piping hot. Optional—add 1 cup pecans.

CLAIRE D. HOLLIER
Opelousas, La.

RICE CASSEROLE

2 cups rice
3 large onions—
   finely chopped
4 large stalks celery—
   finely chopped
1 large green pepper
   finely chopped

½ cup butter
2 teaspoons salt
   (to taste)
1 tablespoon poultry
   seasoning
2 eggs
1 cup chopped pecans

½ cup chopped parsley

Cook rice. While this is cooking, sauté onions, celery, pepper in butter until thoroughly cooked. Add seasonings. Mix well. Beat eggs. Remove onion mixture from heat. Add rice and fold in eggs. Mix well. Add nuts and parsley. Bake in shallow casserole for 25 to 30 minutes at 350 degrees.

Submitted by:
MRS. STEWART CHURCHILL
Belle Alliance Plantation

HAM HOCK SAUERKRAUT PLATTER

4 or 5 ham hocks   2 cans sauerkraut
(remove the skin)   (1 lb., 11 oz. each)
1 medium onion   3 tablespoons brown sugar

Boil ham hocks until tender. Empty drained sauerkraut in skillet; sprinkle with chopped onion and brown sugar. Heat about five minutes, stirring. Pour in a large shallow baking dish and arrange ham hocks on top in nests of sauerkraut. Cover and bake in a slow oven 325 degrees about 45 minutes. Good New Year's dish.

MRS. HENRY P. ALLENDORPH
Oscar, La.

SAUERKRAUT WITH PORK RIBS

1½ pounds beef short ribs,   1½ pounds fresh Kraut
or slab pork ribs   or 1 large can of
cracked in half   sauer kraut
Dash celery seeds   1 tablespoon light brown
½ cup chopped onion   sugar

Sauté the ribs to light brown, add a small amount of water, and cook until tender—about 1 hour. Add the kraut, light brown sugar, a small amount of celery seeds and the onion. Place this kraut mixture on top of meat, cover, and cook 1 hour. Boil separately, Irish potatoes (one per person). Boil separately 2 packages Kosher Knockwurst. Serve on large platter— meat on one end, Knockwurst on the other, kraut and potatoes in the center. Drizzle melted butter over potatoes, and garnish with sprigs of parsley.

MRS. B. N. SWEENEY
Rayne, La.

SPINACH WASHINGTON
Serves 6

2 cups fresh corn,   1½ cups chopped,
cooked, and drained   cooked and seasoned
1 cup medium, white   spinach
sauce, seasoned   ½ cups grated swiss
2 tablespoons grated   cheese
Parmesan cheese

Butter the bottom of a 3 quart casserole. Add the corn to the white sauce. Spread a thin layer of spinach on the bottom of the casserole. Pour part of the creamed corn over the spinach. Repeat layering process with spinach and corn, ending with corn on top. Sprinkle top of casserole evenly with grated cheeses. Place casserole in a shallow pan containing boiling water. Bake for about 20 minutes in preheated oven at 350 degrees F. or until heated through. If desired, brown the top of casserole by placing under broiler.

MRS. DEAN MOSELY

SQUASH CASSEROLE
Serves 4-5

2½ to 3 pounds white squash	½ small jar pimiento, cut
	½ cup cracker crumbs
½ stick butter or oleo	2 eggs, beaten
1 medium onion	Several drops Tabasco
1 medium bell pepper	Salt and pepper
½ cup celery	to taste

Wash squash and cut into quarters. Peel, remove seeds and cut into small pieces. Cook in boiling, salted water until tender. In the meantime, sauté onion, bell pepper and celery in butter or oleo. Drain cooked squash, mash and add to skillet of sautéed vegetables. Cook a few minutes, stirring constantly. Add remaining ingredients and cook a little longer. Pour into shallow pyrex dish, dot with small pieces of bacon (seasoned bread crumbs may also be added) and bake at 350 degrees for 20-30 minutes.

MRS. W. M. GORDON

BAKED SPINACH I

2 bunches spinach	1 tablespoon butter
2 tablespoons flour	½ cup bread crumbs
1 egg	Sherry, salt & pepper
1 cup milk	to taste

Make a roux with flour and butter, then add milk and beaten egg. Add spinach and seasonings, put in a buttered baking dish, sprinkle with buttered bread crumbs, and bake in moderate oven for 15 or 20 minutes. Serve hot.

Submitted by
MRS. GRAHAM BIENVENU
With permission of the family of
Natalie Scott

BAKED SPINACH II

1 package chopped
   frozen spinach
2 strips fried bacon

1 package (3 oz.)
   cream cheese
   (you can use the low
   calorie cream cheese)

Cook spinach in boiling salted water until done. Drain. Mix the cream cheese and crumbled bacon until it is of creamy consistency. Add salt and pepper to taste. Put in greased casserole and top with seasoned bread crumbs and dots of butter. Bake about 15 minutes or until crumbs are crunchy. (Do not let dry out too much)

MRS. BENTON HARELSON

SPINACH WABASH

2 packages frozen,
   chopped spinach
4 hard-boiled eggs,
   finely chopped

½ cup finely chopped
   green onions
½ cup crumbled, crisp-
   cooked bacon

1 stick butter or oleo

Cook spinach as directed on package and drain thoroughly. Blend in butter while hot and season to taste with salt and pepper. Place in serving dish and cover top of spinach with green onions, then bacon, and finally the chopped eggs.

MRS. E. H. TAUSSIG
Lake Charles, La.

YELLOW SQUASH AND DEVILED HAM

14 yellow squash, cut up
1 teaspoon salt
½ stick butter
1 large onion chopped
1 stalk celery chopped
½ bell pepper chopped

Few sprigs parsley minced
1 large can deviled ham
1 clove garlic
1 teaspoon monosodium
   glutamate
Seasoned bread crumbs

½ stick butter

Boil squash in water with salt and butter until tender. Sauté onion celery, bell pepper and parsley in other half stick butter. Add to squash, along with deviled ham, garlic salt and Accent. Put mixture in baking dish, sprinkle with bread crumbs, dot with butter and bake in 350 degree oven until bubbly.

MRS. ANDREW P. GAY
Plaquemine, La.

BEEF SPINACH

1 pound heavy beef, ground once	2 onions
	Parsley
2 pounds spinach or 1 package frozen spinach	1 clove garlic
	6 eggs
	Salt and pepper

Sauté onions, garlic and parsley in bacon fat—do not brown. Add ground beef and cook until pink disappears. Add cooked spinach that has been drained and chopped to the above while cooking, and mix thoroughly. Add eggs, one at a time, stirring all the while and serve immediately.

THE EDITORS

SQUASH ROCKEFELLER

12 small yellow squash	1½ cups Italian style bread crumbs
2 packages frozen chopped spinach	½ pound butter or margarine
1 bunch parsley	Salt
1 bunch green onions	Tabasco sauce
4 pieces celery	2 teaspoons anise seed
1 clove garlic	

½ cup boiling water

Mix anise seed in boiling water and let stand for fifteen minutes. Cut squash in half long way. Steam until almost tender. Remove seeds. Grind other vegetables in meat grinder. Sauté in butter 5 minutes. Cook and drain spinach. Add ground vegetables and bread crumbs, salt, Tabasco, and strained anise water. Stuff the squash halves with spinach mix and bake in 350 degree oven 20 minutes or until well heated. The Rockefeller filling may be frozen. Keeps well.

MRS. ERNEST D. WILSON

STUFFED SQUASH

6 crooked neck squash	1 medium onion
2 tablespoons bacon fat	½ bell pepper
2 stalks celery	½ cup bread crumbs

Parboil squash until tender enough to scoop out center (cut lengthwise) and being careful not to break shells. Sauté celery, onion and bell pepper in bacon fat. Add plain bread crumbs and squash and put in blender until well mixed. Season with salt and pepper to taste and stuff shells. Sprinkle with bread crumbs and place small piece of bacon on each. Bake at 350 degrees for 20 minutes before serving.

MRS. HAMILTON CRAWFORD

SWEET POTATO CHEW-CHEWS
Serves 4-6

2 cups mashed sweet
  potatoes
½ cup chopped nuts
2 tablespoons softened
  butter

3/4 cup drained pineapple
  tid bits or crushed
  pineapple
1 teaspoon salt
½ cup crushed corn flakes

1 can flaked coconut

Combine potatoes, nuts, coconut, butter, pineapple and salt and mix well. Shape into 8 or 10 croquettes, roll in the crushed corn flakes and bake in 375 degree oven until lightly browned—about 20 minutes. Serve warm. Nice companion dish for pork or lamb roast.

MRS. HUNTLEY B. FAIRCHILD
Manchac Plantation
Sunshine, La.

BAKED SQUASH

2 pounds yellow squash
¼ cup onion, chopped
¼ cup water
1/8 teaspoon pepper

1½ teaspoons salt
2 hard cooked eggs
3 tablespoons butter
½ cup cracker crumbs

Paprika

Slice squash thin, place in saucepan. Add onions, water and salt. Cover. Cook until steaming freely, then turn burner on low and cook for 20 minutes. Drain off any liquid and mash squash. Add chopped egg whites, pepper, butter and cracker crumbs. Pour into butter-greased baking dish. Run egg yolks through a sieve and sprinkle over top. Sprinkle with paprika. Bake at 357 degrees for 25 minutes.

MRS. ESTELL GORDON CURRIE

SQUASH SOUFFLE
Serves 10

3 pounds yellow squash,
  cut up
Salt
Pepper
Onion

Bread crumbs
3 eggs, well beaten
Milk, about 1 cup
Sharp Cheese, grated
Butter

Boil squash until tender in waterless cooker. Mash squash, add salt and pepper to taste and stir in grated onion to taste. Add bread crumbs from about 4 slices of bread. Add beaten eggs and enough milk to make the mixture "soupy." Pour into a well greased casserole. Cover top with grated sharp cheese and stir the cheese into squash mixture. Dot top generously with butter. Bake in 350 degree oven for about 30 minutes or until firm and lightly browned.

MRS. LLOYD ERMATINGER

SWEET POTATOES WITH CRANBERRIES

4 large yams, boiled	1/3 cup sugar
1 cup cranberry sauce	2 tablespoons butter
½ cup pecans	

Scoop out hollow in each half potato. Fill with cranberry sauce mixed with pecans. Dot with butter and sugar. Bake 10 minutes.

MRS. DOUGLAS M. WARRINER

SWEET POTATO PONE

3 medium sweet potatoes	¼ stick butter
1 cup sugar	¼ teaspoon baking powder
½ cup brown sugar	2/3 cup evaporated milk
1 egg	½ teaspoon vanilla

Grate raw potatoes and mix with other ingredients, adding melted butter last. Grease baking dish, pour mixture into it, and bake for about 30 minutes in a hot oven.

MRS. ROLAND B. HOWELL

BAKED APPLE-YAM CASSEROLE
Serves six

6 thin slices Canadian bacon (or regular kind)	1 cup seedless raisins Brown sugar Butter
6 medium sweet potatoes or yams	Lemon slices 6 medium tart apples

Put bacon slices in the bottom of a deep baking dish. Cover with an inch of water. Place cored apples that have been stuffed with raisins on top of bacon. Fill all empty places in dish with yams, peeled and sliced thin. (Sometimes I slice apples too and alternate with yams.) Sprinkle top with brown sugar and dots of butter. Cover with lemon slices. Bake in a covered dish in a slow oven (300-350 degrees F) about an hour.

MRS. DOUGLAS M. WARRINER

SWEET POTATOES IN ORANGE CUPS
Serves 6

4 medium size sweet potatoes
2 tablespoons butter
1½ to 2 tablespoons orange juice

2 tablespoons brown sugar
¼ teaspoon vanilla
6 scooped out orange halves
¼ cup chopped pecans
6 marshmallows

½ teaspoon salt

Wash, boil, peel and mash sweet potatoes. Add salt, butter, vanilla and only enough orange juice to keep potatoes fluffy. Fill orange cups with mixture, sprinkle with pecans and top with a marshmallow. Bake in 350 degree oven for 15 to 20 minutes until potatoes are heated through and marshmallows slightly brown.

ADELE LAWLER

SWEET POTATO BALLS

3 cups mashed sweet potatoes
1 teaspoon salt
3 tablespoons melted butter

1 egg
1 tablespoon cold water
2 tablespoons light brown sugar
8 marshmallows

Corn flake crumbs

It is better if fresh potatoes are boiled, peeled and mashed, than to use canned ones. Season potatoes, add butter, and mold in a ball around each marshmallow. Beat egg and cold water together, dip each ball in egg and roll in corn flake crumbs. Place on oiled baking sheet and bake 25 minutes, or until lightly browned.

MRS. B. N. SWEENEY
Rayne, La.

SWEET POTATO PUDDING

3 medium sweet potatoes (grated)
1 cup syrup
¼ cup milk
2 eggs

½ cup sugar
¼ cup flour
½ teaspoon cloves
½ teaspoon all spice
1 teaspoon salt

2 tablespoons butter

Mix ingredients. Beat well. Pour into greased pan and bake in 350 degree oven until brown.

MRS. OSCAR VOORHIES
Alexandria, La.

SWEET POTATOES IMPERIAL

5 or 6 sweet potatoes
½ cup sugar

Butter
½ cup Jamaica rum

Boil sweet potatoes; cool, peel and slice. Brown lightly in butter in a frying pan. Place in chafing dish, sprinkle with sugar, add ¼ cup butter and mix lightly. When thoroughly hot pour in rum, set on fire and baste with the syrup and the flaming rum.

MRS. DOUGLAS M. WARRINER

PANNÉ SWEET POTATOES

Sliced cold boiled yams
¼ cup flour

½ cup vanilla wafer
crumbs

Beaten egg

Combine flour and crumbs. Dip potato slices in egg, then in the crumbs. Fry in hot fat.

MRS. DOUGLAS M. WARRINER

CREAMED TURNIPS
Serves 4

6 medium turnips
3 tablespoons butter or oleo
3 tablespoons sugar—
   or to taste

3 tablespoons breakfast
   cream
Salt
Black pepper

Peel, slice and boil turnips until tender. Remove from fire, drain and mash well. Add other ingredients and return to low fire for 15 or 20 minutes, stirring often.

MRS. JACK JONES

TURNIP AND PEA CASSEROLE

6-8 turnips cooked in salt
   water until tender
½ cup liquid from turnips
1 cup milk
1 full tablespoon flour

1 full tablespoon butter
Salt and pepper to taste
1 can (or more, if neces-
   sary) small peas
Grated cheese and paprika

Make a cream sauce with the liquid, milk, flour, butter, salt and pepper. Grease a casserole dish and layer the sliced turnips then the peas, to which a small amount of onions and crumbled bacon may be added, if desired. Cover with the cream sauce and repeat the layers. Cover top with grated cheese and paprika and place in 350 degree oven until it bubbles.

MRS. JOHN C. HUTCHINSON, JR.

STEWED TOMATOES

8 to ten medium tomatoes
1 onion chopped
1 tablespoon
   Lou Ana oil
1 teaspoon sugar

¼ to ½ cup seasoned
   bread crumbs
Salt and pepper to taste
Pinch each of thyme
   and parsley flakes

1 bay leaf

Chop onion fine and soften in oil. Add peeled chopped tomatoes and let cook down. As this is cooking, stir and add sugar, salt, bay leaf, pepper and thyme, and parsley. Cook until slightly brown then add bread crumbs to thicken. A small amount of chopped raw bacon browned in onions is a good flavor addition.

MRS. ROBERT KENNON, JR.

TOMATO STACK-UPS

3 large tomatoes cut in
   3/4 inch slices
1 10-ounce package spinach
   or broccoli

4 ounces Swiss Cheese,
   grated (reserve 4
   tablespoons)
¼ cup grated onion

Salt and pepper to taste

Cook, drain and mash broccoli or spinach. Combine cheese, except 4 tablespoons, vegetable and onion. Place tomato slices, salted and peppered, on baking sheet and spoon vegetable mixture over each slice. Sprinke with remaining cheese and place in 300 degree oven until slightly brown.

MRS. ALDRICH STROUBE

PISSALADIERE

1 pound of white flour
15-20 grams of yeast

1 glass of olive oil
1 bowl of milk

1 pinch of salt (for pastry)

Pour yeast in a bit of water. Put flour in a bowl. Dig a hole in the middle of the flour and pour the glass of olive oil and yeast, then the salt. Kneed dough with a bit of milk, let it rest in a ball until the dough has risen 3/4 of its volume.

SAUCE PREPARATION

Peel 3 to 4 onions and cook till golden brown in oil. Add 3 to 4 spoonsful of concentrated tomato or use 4 fresh tomatoes.

Put dough in an oiled plate spreading to thickness of 1 centimetre. Pour sauce over dough, add a few anchovies, garlic and olives.

Put in moderate oven and cook for approximately 20 minutes to half an hour. Serve cold.

H. S. H. PRINCESS GRACE
DE MONACCO

Cheese & Eggs

OEUFS AU PLAT AU GRUYÈRE

A portée de la main:

50 grs de beurre	**4 oeufs**
50 grs de gruyère	**poivre & sel**

Durée de la préparation: ¼ d'heure.

Dans un grand plat à oeufs faites fondre sur feu moyen 50 grs de beurre. Ajoutez deux cuillerées à potage de gruyère rapé. Cassez aussitot 4 oeufs. Saupoudrez de gruyère, poivrez et salêz. Mettez au four quelques minutes et servez très chaud.

EGGS GRUYÈRE

Have on hand:

2 oz. of butter	**4 eggs**
1 cup of gruyère cheese	**Pepper and salt**

Time required: ¼ hour. Melt butter in large egg plate. Add 2 soupspoons of grated gruyère cheese. Break 4 eggs over cheese. Powder (cover) with cheese, salt and pepper. Place in oven a few minutes and serve very hot.

DANIELE FAGAN WRIGHT
Hammond, La.
Formerly Le Havre and Paris

EGGS CRÉOLE
Serves 6-8

8 hard boiled eggs, sliced	**½ cup celery, chopped**
1 tablespoon butter	**1 can tomatoes**
½ cup green pepper, chopped	**1 can mushrooms**
½ cup onions, chopped	**1 tablespoon butter**
	1 tablespoon flour
1 cup milk	

Sauté green pepper, onion and celery in butter until tender but not brown. Add tomatoes and mushrooms and simmer for a few minutes. Make a white sauce of the butter, flour and milk. When thickened, season well with salt, pepper, Worcestershire sauce and a few drops of Tabasco. Mix white and tomato sauces. Add sliced eggs. Put in greased casserole, sprinkle with buttered bread crumbs and bake in 350 degree oven until hot. A delicious dish for brunch.

MRS. WALTER H. CLAIBORNE
Bella Vista Plantation
Batchelor, La.

HUEVOS RANCHEROS

1 can tomatoes	1 teaspoon
½ cup chopped green	Worcestershire sauce
onions	¼ teaspoon red pepper
Juice of ½ lemon	1 teaspoon chili powder

Mix all the above in saucepan and simmer for 20 minutes. Fry 1 dozen eggs. Serve eggs individually on slice of cheese toast. Put on large serving platter and spoon sauce on top. (This is wonderful for Sunday brunch).

MRS. THOMAS BRYAN PUGH, III

CHEESE SOUFFLE I
Serves 4

4 tablespoons butter	Paprika
4 tablespoons flour	1/8 teaspoon soda
2 cups milk	3 egg yolks, well beaten
2 cups grated cheese	3 egg whites, beaten
½ teaspoon salt	until stiff

Pinch of dry mustard

Melt butter, add flour slowly, stir till smooth, then add milk, salt, mustard, paprika and soda. When thick add grated cheese. Stir until smooth. Pour over beaten yolks. Fold in beaten whites. Put in a greased casserole. Sit this dish in a pan of hot water. Preheat oven to 375 degrees. Bake 45 or 50 minutes.

MRS. JOHN W. BARTON

CHEESE SOUFFLE II
Serves 6

4 tablespoons butter	Dash cayenne
4 tablespoons flour	1 teaspoon baking powder
1½ cups hot milk	½ pound sharp cheese
1 teaspoon salt	(grated)

6 eggs

Melt butter, add flour and blend. Add milk and cook until thickened, stirring constantly. Add seasonings and cheese. Beat until cheese is melted. Add beaten egg yolks and cool. Fold in stiffly beaten egg whites. Mix well. Bake in a two quart baking dish. Bake at 300 degrees for approximately 1¼ hours.

MRS. HOWARD DE LAUREAL
New Orleans, La.

EGGS A LA HERZBERG

6 eggs   **6 strips bacon**

In a regular size muffin ring, line rings with bacon and cook in oven until almost crisp. Remove and drain most of the bacon fat out of each hole. Drop egg in each ring and return to oven until eggs are set. Remove and serve on round of buttered toast . . . Garnish with parsley. Good for brunch or lunch.

From the file of
MRS. LEE HERZBERG

BAKED CHILIS RELLENOS
Serves 6

1 small can (4 ounce)   2 eggs
  green chili peppers   2 cups milk
½ pound sharp   ½ cup flour
  cheddar cheese   1 teaspoon salt

Cut chili peppers into 2-inch squares and place in the bottom of a buttered casserole. Cut the cheese into long fingers and arrange in an even layer over the layer of peppers. Beat eggs slightly then beat in the milk flour and salt. Pour over cheese and bake in a 350 degree oven for 45 to 50 minutes, or until custard is set.

MRS. H. R. JONES
Ruston, La.

SWISS FONDUE FOR FOUR

1½ pounds Swiss cheese   1 jigger Kirsch (or
  (grated)   slivovitz or cognac)
2 cups dry white wine   1 teaspoon cornstarch
  (Rhine)   2 tablespoons flour

Rub heavy iron saucepan with a clove of garlic. Heat wine (medium heat) until a bubbly froth forms on top. Toss cheese with flour, and add VERY slowly, handful by handful, stirring constantly with a wire whisk or wooden spoon, until cheese is nearly melted and mixture begins to thicken. Dissolve the cornstarch in the Kirsch and add. Continue stirring vigorously until mixture has thickened and looks almost rubbery. Sprinkle with nutmeg & a little fresh ground pepper. Serve in chafing, dish, with crusty bread cut into 1-inch chunks. Each participant should spear bread with fork and give the fondue a complete stir around the sides of the pot to get the thickest cheese and keep fondue stirred.

MRS. DANIEL HENDERSON

QUICHE LORRAINE

Pastry   4 eggs
1 cup ham (diced)   2 cups milk
2 onions (diced)   Nutmeg—to taste
2 tablespoons butter   Dash of cayenne

Line a 10-inch pyrex pie pan with a thin layer of your favorite pastry dough. Over this sprinkle a cup of finely diced ham. Sauté onions in butter until soft and spread over ham. Beat eggs with salt, nutmeg and cayenne. Very gradually stir hot milk into the eggs. Heat mixture over low fire and stir until it begins to thicken. Pour the custard carefully into pie shell. Bake the Quiche in 375 degree oven about 30 minutes, or until it is set and brown on top. Serve hot directly from the pan. Delicious!

EMMY-LOU BIEDENHARN
Monroe, La.

EGGS WITH MUSHROOM SAUCE
AUX FINES HERBES

Saute 8 mushrooms, washed and chopped in 4 tablespoons of butter. Add 1 green onion and stew for 5 minutes. Stir in 1 tablespoon of flour and gradually add ½ cup of hot consomme. Add salt, pepper and 1 teaspoon of tomato paste and cook another 5 minutes. Just before serving, add 1 teaspoon each of finely chopped parsley, chervil and tarragon (if dried herbs, use ¼ teaspoon) and a little dry white wine. On toasted halves of English muffins place a thin slice of ham or Canadian bacon. Top with one or two poached eggs, then spoon over the mushroom sauce.

MRS. RALPH H. SIMS

This is a fine luncheon or supper dish and is excellent with a chilled bottle of rosé wine. Although this recipe serves two, it can be increased easily to serve more if you can manage the egg poaching for several at one time.

Breads

BREAD

3/4 cup sugar
½ cup shortening
1½ tablespoons salt
1 pint water

1 pint milk
2 cakes yeast dissolved
    in 1/3 cup lukewarm
    water

12½ cups flour

Dissolve yeast in 1/3 cup lukewarm water. Mix milk and water and scald. In a large bowl, put shortening, sugar, and salt. Add scalded milk and water and let cool. Add dissolved yeast and add flour. Knead on floured board and let rise until double. Knead again. Divide dough into six parts and put in well-greased loaf pans. Let rise about 2 hours. Preheat oven about an hour at 375 degrees. Bake loaves for 45 minutes. Allow to cool overnight. Slice thin, butter, and wrap in foil. Keep in freezer until ready to use, then heat in foil.

MRS. GEORGE H. REYMOND

WHITE BREAD

1 cup milk, scalded
1 cup boiling water
1 tablespoon Lou Ana oil
1 tablespoon butter
2½ teaspoons salt

1 package, plus 1 teaspoon
    yeast dissolved in ¼
    cup warm water
6 cups flour
6 tablespoons sugar

In bowl, place milk, water, oil, butter, salt and sugar. Stir to dissolve sugar. Cool to lukewarm. Add 3 cups flour and stir. Add 3 more cups flour and stir again. Knead until dough is not sticky. Grease bowl and top of dough, cover and let rise until double in bulk. Divide in two and place in 2 well greased bread pans, then let rise again. Bake 15 minutes in 400 degree oven, then reduce heat to 325 degrees and bake 20 to 25 minutes more.

MRS. ELENA HULINGS

MONKEY BREAD

2 packages Powdered Yeast
¼ cup very warm water
1 teaspoon salt
3 tablespoons sugar

4 eggs
2 cups milk
6 cups flour
1 stick melted butter

In ¼ cup very warm water, dissolve two packages of yeast. Let stand a few minutes, then add sugar, salt and eggs. Beat thoroughly, add milk and flour alternately. When well combined, add melted stick of butter, blend well and let stand to rise until about doubled in size (about an hour and a half). Roll out, or press out with fingers on heavily floured surface. I use wax paper on a counter. Thickness about ½ inch. Cut dough in 2 inch long strips. Dip in 1 pound of melted butter, and place end over end in ring molds, two or three layers, and let rise again a short while. Bake in 350 degree oven for about 30 minutes. Makes about 5 or 6 molds of bread and requires no buttering or cutting. Just pull off and eat very hot. May be frozen, wrapping tightly in foil. I use rubber gloves (floured) and it's less sticky. Real good party bread. Oleo substitutes well for butter.

MRS. LUCILLE DUTTON

SOFT GRAHAM BREAD

3 cups graham flour	2 tablespoons butter
1 cup white flour	3/4 yeast cake
1 teaspoon salt	3/4 cup warm water

Dissolve the yeast with a little of the luke warm water. Mix the other ingredients in order given and add sufficient warm water to make a soft dough. Cover bowl and set in a warm place. When the dough is light beat it and pour into bread pans, filling half full. When raised and light, bake in moderate oven.

MRS. HUGH A. NEAL

BATTER-BREAD

2 eggs well beaten	2 cups milk
2 cups corn meal	1 teaspoon Lou Ana oil
2 cups boiling water	Pinch seasoned salt

Boil the water, pour in half the cornmeal, then all the milk, then the rest of the cornmeal, and the beaten eggs. Then add the oil and stir. Pour batter into a well buttered and heated dish and bake in a moderate oven.

MRS. WALTER PARLANGE
Parlange Plantation
Mix, La.

IRISH BREAD

1 egg	2 tablespoons sugar
1 yeast cake	1 pint milk
Lard, size of egg	½ cup warm water

Add flour enough to make a stiff batter. Stir and allow to set and rise over night. Pour into pie plates to rise again. Bake, split and butter, and serve with syrup.

MRS. JESSE COATES, SR.

BREAD BAKED IN 1½ HOURS
Four small loaves

YEAST MIXTURE

1 cup warm water
  (warm to wrist)
    2 packages yeast or
    2 tablespoons dry yeast
1 tablespoon honey

Mix and let stand 10 minutes.

SPONGE MIXTURE

3 cups hot water (hot
  to your touch)
    1½ cups whole wheat
    flour
1/3 cup honey

Mix and let stand until yeast is ready.

Approximately 7 cups
  flour, or enough to
  make bread dough
  consistency
    4 tablespoons Lou Ana oil
    1½ teaspoons salt

Batter must be lukewarm before yeast is added. Add yeast mixture. Make a good stiff batter. Let stand 15 minutes. Add salt and oil. Waiting period builds good bread, cuts down amount of flour needed. Dough must be soft—not too stiff. Knead 8 to 10 minutes or until smooth. Place into greased pans. Place in a cold oven set at 250 degrees for 25 minutes, then turn oven to 350 degrees until bread is done.

MRS. DANIEL COHN

MOTHER'S SALT RISING BREAD

① 1 cup sweet milk
  1/8 teaspoon soda
  Meal to make very thin
    batter

② 1 cup milk (scald)
  1 cup water—lukewarm
  2 tablespoons sugar
  Flour to make medium
    batter

③ 6-8 cups flour
  2 teaspoons salt
  1 tablespoon sugar

Mix first group of ingredients and let sit all night. In the morning add the second group of ingredients to first group. Set container in a pan of hot water and keep warm by changing water as it cools. When double in size pour into a large mixing bowl and add third group of ingredients.

Knead into loaves. Place into pans and set pans into hot water and let rise about one inch. Then place pan in cold oven. Cook 40-45 minutes at 375 degrees until browned.

MRS. G. LOCK PARET, JR.
Lake Charles, La.

CORN BREAD

2 cups white meal	½ cup molasses
½ cup flour	1 teaspoon salt
2 cups buttermilk	2 tablespoons melted
2 well beaten eggs	butter or fat

1 teaspoon soda

Mix meal, flour and milk gradually. Add melted butter, molasses and salt, then beaten eggs. Mix soda with a little milk. Add to mixture and beat thoroughly. Bake about 45 minutes in deep pan or black skillet.

THE EDITORS

This is a recipe from the old St. Charles Hotel in New Orleans.

FANNIE'S SWEET CORN BREAD

1½ cups corn meal	½ cup flour
½ cup boiling water	1 tablespoon butter
½ cup sugar	1 teaspoon baking powder
2 eggs	Pinch of salt

1 tablespoon Lou Ana oil

Scald meal with hot water. Add sugar, eggs, flour, butter, baking powder and salt. Mix well. Heat oil in baking pan until very hot. Pour in batter. Bake in hot oven (425-450 degrees) about 25 minutes.

MRS. WALTER CLAIBORNE
Belle Vista Plantation

HUSH PUPPIES

1½ cups yellow cornmeal	2 eggs
3/4 cup flour	3/4 cup milk
4 teaspoons baking powder	2 tablespoons lard
3/4 teaspoon salt	(melted)

Sift dry ingredients. Beat eggs, add milk and beat in dry ingredients. Let stand 15 minutes. Drop by spoonful in deep fat and cook until brown. Makes from 1½-2 dozen.

MRS. CHARLES HUSTMYRE

TEXAS CORNBREAD

1 cup corn meal
1/4 cup flour
1 egg
1 cup milk
1/2 teaspoon salt
1/2 teaspoon sugar
1 tablespoon baking powder
3 to 4 tablespoons Lou Ana oil

Sift dry ingredients into mixing bowl, add egg and milk and beat well by hand. Preheat oven to 425 degrees. Put 3 to 4 tablespoons Lou Ana oil in 8 to 9 inch square black pan if brown corners of bread are desired. Otherwise, use an aluminum pan for softer more moist bread. Heat oil until very hot, near smoking, and pour in mixture. Bake as brown as desired.

MRS. JOE E. McDOWELL

MEXICAN CORNBREAD I

1 1/2 cups cornmeal
1 can cream corn
1 1/2 onion chopped fine
1 cup grated, sharp cheese
3 eggs
1 teaspoon baking powder
1 hot, chopped pepper
1/2 cup Lou Ana oil
1/2 cup milk
Salt and garlic powder to taste

Mix together all ingredients and bake in Bundt pan at 350 degrees for 1 hour.

MRS. STEVE ALFORD

MEXICAN CORNBREAD II

1 cup sour cream
2 eggs, beaten
1 cup cream style corn
1/3 cup Lou Ana oil
1 1/2 cups cornmeal
3 teaspoons baking powder
1 pimiento chopped
1 1/2 to 2 teaspoons salt
2 tablespoons chopped bell pepper
2 Jalapeno peppers, chopped
1 cup sharp cheese, grated

Put together in order given (except cheese). Pour half the batter in baking dish, then half the grated cheese, then rest of the batter, and rest of the cheese on top. Bake at 375 degrees for about 30 minutes. If you want to use this as an hors d'ouvres, place in a larger pan to make bread thin, and this will change the time of baking.

MRS. FRED BLANCHE, JR.
MISS BETH PUGH
New Orleans, La.

SALLY LUNN I

2 cups plain flour
½ cup sugar
3 teaspoon baking powder
½ teaspoon salt

2 eggs beaten
separately
3/4 cup milk
2 tablespoons melted butter

Add sugar to beaten egg yolks. Mix other dry ingredients and mix alternately with milk into egg and sugar mixture, then add melted butter. Beat egg whites until stiff, fold in. Bake in well greased oblong or square pan or muffin tins. For the loaf allow 40 minutes in a moderate oven.

MRS. BERTRAND HARALSON
St. Francisville, La.

SALLY LUNN II

1 yeast cake
¼ cup warm water
4 eggs
1 cup melted butter

1 cup milk
3 tablespoons sugar
1 teaspoon salt
4 cups sifted flour

Soak yeast in lukewarm water. Beat eggs well until light in color. Add milk and butter after milk has been heated to lukewarm temperature. Add sugar, salt, yeast and flour. Let double in size in bowl. Then beat well and put in oiled angel food cake pan and allow 1¼ hours to rise. Bake 25 minutes at 350 degrees. Serve hot.

MRS. CHARLES KENNON
Shreveport, La.

LEMON BREAD

½ cup butter
2 eggs
½ cup milk
1 teaspoon baking powder
Dash of salt

1 to 2 cups nuts,
chopped
1 cup sugar
Grated rind of 1 lemon
1½ cups sifted flour

Cream butter and sugar until light. Beat in eggs and rind. Sift together flour, baking powder and salt—add 1/3 at a time, alternately with the milk, to the egg and sugar mixture. Fold in nuts. Pour into buttered loaf pan (8X4X2). Bake at 350 degrees for 45 to 55 minutes. While hot and still in the pan pour over it a mixture of ½ cup sugar and juice of 1 lemon. Leave in pan 10 minutes then turn out to cool, glazed side up.

MRS. WILLIAM Y. LOBDELL

SPOON BREAD

1 stick butter
2 cups milk
½ cups yellow corn meal

½ teaspoon salt
1 teaspoon sugar
3 eggs

Scald milk and add corn meal. Cook until thick, stirring constantly. Remove from heat, add seasonings and the 3 eggs well beaten, Bake at 375 in shallow baking dish (casserole rectangle) until golden brown. Serve immediately.

MRS. W. J. OLIVER, JR.

ORANGE MARMALADE NUT BREAD

2½ cups all-purpose flour
1 tablespoon baking
  powder
1 teaspoon salt
2 tablespoons butter

3 eggs
1 cup orange marmalade
Grated rind of one orange
1 cup chopped walnuts
  or pecans

½ cup honey

Cream butter, add honey, then eggs, orange marmalade and rind. Beat until well mixed. Stir in other ingredients and nuts. Mix well. Pour into greased bread pan (9" X 5" X 3") and bake in 350 degree oven for 50 or 55 minutes.

MRS. JOE DURRETT
Monroe, La.

LIZZY'S BREAD

1 cup milk
½ cup sugar
½ cup Lou Ana oil
1 tablespoon salt

2/3 cups mashed potatoes
3 eggs
2 packages yeast
5½ cups flour

1 cup Lou Ana oil

Bring milk, sugar and half cup oil to boiling point. Cool. Dissolve yeast in 1/3 cup warm water. Add yeast, beaten eggs and mashed potatoes to milk mixture. Stir in flour (this is a soft dough). Pour 1 cup oil over dough, cover with a cloth and let rise at room temperature until double in bulk. Knead on floured board until elastic, then form into 4 loaves. Place in well oiled loaf pans and let rise 30 minutes. Bake at 350 degrees for 30 minutes. Yields 15 slices in each loaf.

MRS. W. T. BAYNARD

ORANGE BREAD

1 large orange (juice and ground rind)	2 tablespoons shortening
1 cup dates or raisins	1 beaten egg
1 teaspoon soda	2 cups flour
1 cup sugar	1 teaspoon baking powder
	½ teaspoon salt

½ cup pecans

Add dates to ground orange peel to make 1 cup. Add boiling water to orange juice to make 1 cup. Stir in soda, sugar and shortening. Add beaten egg, then flour sifted with baking powder and salt. Stir in nuts, dusted with a little of the flour. Bake in greased loaf pans at 350 degrees for about 50 minutes.

MRS. FOSTER PROVOST

MRS. PETE'S PUMPKIN BREAD

3½ cups all purpose flour	1/3 cup water
1½ teaspoons salt	1 cup Lou Ana oil
1 teaspoon cinnamon	4 eggs slightly beaten
1 teaspoon nutmeg	3 cups sugar
2 teaspoons soda	1 can pumpkin (2 cups)

Using a large bowl, mix all the dry ingredients. Make a well and add all other ingredients. Mix until smooth. Grease and flour 3 loaf pans or 4 or 5 smaller pans and divide the batter to fit pans. Bake at 350 degrees about one hour. Cool slightly in pans, remove and allow to get cold. Wrap in plastic bags or foil and freeze. Will keep in refrigerator for 3 or 4 weeks. Chopped nuts may be added, if desired.

MRS. FELIX SPILLER

FLAT BREAD

2 cups sifted flour	4 tablespoons butter
½ cup yellow corn meal	(necessary)
½ teaspoon salt	2/3 cup warm water

Mix like pastry and chill. Roll dough thin. Place on ungreased cookie sheet and bake until light brown at 375 degrees. Can be rolled out on cookie sheet and marked with knife in squares or other shapes to be broken when cool. When baked in one sheet, break up.

MRS. ROY FIELD

This flat bread is delicious with any salad.

DATE-NUT BREAD

3/4 cup pecans chopped   2 eggs
1 cup dates   1 teaspoon vanilla
1½ teaspoons soda   1 cup sugar
3 tablespoons butter   1½ cups sifted flour
3/4 cup hot water   ½ teaspoon salt

Mix nuts, dates, soda, salt and butter, add boiling water, and let stand for 20 minutes. Beat eggs, add flavoring, sugar and flour. Combine with date mixture. Bake in a greased and floured 9 X 5 X 3 inch pan at 350 degrees for 1 hour. You may also divide and bake in smaller greased and floured pans.

MRS. L. O. GAHAGAN
Ruston, La.

PRUNE BREAD

2 cups sugar   2 cups flour
1 cup Lou Ana oil   ½ teaspoon salt
3 eggs   1 teaspoon soda
1 cup buttermilk   1 teaspoon cinnamon
1 cup chopped, cooked   1 teaspoon allspice
    prunes   1 teaspoon cloves
1 teaspoon baking powder   1 teaspoon vanilla

1 cup chopped nuts

Mix sugar, oil, eggs, buttermilk and chopped prunes together. Sift flour and remaining ingredients together and add to the first mixture. Bake 1 hour at 350 degrees in well oiled loaf pans. Freezes well.

MRS. ETHEL BOWMAN
Jennings, La.

CINNAMON BREAD

1 package dry yeast   3/4 cup sugar
1 teaspoon sugar   1/3 cup margarine
Dash of ground ginger   1 cup raisins
¼ cup lukewarm water   3½ cups flour
3/4 cup milk, scalded   1 teaspoon salt

Dissolve the yeast, sugar and ginger in the warm water. Dissolve the sugar and margarine in the scalded milk and let cool. Wash, drain and set aside the raisins. Mix flour and salt and stir the cooled milk into the yeast mixture. Beat in half the flour-salt mixture. Cover and let rise until double. Stir dough down and beat in the rest of the flour. Turn out on floured board and knead, working in raisins, until smooth and elastic, about 7 minutes. Place in greased bowl, cover with clean towel, and let rise in warm place until your finger makes an impression in the dough. Then, mix together:

2 tablespoons softened butter	¼ teaspoon nutmeg
1 teaspoon cinnamon	6 tablespoons brown sugar, packed

Turn out dough and roll into rectangle. Spread with cinnamon mixture. Roll up and shape into loaf. Place in greased loaf pan, cover with wax paper and let rise in a warm place. When double, place in a preheated 350 degree oven and bake 45 minutes, or until it is brown and makes a hollow thump when tapped. (This is the bread I make for Christmas gifts each year. You can multiply ingredients by 4 and make 4 loaves at a time, or, it makes great miniature loaves for party sandwiches. Freezes beautifully, although I don't know how long it lasts. Never had any left long enough to find out.

MRS. CHARLES D. BALDRIDGE, JR.

BANANA BREAD

1¼ cups sugar	3 mashed bananas
½ cup butter	2 cups sifted flour
2 well beaten eggs	1 teaspoon soda
½ cup nuts	

Cream sugar and butter. Add eggs and bananas. Sift flour and soda and add. Beat well. Fold in nuts. Pour into well greased loaf pan or small ring. Bake 45 minutes at 375 degrees.

MRS. RICHARD L. MERRITT, JR.

GINGERBREAD

½ cup butter	1½ cups cake flour
½ cup cane syrup	½ cup sugar
½ teaspoon soda	½ cup buttermilk
½ teaspoon ginger	½ teaspoon baking powder
¼ teaspoon salt	½ teaspoon cinnamon
1 egg	

Cream butter and sugar well. Add all other ingredients except milk and flour. After mixing well, add to this the milk and flour alternately. Bake in greased pan lined in bottom with paper, at 350 degrees.

MRS. KING MANGHAM
Rayville, La.

BISCUITS

2 cups flour　　　　　　　　1 teaspoon salt
4 teaspoons baking powder　　½ cup shortening
2/3 cup milk

Sift dry ingredients, cut in shortening with a fork until mixture resembles coarse corn meal. Add milk slowly and stir with fork only until slightly mixed. Place on floured board; knead gently. Roll to ½ inch thickness; cut into biscuits. Place on cookie sheet and bake at 450 degrees for 10-12 minutes.

MRS. L. W. WINDSOR
Rayne, La.

CHEESE BISCUITS I

1 stick butter　　　　　　　1 cup flour
½ pound New York cheese　　1 teaspoon salt
1 teaspoon dry mustard

Mix well, cook about 10 minutes at 400 degrees.

MRS. T. J. SINGLETARY

CHEESE BISCUITS II

1 small package (3 ounces)　　1 cup flour
　cream cheese　　　　　　　¼ teaspoon salt
1 stick butter

Mix well, roll out, cut into small biscuits and bake at 425 degrees for 10 minutes.

THE EDITORS

DROP BISCUITS

2 cups flour—　　　　　　　½ teaspoon salt
　measured after sifting　　　2 tablespoons butter
4 teaspoons baking powder　　3/4 cup milk

Sift dry ingredients twice. Work in butter, using tips of fingers, until well mixed. Add milk gradually. Mix quickly with knife. Drop by spoonfuls on greased tin. Bake in hot oven (350 degrees to 400 degrees) about 10 minutes.

Submitted by:
MRS. STEWART CHURCHILL
Belle Alliance Plantation

LINDA'S CHEESE BISCUIT

1 jar sharp cheese spread
    (I use Sharp, Old
    English, 5 ounces)
½ stick butter

3/4 cup all-purpose flour
    (not cake flour)
Dash of Worcestershire
    sauce

Salt and pepper to taste

I mix all this with my electric mixer. Put in the refrigerator to chill for several hours—or overnight. Then roll into small balls about the size of small walnuts. Place on greased baking sheet. Bake in 400 degree oven for about 10 minutes. They do not brown on top so you have to take a spatula and peep under the bottom of some. When brown on bottom they are done.

MRS. CAREY J. ELLIS JR.
Rayville, La.

RAISED BISCUITS

2½ cups flour
1 teaspoon salt
2 tablespoons sugar

½ teaspoon soda
6 tablespoons shortening
1 cup buttermilk

1 package dry yeast

Sift first 4 ingredients together. To this work shortening in with a spoon. Dissolve yeast in buttermilk (room temperature), then add to dry ingredients. Roll out as for biscuits—very thin. Cut into rounds, grease one round and place another on top; press together to grease top round. Let rise for 2 hours or more. Cook at 375 degrees until brown. May be frozen.

MRS. HAMILTON CRAWFORD

ORANGE BISCUITS

2 cups flour
2 tablespoons shortening
1 teaspoon salt

½ cup sugar
Juice and grated rind of
    1 orange

4 teaspoons baking powder

Mix part of rind, a couple of spoonsful of the juice with a little sugar and save for topping. To the remaining juice and rind add milk to make 3/4 cup of liquid. After sifting flour, baking powder, salt and sugar together, add liquid. Roll and cut biscuits. Brush tops with sugar and rind mixture. Bake in 450 degree oven for 10 to 12 minutes.

MRS. WILLIAM Y. LOBDELL

FEATHER-BED ROLLS

1 package yeast
2½ cups milk, scalded
2 tablespoons sugar

½ cup Lou Ana oil
2 teaspoons salt
5 cups flour

Mix yeast and scalded, cooled milk. Cream shortening and sugar. Add the salt and yeast mixture, add flour and beat with spoon until smooth. Let rise, place spoonful of dough in greased muffin tin, being careful not to release much gas from dough. Fill cups 2/3 full. Let rise until double. Brush rolls with melted butter after removing from oven. Bake in a 425 degree oven. Yields 2½ dozen medium sized rolls. This is our very favorite recipe.

MRS. AMY McNUT
Gallagher's ranch
Helotes, Texas

POTATO ROLLS

1 yeast cake
½ cup lukewarm water
½ cup shortening
2 teaspoons salt

½ cup sugar
1 cup mashed potatoes
1 cup scalded milk
2 eggs

6-8 cups flour

Mash potatoes. Add shortening, sugar, salt, eggs, and cream well. Dissolve yeast in warm water. Add to milk (that has been scalded and cooled to lukewarm), then add to mixture.

Sift flour, stir into mixture to make a stiff dough. Knead well on floured board. Put in large bowl. Let rise double in bulk. Knead again. Rub over dough with melted butter, cover and put in icebox. After removing from icebox, shape into rolls and let rise at least 1½ hours. Bake at 450 degrees.

From the file of
MRS. FRANK E. POSEY

GOLDEN ROLLS

3/4 cup warm water
1 package yeast
½ cup sugar
½ teaspoon salt
3 eggs

1 egg yolk (reserve white
for brushing rolls
later)
½ cup soft butter
3½ cups all-purpose flour

In mixer bowl, dissolve yeast in water. Add sugar, salt, eggs, egg yolk, butter and half the flour. Beat 10 minutes with mixer on medium speed (or by hand), scraping sides of bowl frequently. Blend in remaining flour. Cover and let rise in warm place (85 degrees) until double in bulk—about 1 hour. Stir down batter by beating 25 strokes. Cover tightly and refrigerate over night. In the morning, stir down batter and place on floured surface. Flour rolling pin and roll out dough. Cut and shape for Parkerhouse, clover-leaf, or whatever you like, brush tops with mixture of egg white (slightly beaten) and 1 tablespoon sugar. Let them rise in warm place until double—about 40 minutes—and bake in preheated 375 degree oven for 15 to 20 minutes. Makes 4 dozen small rolls.

MRS. WARREN MUNSON

OATMEAL MUFFINS

1 cup quick oats	½ cup Lou Ana oil
3 tablespoons brown sugar	1 cup flour
1 cup buttermilk	4 teaspoons baking powder
2 eggs	½ teaspoon soda

Mix first five ingredients. Sift together dry ingredients. Add, stirring until just barely mixed. Put in greased muffin pans and bake at 400 degrees 25-30 minutes. Makes 12 muffins.

MRS. FRANK RICKEY

SWEET POTATO MUFFINS

1 cup sweet potato	½ cup milk
1 tablespoon butter	2 eggs
1 tablespoon salt	2 cups flour
2 tablespoons baking powder	3 tablespoons sugar

Boil potato until soft. Mash thru a colander. Add butter, salt and milk. Mix thoroughly. Add eggs, well beaten. Add sifted dry ingredients. Bake in greased muffin tins moderately.

THE EDITORS

PAIN PERDU

1 cup milk	1 cup sugar
2 eggs	6-8 slices stale bread

Beat eggs well. Gradually add sugar and then milk. Dip bread on both sides in mixture and fry on both sides in half butter and half Lou Ana oil until golden brown.

Note: Use just a little of the butter and oil at a time.

MRS. W. V. LARCADE
Crowley, La.

CREPES

2 cups flour	2 teaspoons baking powder
2 eggs	1 teaspoon salt

Add milk until batter is thin

Pour into small skillet (oiled with one teaspoon Lou Ana oil) one demi-tasse cup of batter and tilt until bottom is covered. Cook quickly on both sides. Place lump of butter in center soon as removed from skillet and roll. Place on hot plate and serve when 4 or 5 have been prepared. These are good with cane syrup, honey or maple syrup. Rolled and stuffed with creamed chicken, lobster or crab meat with your favorite sauce—they make a full luncheon dish. With fruit, topped with a buttery brandy sauce they make a good dessert.

MRS. GEORGE M. SIMON, JR.

SAUCE FOR CHEPES
STUFFED WITH CREAMED CHICKEN

1 cup hot chicken stock	1 tablespoon butter
½ cup cream	1 tablespoon flour
1 cup chicken cut into	¼ teaspoon salt
small pieces	Pinch cayenne
1 tablespoon parsley	2 egg yolks

Melt butter, add flour, salt and cayenne. Add hot chicken stock (slowly) and cream, chicken and parsley. Add hot mixture to beaten egg yolks. Return to heat and stir one minute and serve.

MRS. GEORGE M. SIMON JR.

CINNAMON MUFFINS

1 stick of melted butter	2½ cups cake flour
1 cup sugar	(measure after sifting)
2 whole eggs (little salt)	1 teaspoon cinnamon
1 teaspoon soda	1 cup buttermilk

Beat eggs until light color. Add sugar, continue to beat. Add butter and mix thoroughly. Sift flour and cinnamon together. Add soda to buttermilk. Add the flour mixture alternately with the buttermilk mixture to egg mixture. Beat until smooth. Place in buttered muffin tins and bake at 400 or 425 degrees for about 20 or 25 minutes. Makes 24 small muffins.

MRS. ROBERT B. WALLACE

HOT CAKES

1 slice of bread dissolved in warm water	½ teaspoon soda
	½ teaspoon salt
1 whole egg	1 cup milk
1 heaping teaspoon sugar	1 cup flour plus
1 heaping teaspoon baking powder	little more
	2 tablespoons Lou Ana oil

Mix together and bake on hot griddle. This is a very old recipe and makes light cakes.

MRS. FRANK CONTOIS
Lake Charles, La.

FRENCH PANCAKE

½ cup flour	4-6 tablespoons butter
½ cup milk	2 tablespoons confectioner's
2 eggs lightly beaten	sugar
A pinch of nutmeg	Juice of ½ lemon

Preheat oven to 425 degrees. Combine flour, milk, eggs and nutmeg. Beat lightly, leaving the batter a little lumpy. Melt butter in a 12-inch heatproof skillet or baking pan, and when very hot, pour in the batter and bake 15 to 20 minutes, or until golden brown. Sprinkle with sugar and return to oven briefly. Sprinkle with lemon juice and serve immediately. Recipe may be doubled successfully. This is delicious served with crisp bacon curls and home made applesauce.

MRS. BEN R. MILLER

GERMAN POTATO PANCAKES

6 medium sized potatoes	2 tablespoons flour
½ of small onion (grated)	2 eggs
	Pinch of black pepper
½ cup Lou Ana oil	

Peel potatoes and cover with water. When ready to prepare mixture grate potatoes and drain off any excess water. Add onion, flour, salt, pepper and well beaten eggs—mix well. Heat oil in large skillet, about ½ inch deep, put tablespoons of mixture into the hot oil and let brown quickly. Keep hot and serve with applesauce.

MRS. ERICH STERNBERG

BUTTERMILK PAN CAKES

1 cup buttermilk	1 teaspoon salt
1 egg	½ teaspoon soda
4 tablespoons Lou Ana oil	Flour to thicken

Combine buttermilk, egg, cooking oil and salt. Add sifted flour to consistency desired for pancakes. Put soda in small amount of hot water and add to pancake mixture. Cook on ungreased griddle.

MRS. D. M. PIPES
Jackson, La.

THIN CORNMEAL BATTER CAKES

1 cup cornmeal	1 teaspoon salt
boiling water	1 egg
1 tablespoon flour	Milk to make thin batter

Scald cornmeal with enough boiling water to dampen well. When cool, sift in flour and salt. Add beaten egg and milk to make **thin** batter. Beat well. Have griddle very hot and **well** greased. This makes a cake with a nice crispy edge.

MRS. WILLIAM HEARD WRIGHT

CREPES "A LA MAISON"

2/3 cup flour	2 tablespoons melted butter
2 whole eggs	1 cup milk
2 egg yolks	3/4 cup chicken broth
Pinch of salt	

Sift dry ingredients. Add eggs and egg yolks, stir in milk, broth and melted butter. Be careful not to beat mixture too much. Let stand for 2 hours, or over night. Use a heavy skillet with the bottom the size you wish the crepes to be. Heat, brush lightly with butter. When hot, pour in 1 3/4 to 2 ounces of batter and quickly roll it around to cover the entire bottom of the skillet. When brown (about 1 minute or more) turn once, brown and stack on flat plate or tray. These may be frozen, if desired.

FILLING

Cooked chicken meat, oysters, lump crab meat, or mushrooms in a light sauce made with wine, butter, chicken fat, or oil, flour and seasoned with parsley, onion powder, and your favorite herbs and seasoned salt. Place several spoonsful on a crêpe, fold and place in buttered baking pan. Repeat this until desired number is reached.

MRS. CARLTON BATES

Sweets

CHOCOLATE FUDGE SAUCE

1½ sticks oleo	Pinch of salt
6 tablespoons cocoa	1½ cups evaporated milk
1½ cups sugar	2 teaspoons vanilla

Combine cocoa and sugar. Melt oleo in large boiler and add all ingredients. Bring this to a boil and stir constantly over medium heat for exactly 7 minutes. Remove from heat and cool. Serve warm over ice cream.

MRS. NELSON D. ABELL
Monroe, La.

RASPBERRY SAUCE

1 box frozen raspberries	2 tablespoons brandy
1/3 cup sugar	2 tablespoons corn starch
½ cup water	1 tablespoon butter
1 tablespoon lemon juice	½ cup red current jelly

Heat berries and water. Mix sugar and cornstarch. Add to berries. Cook over low heat until slightly thick. Put through sieve to remove suds. Add lemon juice, butter and slowly add brandy.

Serve 2 tablespoons over serving of ice cream. Keep refrigerated.

MRS. TED DUNHAM

NESSELRODE SAUCE

1 No. 2 can sliced pineapple	½ cup sliced Brazil nuts
1 cup sugar	1 cup candied cherries,
1/3 cup Jamaica rum	cut in half

Drain pineapple; add water to pineapple juice to make one cup. Cut pineapple in small pieces. Combine pineapple, liquid, sugar and cherries in saucepan. Simmer, uncovered, about half an hour. Cool; add rum and nuts. Chill. Serve on vanilla ice cream.

MRS. LEWIS HESS

HARD SAUCE

1/3 cup butter	1 cup powdered sugar
	Brandy or whiskey to taste

Cream butter until very soft. Add powdered sugar gradually until very smooth. Add brandy or whiskey and keep in cool place until served. Will keep indefinitely in the refrigerator.

THE EDITORS

LEMON-ORANGE SAUCE

2 eggs
3/4 cup of sugar
Juice of 1 lemon
1 cup fresh orange juice

Moisten 2 tablespoons
of cornstarch
Dash of salt
1 cup whipped cream

Mix all together except the cream and cook slowly until thick. Cool and fold in the whipped cream.

MRS. CHARLES KEAN

VANILLA SAUCE

½ cup sugar.
1 tablespoon cornstarch
2 tablespoons butter

1½ tablespoons lemon juice
Nutmeg
Salt

Mix sugar and cornstarch and add to this gradually stirring constantly 1 cup boiling water. Boil 5 minutes. Remove from fire and add butter, lemon juice (or 1 teaspoon vanilla), a few gratings of nutmeg and a dash of salt. This is especially good as a topping for butter cakes.

MRS. JOHN GODFREY
Monroe, La.

CREPES IN ORANGE SAUCE

1 egg, separated
2/3 cup milk
½ cup flour

Dash of salt
½ teaspoon grated
lemon rind

1 tablespoon sugar

Beat egg yolk well; stir in milk. Add flour and blend until smooth. Stir in sugar, salt, lemon rind. Fold in stiffly beaten egg white. Pour onto hot lightly greased griddle to make crepes about 4" in diameter. When brown, turn and brown other side. Roll up. When ready to serve carefully add crepes to orange sauce, cover and heat slowly, basting with sauce several times.

SAUCE

1 medium size orange
2 tablespoons butter
½ cup orange juice

½ cup brandy (optional)
3 tablespoons powdered
sugar

To make sauce: Cut orange rind in slivers, removing all membrane. Add to butter in skillet with powdered sugar and orange juice, plus brandy if desired. Heat to boiling.

MRS. T. L. DANIELSON

LA COUPE ENCHANTEE

Dans un saladier, coupez en morceaux ou en rondelles les fruits très juteux tels que: peches, oranges, prunes très mures . . . (fruits épulcheés bien entendu). Saupoudrez-les de sucre et laissez-les macérer pendant au moins une heure. A ce moment, vous observerez que le jus des fruits est devenu très abondant; ajoutez alors à ce moment les fruits à pulpe plus ferme: bananes, abricots, grains de raisins frais, poires, etc. . . . Laissez macérer à nouveau, sans ajouter de sucre. Mélanger doucement tous les fruits et, recommandation essentielle, égouttez une partie du sirop qui s'est formé, remplacez-le par une meme quantité de liqueur. Laissez encore reposer au frais avant de servir dans des coupes de cristal. Vous avez ainsi une vraie salade de fruits à la liqueur (et non au sirop) des coupes de fruits.

ENCHANTED FRUIT CUP

In a salad bowl, cut up into pieces or rings very juicy fruit, such as peaches, oranges, very ripe plums (peeled, of course). Sprinkle them with sugar and let them soak for at least an hour. At this point you will notice that the juice has become abundant, so add firmer fruit now: bananas, apricots, grapes, pears, etc. Let them soak again, without adding sugar. Gently mix all fruit and drain out part of the syrup which has formed and replace with equal amount of liqueur. Let this stand and cool before serving in crystal dish.

DANIELE FAGAN WRIGHT
Hammond, La.
formerly LeHavre and Paris

MERINGUE SHELLS
Serves 12

6 egg whites (3/4 cup)	1½ teaspoon lemon juice,
2 cups sugar	or ½ teaspoon cream of tartar

Heat oven to 400 degrees. Beat egg whites and lemon juice until frothy. Gradually beat in sugar, a little at a time. Beat until stiff and glossy. Drop by small spoonfuls in a circle on brown paper on baking sheet, or heap into a high mound and hollow out with the back of a spoon. Place meringue in oven, close door, turn oven off. (Don't peek) Let stand over night in the oven. Serve filled with ice cream and fresh fruit.

MRS. CHARLES KEAN

LIME MERINGUES

3 egg whites   1/8 teaspoon salt
¼ teaspoon cream of tartar   3/4 cup sugar

Beat egg whites to foamy stage. Add cream of tartar and salt. Beat stiff but not dry. Then add sugar gradually. Beat until stiff. Cover baking sheet with buttered brown paper. Pile meringues into 6 mounds about 3 inches in diameter. Make 2 inch depression in center of each. Bake at 225 degrees for one hour. While baking make filling.

FILLING:

¼ cup sugar   1½ teaspoons grated
4 tablespoons fresh   lime rind
    lime juice   1 cup whipping cream
3 egg yolks

Beat egg yolks and add the ¼ cup sugar and 4 tablespoons lime juice. Cook over boiling water stirring constantly so egg yolk does not curdle, until thickened. Remove from heat and add grated lime peel and chill in refrigerator. When meringues are cool, whip cream and fold custard (chilled) into it. Fill the meringues and place in refrigerator 6-12 hours or longer. Garnish with desired fruit or minted cherries.

MRS. CARL CAMPBELL

BUTTERSCOTCH SAUCE

5/8 cup brown sugar   1/3 cup white corn syrup
2 tablespoons butter   3/8 cup cream

Cook brown sugar, butter and corn syrup together until thick and then add 3/8 cup cream. This is a really delicious sauce over most any kind of cake. Originated in Kentucky.

MRS. A. E. MONTGOMERY, SR.
Monroe, La.

MERINGUE SHELLS

4 egg whites   1 cup of sugar
Pinch of salt   ½ teaspoon vanilla

Add salt to eggs and beat until stiff. Add sugar gradually and continue beating until all is used, then add in vanilla. Cover a baking sheet with unbuttered paper. With a tablespoon drop the mixture on the paper in mounds with about 2 heaping tablespoons in each. Bake at 250 degrees for 1 hour. Keep in dry place if not served immediately. Serve with favorite ice cream or sauce.

MRS. GEORGE HILL
Homestead Plantation

CURRIED FRUIT BAKE
Serves 4

1 no. 2½-can fruit salad 2 bananas—cut bite size
½ cup maraschino cherries 1 cup black cherries

This is the basic recipe. We use fresh fruit, if possible. Bananas are a must.

½ cup sugar ¼ cup butter
1 tablespoon curry (or less) 2 tablespoons cornstarch

Drain fruit. Mix curry powder, sugar, cornstarch and melted butter. Toss lightly into fruit, which has been cut bite size. Bake in greased casserole—30-40 minutes at 350 degrees until slightly browned.

MRS. RALPH M. FORD

SHERRIED FRUITS
Serves 10-12

1 can sliced pineapple 1 can apricots (halves)
1 can peaches (halves) 2 tablespoons flour
1 can pears (halves) ½ cup brown sugar
1 jar spiced apple rings 1 stick butter
1 cup dry sherry

Use all medium size cans of fruit. In a shallow casserole place fruit which has been well drained. I suggest placing the pineapple rings first, then placing a peach half in the center of each pineaple ring. Arrange pears in between the pineapple. Then make another layer of apple rings and place the apricots in the center of the apples. In a double boiler combine butter, sugar, flour, and sherry, stirring over hot water until thick and smooth. Pour this sauce over the fruits. Cover and refrigerate several hours—preferably overnight so the flavors can be absorbed. To serve heat in 350 degree oven about 20 minutes. Serve hot. This dish is excellent with any curry. Charcoal broiled chicken, pork, or ham are also delicious with the fruits.

From the files of
BARRON AND BARONESS
VON BRENNIG through their
grandson and his wife
Mrs. Charles Coudart Brennig, Jr.

FOOD OF HEAVEN

1 cup sugar	3/4 pound dates (chopped)
2 eggs	1 cup pecans (chopped)
2 tablespoons flour	3 bananas
1 teaspoon baking powder	3 oranges
	Whipped cream

Beat sugar and eggs well. Add flour and baking powder. Chop dates and pecans very fine and add to mixture. Bake in well buttered pan for about 30 minutes at 350 degrees. You may have to stir in order that the sides and top will not burn before the center is done. Cut 3 bananas and 3 oranges and add to warm mixture. Allow to cool. Serve with whipped cream. Do not use pitted dates; they are too dry.

MRS. WALLACE PEARSON
Lafayette, La.

HOT CURRIED FRUIT
Serves 8

1 #2½ can fruit for salad	2 bananas cut
	½ cup light brown sugar
½ jar (med.) cherries	2 teaspoons cornstarch
1 can dark bing cherries	¼ teaspoon curry powder
	½ stick melted butter

Drain fruit. Mix dry ingredients. Add butter. Mix with fruit. Bake 350 degrees 30 to 40 minutes.

From the files of
BARON & BARONESS VON BRENNIG
through their grandson & his wife
Mrs. Charles Coudart Brennig, Jr.

CURRIED FRUIT

½ cup butter	1 can pineapple chunks or slices
1 cup light brown sugar	
4 teaspoons curry powder	2 cups plums or prunes
1 No. 2 can pear halves	1 can or jar dark Bing cherries
1 No. 2 can peach halves	

Drain and dry fruit. In shallow casserole, place butter, brown sugar, curry powder, and arrange fruit on top. Bake 45 minutes to an hour in a 350 degree oven.

MRS. OMER J. HEBERT
Plaquemine, La.

A ROYAL RICE PUDDING
Serves 6

½ cup seedless raisins	3 tablespoons sugar
½ cup sherry	¼ teaspoon salt
¼ cup uncooked rice	1 teaspoon vanilla
½ cup rich milk	2 egg whites
2 egg yolks, well beaten	3 or 4 tablespoons sugar

Soak raisins in sherry overnight. Cook rice and milk together about 1 hour over boiling water until tender. Into beaten egg yolks stir 3 tablespoons sugar, salt, then stir in hot rice mixture slowly. Return to slow boil and cook 2 minutes longer, stirring constantly. Partially cool. Stir in vanilla and soaked-in-sherry raisins. Beat egg whites until frothy, then stir in 3 or 4 tablespoons sugar gradually until whites are stiff and glossy. Fold into rice custard mixture. Chill. Serve with cream.

MARIE COUDERT BRENNIG SANDS
Daughter of Baron and Baroness
von Brennig of Vienna, Austria

ENGLISH TRIFLE
Serves 8

1 dozen ladyfingers	2 tablespoons sherry
2 cups English custard	1 dozen almond macaroons
(see below)	1 cup whipping cream,
2 tablespoons currant jelly	whipped

toasted almonds

Place one-half of ladyfingers in shallow bowl and sprinkle with one-half of the sherry. Pour custard over ladyfingers. Roll out macaroons to coarse crumbs. Sprinkle over custard. Add jelly in bits and dabs. Cover with remaining ladyfingers and sprinkle with sherry. Top with sweetened whipped cream and sprinkle toasted almonds over all. Chill well. An easy and delicious dessert.

BOILED ENGLISH CUSTARD

4 egg yolks	½ teaspoon vanilla
1 cup milk	½ cup sugar
Pinch salt	1 cup cream

Beat yolks and sugar. Add vanilla, milk and cream and cook over hot water, stirring constantly. Strain and cool. When thickened makes 2 cups.

MRS. JOHN MCKOWEN

PLUM PUDDING

1½ cups grated bread crumbs	½ cup citron
1½ cups butter or suet finely chopped	½ cup sweet milk
1½ cups raisins	4 eggs
1½ cups currants	2 cups flour
1½ cups sugar	1 teaspoon each—baking powder, cinnamon, cloves and nutmeg

½ cup orange marmalade

Mix ingredients and pour into well greased vessel. Set in pan of water half-way up the vessel and steam for 3½ hours. Serve with wine sauce or hard sauce flavored with whiskey.

From the files of
MRS. W. E. GLASSELL
(Nee Jane Richmond Adger)
Shreveport, La.

ENGLISH PLUM PUDDING

1 cup flour	2/3 cup sugar
1/3 cup shortening	3 eggs
1 cup bread crumbs	½ teaspoon nutmeg
1 cup raisins	½ teaspoon cinnamon
1 cup currants	¼ cup candied peel
½ cup Rum or Brandy	(lemon or orange)

Mix well, put in ovenware bowl, cover with foil and steam for 3½ hours. Serve hot with hard sauce made with butter, confectioners sugar and teaspoon of vanilla.

MRS. ELENA H. HULINGS

DATE PUDDING

1 8-ounce package of dates	1 cup brown sugar
1 cup white sugar	1 cup sifted all purpose flour
1 cup water	
1½ cups rolled oats	½ teaspoon soda
1 teaspoon vanilla	½ teaspoon almond extract

½ cup shortening

Mix dates, white sugar and water in a sauce pan and cook over low heat, mashing dates as mixture cooks. Cook until sugar is dissolved and dates are soft. Blend oats, brown sugar, flour, soda, and shortening until they resemble coarse crumbs. Add vanilla and almond extract. Lightly grease a 9X6-inch baking dish and place half the dry ingredients in the bottom. Put the date mixture

on top of this, then finish with a layer of the first mix.
Bake at 350 degrees for about 30 minutes, or until lightly
browned. Cool. Serve with ½ pint whipping cream to
which has been added ¼ cup sugar and 1 teaspoon
vanilla.

MRS. OLLIE DYER, JR.

STUFFED ORANGES
Will fill 6 or 8 orange halves

Select large oranges
1½ cups orange juice
½ cup sugar
½ tablespoon gelatin
2 tablespoons water

1 cup whipping cream
½ cup chopped pecans
¼ cup confectioners sugar
Curacao or Grand
Marnier

Cut oranges in half and scoop out centers, saving
juice. Oranges may be notched around edges for a dec-
orative touch. Meanwhile, combine 1½ cups orange juice
and sugar, stirring until the sugar is dissolved. Soften
gelatine in water. Dissolve over hot water. Add to orange
juice. Whip cream until it thickens and begins to hold
its shape. Then fold in nuts and confectioners sugar.
Add orange juice. Add Curacao or Grand Marnier for
flavor, to taste. Fill orange cups and freeze. Before serving, thaw slightly and cover with whipped cream, sweetened. Garnish with fresh whole strawberry or fresh
cherry.

MRS. JAMES W. MCLAURIN

CHOCOLATE BLANC MANGE

4 tablespoons corn starch
3/4 cup sugar
¼ teaspoon salt
3 eggs

1 quart milk
3 ounces bitter chocolate or
1/3 cup cocoa
1 teaspoon vanilla

Mix cornstarch, sugar together with a little milk.
Put rest of milk on to boil with chocolate. When chocolate
is melted stir all together and cook until thick. Add egg
yolks and set over hot water and cook 20 minutes. Add
vanilla and beat egg whites until stiff. Fold in chocolate
mixture.

From the file of
MRS. ESTELLE LEWIS CORBETT

WALNUT SPOON PUDDING
Makes 8 servings

1 cup California walnuts	1 cup soft, dried dark
¼ cup soft butter	or golden figs
2/3 cup brown sugar,	1 egg beaten
packed	3/4 cup sifted all purpose
¼ teaspoon cinnamon	flour
1/8 teaspoon cloves	1/4 teaspoon soda
1/8 teaspoon nutmeg	½ teaspoon salt

Chop walnuts; clip stems from figs and cut fruit in small pieces. Cream butter, sugar, spices, and egg together until well blended and fluffy. Resift flour with soda and salt. Add to creamed mixture; beat until blended. Stir in fruit and walnuts. Turn into buttered 8 or 9 inch square pan. Bake at 350 degrees for 20 to 25 minutes. Spoon, while warm, into serving dishes. Serve warm with fluffy **Bourbon Sauce.**

FLUFFY BOURBON SAUCE

2 egg yolks	Pinch of salt
1 cup sifted powdered	3 or 4 tablespoons of
sugar	Bourbon

1 cup whipping cream

Beat eggs and add sugar and salt. Beat and stir in Bourbon. Gently fold in whipped cream. Chill until ready to serve. Stir before using.

MRS. BEN BOGARD
Ruston, La.

BREAD PUDDING WITH WHISKEY SAUCE

2 cups milk	2 eggs, slightly beaten
4 cups coarse bread crumbs	¼ teaspoon salt
¼ cup melted butter	½ cup seedless raisins
½ cup sugar	1 teaspoon cinnamon

Scald milk and pour over bread crumbs. Cool and add remaining ingredients, mixing well. Pour into a 1½ quart casserole. Place casserole in pan of hot water (1 inch deep) and bake at 350 degrees for one hour, or until a silver knife inserted into pudding comes out clean.

WHISKEY SAUCE

1 stick butter or oleo	1 cup sugar
1 egg	¼ cup whiskey

Cook butter and sugar together in double boiler until mixture is very hot, thick and sugar dissolved. Add

egg quickly and beat. Cool slightly and add whiskey.
Serve hot or cold over pudding.

MRS. ANTHONY J. DOHERTY

SHERRY DATE PUDDING

1 cup sifted flour	1 cup chopped dates
2 teaspoons baking powder	½ cup chopped pecans
¼ teaspoon salt	3 tablespoons butter
2/3 cup sugar	3/4 cup water
½ cup milk	3/4 cup sherry

3/4 cup brown sugar

Sift flour with baking powder, salt and sugar. Add
milk, dates and pecans; blend well. Grease 8" square
baking dish and spread mixture evenly over bottom.

Combine water, sherry, brown sugar and butter in
saucepan; bring to a boil. Pour this syrup over batter in
baking dish. **Do not stir.**

Bake at 350 degrees F. for about 1 hour. Serve warm
with whipped cream or vanilla ice cream. Pudding will
have a cake-like layer on top, with a rich-flavored sauce
beneath it.

MRS. LEWIS HESS

SYLVINITE PUDDING

1 package unflavored gelatine	3/4 cup sugar
	1 cup boiling water
¼ cup cold water	3 egg whites

Sprinkle gelatine over ¼ cup cold water. Dissolve
sugar in boiling water, cool, put all in the mixing bowl
and whip until very stiff. Pour in pan and chill in refrigerator over night. To serve, turn out, cut in squares,
roll in graham cracker crumbs and serve with lemon
butter sauce:

SAUCE

3 egg yolks	Juice of 1 lemon and
1/3 cup sugar	grated rind

1/3 cup melted butter

Whip well together over hot water until slightly
thickened. Fold in 1/3 cup heavy cream, which has been
whipped. A tasty dessert after a rich dinner.

MRS. AMY McNUT
Gallagher's Ranch
Helotes, Texas

WOODRUFF PUDDING

3 eggs (beaten separately)
1 cup sugar
Butter size of an egg
3/4 cup flour
1 cup blackberry jam

1 teaspoon soda
3 tablespoons buttermilk
½ teaspoon cloves
½ teaspoon all spice
1 cup chopped nuts

Cream egg yolks and sugar together, add butter and flour and cream well. Mix together with other ingredients and put in casserole or baking dish and bake at 350 degrees for about 30 to 40 minutes.

MRS. FRANK M. WOMACK

MARSHMALLOW PUDDING
Serves 12

1 pound marshmallows
2 tablespoons cold water
1 can grated pineapple
    (8½ ounces.)

2 chopped bananas
½ cup chopped pecans
4 beaten egg whites
Whipped cream

Put marshmallows and cold water in top of double boiler and melt stirring constantly. Add pineapple after draining off juice. Add bananas and pecans. Beat egg whites until stiff and add to above ingredients. Put into mold or individual molds and place in refrigerator until set. Top with whipped cream and garnish with cherry.

MRS. ROBERT KENNON

FLOATING ISLAND CUSTARD
(From My Mother's "Marian Harland" Recipe Book)

1 quart of milk
5 eggs-whites and yolks
    beaten separately
½ cup currant jelly

4 tablespoons (heaping)
    white sugar
2 teaspoons extract bitter
    almond or vanilla

Beat the yolks well, stir in the sugar and add the hot, not boiling milk, a little at a time. Boil until it begins to thicken. When cool, flavor and pour into a glass dish, first stirring it up well. Heap upon it a meringue of the whites into which you have beaten, gradually, half a cup of currant, cranberry, or other bright tart jelly. Dot with bits of jelly cut into rings or stars, or straight slips laid on in a pattern.

MRS. ROBERT L. PETTIT

LADY FINGER AND ALMOND MACAROON ICE BOX DESSERT

Grease large aluminum ring and line sides with split lady fingers. In bottom of pan put almond macaroons and layer of cream custard filling, layer of macaroons, until pan is filled and custard on top. Make this the day before if possible and refrigerate overnight. When ready to serve turn onto large round platter, cover with whipped cream. If strawberries are in season decorate with them; if not, use maraschino cherries.

CUSTARD FILLING

6 eggs	1 pint milk
2 sticks butter	Sugar to taste (½ cup)
1 pinch salt	Vanilla
1 pint whipping cream	2 tablespoons gelatine

Melt butter in scalded cream and milk. Mix the slightly beaten eggs with the sugar and salt. Add the scalded milk and cream gradually to the eggs. Cook in a double boiler, stirring constantly, until the mixture thickens and coats a spoon. Remove from the heat at once and add the vanilla and the gelatine, which has been softened in water. Cool slightly before putting in ring.

MRS. MONROE J. RATHBONE, SR.

CALINE'S FRESH PEACH ICE CREAM

Make boiled custard using:

3 eggs	1 quart milk
1 cup sugar	¼ teaspoon salt
whipping cream	

Use about 12 to 16 peaches that are real ripe. Peel, remove seeds and either put thru a colander or use a blender. (I use my blender as it is faster). Sweeten to taste. (Will take 1 to 1½ cups sugar).

Mix peaches and custard, then add 1 or 2 cups whipping cream. (1 cup makes it good—2 cups lots better).

We do all this mixing right in the freezer. Pour the custard in, then peaches, then cream. This should come to about 2 or 3 inches from top of 1 gallon freezer. If it is much less than 2 or 3 inches just add a little more milk and stir. Add more sugar if needed. Freeze.

MRS. CAREY J. ELLIS SR.
Rayville, La.

BAKED CUSTARD

4 egg yolks	1 heaping tablespoon flour
1 heaping teaspoon butter	Flavoring
Sugar to taste	1½ cups milk

Beat egg yolks and add sugar, then add milk. Stir this in to the flour so it won't lump. Add flavoring, pour into baking dish, float butter on top, and bake at 350 degrees until an inserted knife comes out clean. It is best to put the baking dish in a pan of water.

From the file of
MRS. GILBERT MILLS
Fair Haven Plantation

FROZEN MINT DESSERT

1 cup sugar	Handful of crushed mint
1 cup water	leaves
Juice of 2 lemons	Juice of 2 oranges

Boil sugar and water for five minutes. Pour over 1 handful of crushed mint leaves and cover. When cooled, strain and add juices from oranges and lemons. Pour liquid mixture over canteloup and watermelon balls. Freeze in ice tray.

MRS. CHARLES NUNN

CRANBERRY ICE

1 quart cranberries	Juice of one orange
1 pint water	Grated rind of 1 orange
2 cups sugar	Juice of one lemon

Wash and pick over the berries and cook with water until all are popped open. Run through a sieve and mash all the pulp out. Add sugar and rind and return to the fire, stirring until sugar is dissolved. Add the juice, cool, freeze to a mush and stir. (Do not allow to freeze hard) and beat in an electric mixer. Refreeze and serve.

Serves about 15 people.

TIP: Save the orange hulls from your breakfast juice, clean out, and fill with Cranberry Ice.

MRS. I. H. RUBENSTEIN

LEMON SHERBERT

1 cup fresh lemon juice	1 quart milk
2 1/3 cups sugar	1 pint whipping cream

Mix lemon juice and 2 cups sugar and refrigerate. Mix well. Add 1/3 cup sugar to milk, mix well, place in freezer and chill slightly. Add lemon juice mixture, then cream. Then place in old fashioned type freezer. Use lots of ice cream salt.

MRS. G. W. JAMES, JR.
Ruston, La.

ICE CREAM PIE

1 8-ounce package	3 egg yolks and whites,
cream cheese	beaten separately
1 scant cup sugar	½ pint whipping cream
Few drops almond extract	¼ teaspoon vanilla extract

Cream sugar and cheese and add egg yolks, one at a time. Add whipped cream and fold in beaten egg whites. Place in graham cracker crust and freeze. Good with crushed strawberries on top.

MRS. R. P. MATHIS

MINT ICE CREAM
(Made in Refrigerator)
Serves 4-6

2 cups sugar	½ pint whipping cream
2 cups water	1 egg white
Juice of 3 oranges	Dash of salt
Juice of 2 lemons	Few drops green fruit
Grated rind of 1 lemon	coloring
3 or 4 sprigs fresh mint	

Boil sugar and water together and let cool. Crush mint leaves and add to fruit juices and let set for about 30 minutes. Strain juices into syrup mixture and put in tray in refrigerator until it becomes mushy. Whip cream with egg white and stir into mushy mixture and return to refrigerator. In order to be creamy it must be stirred several times before it becomes completely frozen.

MRS. STERLING GLADDEN, JR.

CUSTARD ICE CREAM

Chill (almost freeze) ½ large can Pet milk; Beat 10 eggs in bowl; Add 1½ cups sugar, pinch of salt; Beat well; Scald 1 quart milk (in double boiler); Add eggs and sugar mixture to milk; Cook (and stir) about 10 minutes (until it thickens); Cool—Add 1 can condensed milk. Mix well. Whip Pet milk and add to mixture; Add 2 tablespoons vanilla. Freeze in old fashioned type freezer (electric or handcrank freezer). Very rich.

MRS. BERLIN E. PERKINS, JR.

CHARLOTTE RUSSE

2 eggs
½ cup sugar
1 cup milk
2 cups whipping cream
2 tablespoons Rum

2 tablespoons gelatine
2 tablespoons Bourbon
Pound cake or split
lady fingers

In double boiler make a custard of slightly beaten eggs, sugar and milk, reserving some milk in which to dissolve gelatine. Beat cream until stiff. Add gelatine (dissolved) to hot custard. Fold in whipped cream, Bourbon and Rum. When mixture thickens, pour into a bowl or mold lined with cake. Cover top with cake also. Chill until set. Unmold by running knife around edges and turning onto platter. Ice with additional whipped cream. Garnish with nuts and cherries if desired.

MRS. WALTER H. CLAIBORNE
Bella Vista Plantation

RUSSIAN CREAM

1 quart milk
7 tablespoons sugar
4 eggs

3 envelopes gelatine
2 teaspoons vanilla
(or sherry)

Whipped cream and cherries

Dissolve gelatine in 3/4 cup water and heat slowly until dissolved. Beat yolks of eggs with 4 tablespoons sugar until creamy. Add milk, gelatine and cook in double boiler until it thickens or bubbles slightly. Remove from heat and fold in the stiffly beaten egg whites, to which has been added 3 tablespoons sugar. Add vanilla or sherry and refrigerate over night or at least 6 hours. Top with whipped cream and Maraschino cherries.

MRS. J. P. BURTON

STRAWBERRY-RASPBERRY FRENCH PASTRY

4 eggs, well beaten
1 pound vanilla
    wafers, crushed
½ pound ground pecans
1 pound confectioner's
    sugar
3 boxes frozen strawberries

1 stick butter or oleo
1 quart vanilla ice cream
1 large can condensed
    milk, whipped, or 2
    pints whipped cream
3 boxes frozen raspberries

Cook sugar, butter and eggs over boiling water slowly for 1½ hours. Stir occasionally to prevent sticking. Mix nuts and vanilla wafers. Pour sugar and egg mixture over nuts and wafers and mix thoroughly. Line bottom and sides of large pan with crumb mix. Thaw and crush raspberries and put a layer over the crumb mix. Put in freezer until firm, then cover with a layer of vanilla ice cream, thawed enough to spread. Return to freezer until firm. Add a layer of strawberries, thawed and crushed enough to spread. Return to freezer until firm. End with a layer of whipped cream. To make more festive, sprinkle with ground pecans. Cut in squares to serve. May be stored in freezer for weeks. Wrap tightly, with Saran then aluminum foil to store.

MRS. R. O. RUSH

PEACH MOUSSE

2 cups mashed peaches	¼ cup water
(put through sieve)	1 pint whipping cream
½ tablespoon gelatine	½ teaspoon almond extract

Soften gelatine in cold water. Sweeten peaches with sugar to taste. Dissolve gelatine over hot water and add to peaches. Fold into whipped cream. Add flavoring and freeze. Strawberries may be substituted for peaches.

MRS. FRANK S. LOWE

FROZEN FRUIT CAKE (DESSERT)
Serves 12

1 pint cold custard	2 dozen lady fingers
1 cup seedless raisins	(broken)
½ pound marshmallow bits	2 dozen almond macaroons
1 cup pecans	(crumbled)
½ cup sherry	1 pint whipped cream

Add last 6 ingredients to cold custard, fold in 1 pint whipped cream and freeze in refrigerator trays.

THE EDITORS

DATE TARTS

1 cup flour	3 eggs
1 cup dates (chopped)	3 teaspoons baking powder
1 cup nuts (chopped)	1 teaspoon vanilla
1 cup sugar	pinch salt

Beat eggs. Add sugar and beat. Add flour to which baking powder has been added. Add other ingredients. Bake in well greased muffin pans in moderate oven for 20 to 30 minutes.

From the files of
COLLINGSBURG PLANTATION
Bossier Parish

SCHAUM TORTE

7 egg whites	1 cup heavy cream,
2 cups sugar	whipped
1 teaspoon vanilla	1 No. 2 can crushed
1 teaspoon vinegar	pineapple

Beat egg whites until very stiff, gradually adding sugar, vanilla and vinegar. Pour into pyrex plate and bake at 275 degrees for one hour. Cool. Pull off top crust and spread whipped cream over lower crust. Over cream spread drained pineapple. Replace top crust carefully. Cover witih wax paper or plastic wrap and refrigerate. This torte is better made a day or two in advance.

MRS. J. B. HEROMAN JR.

Mc's HAITIAN BANANAS
Serves 6

6 moderately ripe bananas. Peel, split lengthwise, and cut across. (I cook mine whole.) Brush with lime juice. Brown in hot butter, salt very lightly.

Make syrup of one cup sweet red unfortified wine (not port), I use Marsala, one cup brown sugar, ½ teaspoon each cinnamon and nutmeg, ½ teaspoon powdered cloves, 1½ teaspoon fresh finely grated orange rind.

Put bananas into a buttered shallow casserole, turn in spiced syrup and cover with about ¼" layer of crushed macaroons (I use sugar wafers instead) and finely chopped almonds mixed together in equal quantities. Brown in oven about 350 degrees until hot. Just before serving, heat and pour over 1½ tablespoons dark rum, light and bring to the table flaming.

MRS. KATHERINE H. LONG

ORANGE-DATE TORTE

1½ cups snipped dates—	1 teaspoon baking soda
½ pound	½ teaspoon salt
¼ cup hot water	1 cup buttermilk
1 cup sugar	½ cup butter or margarine
2 eggs	1 teaspoon grated
2 cups all purpose	orange rind
flour, sifted	½ cup chopped walnuts

Combine dates with hot water and set aside. In mixing bowl, cream butter and sugar. Beat in eggs and orange peel. Sift together flour, soda, and salt. Add to creamed mixture alternately with the buttermilk. Beat well after each addition. Stir in date mixture and walnuts. Pour into greased 13X9X2 inch baking pan and bake in 350 degree oven for 35 to 40 minutes. Remove from oven and prick with wooded pick or meat fork. Make and drizzle the following sauce over the cake while still warm:

3 tablespoons each orange and lemon juice	½ cup sugar

Stir until sugar has dissolved. Serve with ice cream or whipped cream.

LELA A. TOMLINSON
Ruston, La.

CHOCOLATE TORTE

½ cup butter	5 squares unsweetened
2 cups confectioners	chocolate, melted
sugar	½ cup cognac
4 egg yolks	¼ cup water
1½ teaspoon vanilla	24 lady fingers
1 tablespoon cognac	½ pint whipped cream

1 cup toasted pecans or almonds

Cream butter, add sugar and then egg yolks one at a time, stirring well. Add vanilla and the one tablespoon cognac, blend. Stir in melted chocolate. Now mix ½ cup cognac and ¼ cup water. Dip lady fingers quickly into this mixture removing immediately. Arrange 16 halves on long platter or silver tray and cover with part of chocolate mixture, repeat making 3 layers. Cover top and sides with remaining chocolate. Sprinkle well with 1 cup toasted, crushed pecans or slivered almonds. Chill for a few hours. Pile whipped cream on center of loaf and serve.

MRS. DAVID I. GARRETT, JR.
Monroe, La.

TORTONI

½ gallon vanilla ice cream, softened	½ cup chopped Maraschino cherries
1 cup chopped toasted, salted pecans	1 cup crushed, coconut macaroons (boxed)

1 tablespoon almond extract

Mix all together and spoon into fluted, paper cups placed in muffin tins to freeze. Makes 16-18 cups. May be frozen a week ahead.

MRS. LYTTLETON T. HARRIS

FAVORITE STRAWBERRY SHORTCAKE

Thick short biscuits   Fresh strawberries
Drawn butter   Whipping cream

Make thick short biscuits from your favorite recipe. These are served hot—split in two on individual serving plates. Pour drawn butter over each. Add cut and pre-sugared strawberries. Pour unwhipped whipping cream over all.

From the files of
MRS. LYDIA WICKLIFFE

COCONUT CRUNCH TORTE

4 egg whites   1 cup Graham cracker
¼ teaspoon salt   crumbs
1 teaspoon vanilla   ½ cup moist coconut
1 cup sugar   ½ cup pecans chopped
1 cup whipping cream

Beat egg whites with salt and vanilla until foamy. Add sugar gradually and beat mixture until it is **very** stiff. Fold in other ingredients and bake in greased 9 inch pie plate at 350 degrees for thirty minutes. When cool, spread whipped cream on top.

This dessert may be made a day ahead of time. It is delicious for a luncheon or as a special family treat.

MRS. H. L. HENRY
Ruston, La.

PEACH COBBLER

1 stick butter or margarine   3/4 cup milk
1 cup flour   6 to 8 sliced peaches
1 cup sugar   8 tablespoons sugar
2 teaspoons baking powder   ½ cup water

Pre-heat oven to 350 degrees F. Then melt butter in pyrex dish. In mixing bowl sift together flour, sugar (1 cup), and baking powder. To this mixture, add milk; pour over melted butter. Place the sliced peaches on top of mixture, sprinkle with the 8 tablespoons of sugar. Over this pour ½ cup of water. Bake 50 minutes at 350 degrees.

Blackberries and blueberries may be substituted for peaches.

MRS. A. C. PRINCE
Mount Hope, West Virginia

FROZEN CREAM CHEESE DESSERT

3 3-ounce packages   3 eggs
   cream cheese   ½ pint whipping cream
1 cup sugar   Graham crackers
                Pinch of salt

Cream the sugar and cream cheese with a pinch of salt. Add well beaten egg yolks. Fold in whipped cream and the egg whites stiffly beaten. Line bottoms of two freezing trays with 3 double graham crackers rolled fine. Pour in mixture and sprinkle 3 more double graham crackers rolled fine on top. Freeze, slice and serve.

MRS. JACK THIGPEN

CHOCOLATE CREAM CHEESE CAKE
Serves 16

1 eight ounce package   1 eight ounce pack
   cream cheese   semi-sweet chocolate
6 cups sifted powdered   bits
   sugar   1½ sticks oleo
                1 teaspoon vanilla

Set oleo and cream cheese out of refrigerator for several hours to soften. Put chocolate bits into ½ cup hot water and let melt over very low heat.

Cream oleo and cream cheese together. Add 3 cups sifted powdered sugar and stir well. Add melted chocolate bits and mix. Add 3 more cups of sifted powdered sugar and stir well. Add 1 teaspoon vanilla. Remove to a clean bowl a half of this mixture to use for icing. (About 12 rounded tablespoons).

To original bowl add ½ stick softened oleo and mix well.

3 eggs   1½ teaspoon soda
2¼ cups sifted cake flour   3/4 cup milk

Add eggs one at a time and beat well. Add soda to sifted flour. Alternately add milk and dry ingredients and mix thoroughly. Pour into 3 ten inch cake pans which have been greased and a bottom lining put in. Bake about 30 minutes in a 375 degree oven. Cool and ice with mixture that was set aside.

MRS. WILLIAM SWART

CHEESECAKE
CRUST

1 box unsweetened Zwieback	2 teaspoons cinnamon
1 stick butter	2 teaspoons superfine sugar

Roll Zwieback into fine crumbs. Add cinnamon, sugar and melted butter. Oil baking pan with Lou Ana oil and line sides and bottom with crumbs, reserving a little to sprinkle on top of cake.

CAKE

3 packages cream cheese (8 oz. each)	1½ cups superfine sugar
5 eggs	1 teaspoon vanilla
½ cup coffee cream	Juice of 2 lemons— strained
¼ cup flour	

Have cream cheese and eggs at room temperature. Break cheese in small pieces and mix well. Separate eggs, add one yolk at a time, alternating with sugar, cream and flour. Add vanilla and lemon juice. Beat egg whites stiff and fold into cheese mixture. Pour into cake pan (spring pan).

PLACE IN COLD OVEN, set at 350 degrees, cook 30 minutes. **Do not open door.** Turn off heat and leave in oven 20 minutes more. Open oven door, and leave 15 minutes more. Place cake on top of stove one hour, then cool for an additional 2 hours. Secret of cake is in the slow cooling. Top of cake will be cracked when first taken out of the oven, but will close up in the slow cooling. If cooled too quickly, it will fall.

ICING

1 package cream cheese (8 ounces)	1 cup superfine sugar
	½ pint whipping cream
1 teaspoon vanilla	

Mix cream cheese, sugar and vanilla well. Whip cream and fold into cheese mixture. This will cover top and sides of cake. Chill before taking it out of pan and icing. May be put in deepfreeze.

MRS. L. D. GREMILLION

Cakes--Icing

FOUR MINUTE ICING

1 cup sugar
½ teaspoon cream of
   tarter
3 tablespoons water
¼ teaspoon salt
2 unbeaten egg whites
1 teaspoon vanilla

Combine ingredients except vanilla and put into top of double-boiler over boiling water. Beat constantly with electric beater for four minutes. Take off heat and continue beating for one minute. Add flavoring. Stir in and spread on cake.

THE EDITORS

NEVER FAIL CHOCOLATE ICING

1½ bars unsweetened
   chocolate
1½ cups sugar
7 tablespoons milk
4 tablespoons butter
1 tablespoon corn syrup
¼ teaspoon salt
1 teaspoon vanilla

Put into sauce pan. Bring to full boil slowly so as to allow chocolate bars and sugar to melt without burning. Boil 1½ minutes. Beat until spreading consistency.

MRS. H. F. BRADFORD

LEMON FILLING

2 lemons
2 cups sugar
4 egg yolks
3/4 cup boiling water
3 tablespoons flour
3 tablespoons butter

Use lemon juice and grate peel. Mix above ingredients and cook in double boiler or very heavy boiler until thick and creamy. Cool before spreading on cake. Very delicious on yellow cake.

From the recipe file of
COLLINGSBURG PLANTATION
Bossier Parish

ORANGE GLAZE CAKE

1 cup butter or
   shortening
2 cups sugar
4 eggs—separated
2 tablespoons orange rind
1 teaspoon soda in
1 1/3 cups buttermilk
4 cups flour
1 package dates
1 cup nuts

Cream butter and sugar. Add egg yolks and beat. Add buttermilk and flour alternately, saving ½ cup flour to dredge dates and nuts. Add them with orange rind.

Beat egg whites until very stiff. Fold into cake mixture. Bake in tube pan about $1\frac{1}{2}$ -2 hours in 300 degree oven. Remove from oven and while hot, pour sauce over. Set to cool. If wrapped foil, cake will stay moist and fresh for weeks.

SAUCE

3 cups sugar	Note: this orange rind and
$1\frac{1}{2}$ cups orange juice	juice will require
2 tablespoons orange rind	about four average
1 teaspoon lemon juice	oranges.

Heat just long enough to melt sugar. DO NOT BOIL. Pour over cake immediately. When cool, pick up cake which will be resting on the tube section. Slice from there or serve as you like.

MRS. RATCLIFF ANDERSON

TRIPLE SEED CAKE

3 cups all purpose flour	2 tablespoons grated
$2\frac{1}{2}$ teaspoons baking	orange rind
powder	1 tablespoon grated
3/4 teaspoon nutmeg	lemon rind
1 teaspoon salt	1 cup milk
2/3 cup shortening	1 tablespoon caraway
2 cups sugar	seeds
4 eggs	1 tablespoon poppy seeds

1 tablespoon anise seeds

Sift together the flour, baking powder, nutmeg and salt. Cream shortening and sugar thoroughly, add eggs one at a time, beating 1 minute after each egg. Blend in the orange and lemon rind, mixing very well. Add alternately the dry ingredients and the milk, beginning and ending with the dry ingredients. Blend thoroughly after each addition. Spread one fourth of batter in a tube pan (greased and floured on the bottom only). Sprinkle with caraway seed. Alternate remaining batter with the poppy seed and then the anise seed, ending with last of the batter on top. Bake in 350 degree oven 75 to 80 minutes. Let cool 15 minutes in the pan before turning out and frost while still warm.

FRUIT JUICE GLAZE

$1\frac{1}{4}$ cups sifted confectioner's sugar	2 tablespoons orange juice
	1 tablespoon lemon juice

Beat well and spread on triple seed cake while still warm.

MRS. ROY BOCK

BUTTER MILK CAKE

½ pound butter or margarine (can use 1 stick each)

2 cups granulated sugar

3 cups all purpose flour

¼ teaspoon soda (mix with milk)

1 cup buttermilk with a bit of food coloring added

4 eggs

2 teaspoons vanilla

3/4 teaspoon lemon juice

½ teaspoon baking powder

Cream butter and sugar well. Add a little of the flour, which has been sifted with the baking powder. Then alternate flour and milk and soda mixture. Add eggs one at a time. Beat well after each one. Add vanilla and lemon juice. Beating is secret of success. Bake in oven 350 degrees 1 hour. Use a stem pan lined with a layer of wax paper. Grease paper.

MRS. GEORGE C. BRILEY
Natchitoches, La.
MRS. ROBERT CARR

QUEEN ELIZABETH TEA CAKE

1 cup chopped dates

1 teaspoon soda

1 cup boiling water

1 cup sugar

1 stick oleo

1 egg

1 teaspoon vanilla

1½ cups flour

Pour boiling water over dates and soda, set aside. Mix butter and sugar, cream well. Add date mixture and egg, flour and vanilla. Mix well and bake in 9 X 13 pan at 325 degrees for 35 minutes.

FROSTING

1 stick butter

8 tablespoons cream

8 tablespoons sugar

1 teaspoon vanilla

Boil two minutes and spoon over cut cake in pan.

MRS. LOYD HUVAL

COCOANUT CAKE

1 cup sugar

1 cup butter

4 egg whites

2 cups cake flour

3 teaspoons baking powder

½ teaspoon salt

1 cup milk

1 teaspoon vanilla

½ teaspoon almond

Cream sugar annd butter. Sift flour before measuring. Sift with baking powder and salt. Add alternately with milk to creamed mixture. Beat well. Fold in stiffly beaten egg whites. Pour into three greased layer cake pans. Bake at 375 degrees about 20 minutes. Test with a straw.

FILLING

1 fresh cocoanut (grated)
Milk from cocoanut plus
    sweet milk to make
    1 cup
½ stick butter

½ teaspoon almond
    extract
Dash salt
1 cup sugar
1 teaspoon flour

1 teaspoon vanilla

Combine cocoanut, sugar, flour, salt and milk. Cook over low heat, stirring frequently till liquid is reduced to about half. Remove from heat. Add butter, stir until melted. Cool, add extracts and spread between layers of cake, allowing the juice to soak into the cake. (Have just enough to make the cake moist, but not soggy.)

SEVEN MINUTE ICING FOR COCOANUT CAKE

1 cup sugar
1/8 teaspoon cream
    of tarter
1/3 cup boiling water

½ teaspoon almond extract
Dash of salt
1 egg white
1 teaspoon vanilla

Measure sugar, salt, cream of tarter and water into top of double boiler. Add egg white. Turn mixer to fairly high speed and beat continuously while cooking over boiling water for about seven minutes. Remove from heat and blend in extracts. Enough for large cake. Reserve ½ cup cocoanut to sprinkle over finished cake.

From the files of
MRS. WILLIAM LOUIS VOORHIES
Alexandria, La.

GOLD CAKE

2/3 cup butter or oleo
1½ cups sugar
8 egg yolks

2½ cups cake flour
2/3 cup milk
1 teaspoon cream of tartar

½ teaspoon soda

Cream butter and sugar together. Add well beaten egg yolks and milk. Then add sifted flour, soda and cream of tartar, folding in gently. Bake at 350 degrees for about 35 minutes, or until lightly browned and springing away from edge of pan. This is an excellent cake.

MRS. FREDERIC E. DREW, JR.

FRUIT COCKTAIL CAKE

1½ cups sugar	1 medium can fruit cocktail
2 eggs	2 cups sifted flour
½ cup Lou Ana oil	½ teaspoon salt
2 teaspoons soda	

Cream sugar, eggs, and oil. Mix flour salt and soda, and add to the above. Add one medium can fruit cocktail. Pour into large greased pyrex pan. Sprinkle with ½ cup cocoanut (optional). Bake 45 minutes at 350 degrees. Top with icing.

ICING

1 stick butter or oleo   ½ cup evaporated milk
1 cup sugar

Bring to boil for about one minute. Add 1 teaspoon vanilla and ½ cup nuts. While hot, pour over cake. Cut in squares. Top with whipped cream flavored with rum (if desired) or ice cream.

MRS. CHARLES C. BEADLES
Monroe, La.

OLD FASHIONED JAM CAKE

1 cup Lou Ana oil	1 teaspoon each soda, salt,
2 cups sugar	cloves, allspice,
4 eggs	cinnamon
1 cup buttermilk	1 cup jam
3 cups flour	1 cup nuts

Combine Lou Ana oil and sugar, add unbeaten eggs and beat until fluffy. Add sifted dry ingredients, alternating with buttermilk and beat well. Add jam and nuts. Bake in 3 nine inch pans. 350 degrees. Test for doneness with straw.

FILLING:

#2 can crushed pineapple (drained)	1½ cups sugar
1 tablespoon flour	3/4 stick butter
	1 cup nuts

Combine first four ingredients. Cook over low heat until thick. Add nuts and spread between layers.

CARAMEL ICING FOR JAM CAKE

1 box light brown sugar	4 tablespoons flour
1 stick butter	10 tablespoons evaporated milk
½ teaspoon vanilla	

Mix sugar and flour. Add milk and butter. Stir over medium heat until butter melts. Bring to a boil and cool one minute. Add vanilla and beat until thick enough to spread. Ice top and sides of cake. Work quickly when it starts to thicken it gets hard fast. A few drops of hot water can usually remedy this, however. This cake freezes well.

MRS. W. E. NUTT
Alexandria, La.

MAM-MA'S BLACKBERRY JAM CAKE

1 cup butter
2 cups sugar
3 cups flour
½ teaspoon salt
4 eggs
1 teaspoon soda
½ cup buttermilk
1 cup blackberry jam

1 cup chopped pecans
  (more if desired)
1 wine glass Sherry wine
  or apple juice
1 teaspoon each —powdered
  cinnamon, nutmeg,
  ginger, allspice and
  cloves

Cream softened butter and sugar in electric mixer. Add eggs, one at a time; whip well inbetween at high speed. Sift flour with spices and salt. Add soda to buttermilk and stir well. Fold in flour mixing alternately with buttermilk mixture. Add wine. Lastly, fold in pecans and blackberry jam. Pour into 3 nine-inch, well oiled (Lou Ana) floured pans and bake at 325 degrees for 30 to 40 minutes. At 30 minutes test with straw; when straw is clean, remove from oven. Cool in pans 5 minutes. Invert on cake rack and leave pans over cake for 10 minutes more. This insures a moist cake.

CARAMEL FILLING FOR MAM-MA'S BLACKBERRY JAM CAKE

2 tablespoons white
  corn syrup

3/4 cup milk
½ stick butter

2 cups sugar

Mix sugar, syrup and milk together and cook until it forms a soft ball in water. Remove from heat, add butter. Cook in small pot so this can be placed under electric beater and beaten until creamy and thickened. Spread between layers, on top and sides. In spreading icing, if it thickens too quickly, dip knife into hot water and continue spreading. This icing should never be hard.

MRS. E. O. WARMACK

Comment: This is not meant to be a thick icing; this cake is too important to need one.

THE EDITORS

BANANA CAKE

2¼ cups sifted cake flour
1¼ cups sugar
2½ teaspoons baking powder
½ teaspoon baking soda

½ teaspoon salt
½ cup shortening
1½ cups mashed ripe bananas
2 eggs

1 teaspoon vanilla

Sift together flour, sugar, baking powder, soda and salt into large mixing bowl. Add shortening, ½ cup of the mashed bananas, and the eggs. Beat 2 minutes in electric mixer at medium speed or by hand. Add remaining mashed bananas and vanilla. Beat 1 minute longer. Turn into 2 well greased 8 inch layer pans. Bake in moderate oven, 375 degrees, for about 25 minutes.

ICING

One pint, heavy cream   2 ripe bananas, sliced

Whip cream and spread between layers of the cake. Cover cream with bananas. Spread whipped cream and bananas on top of cake. Chill until ready to serve.

ALTERNATE ICING FOR BANANA CAKE

1 cup butter
4 tablespoons cream
4 cups powdered sugar

2 packages (3 ounce) Cream Cheese
2 teaspoons vanilla

Chopped nuts

Melt butter with cream, add powdered sugar, cream cheese and vanilla. Spread between layers of cake and on top and sides. Sprinkle with chopped nuts.

Mrs. Melvin D. Robinson

ELVA'S ICE BOX CAKE

2 squares chocolate
½ cup sugar
¼ cup water
4 eggs (separated)

1 cup powdered sugar
2 sticks butter
1 pint whipping cream
12 lady fingers

Melt chocolate squares in double boiler, add sugar and water and stir well. Slowly stir in the four well beaten egg yolks until mixture is thick. Remove from fire and let cool. Cream powdered sugar with the two sticks of butter and add to chocolate after it has cooled. Beat egg whites very stiff and fold into chocolate mixture and beat until smooth. Arrange split lady fingers around edge of pan and on bottom of pan. Make alternate layers of chocolate mixture and lady fingers. Place in refrigerator over night. Top with whipping cream about one hour before serving.

MRS. FRANK M. WOMACK

CARROT CAKE

2 cups regular flour
2 teaspoons baking powder
1½ teaspoon soda
2 teaspoons cinnamon
1 teaspoon salt
4 eggs

2 cups sugar
1½ cups Lou Ana oil
2 cups grated carrots, lightly packed
1 small can crushed pineapple

½ cup chopped pecans

Sift together the dry ingredients. Mix eggs, oil and sugar. Add dry ingredients—a little at a time and beat well after each addition. Fold in carrots, pineapple and nuts. Bake 350 degrees in three 9-inch layers.

FROSTING

1 box sifted powdered sugar
1 stick butter

1 8 ounce package cream cheese
1 teaspoon vanilla

Cream well. Spread between layers and cover top and sides of cake.

MISS BETH PUGH
New Orleans, La.
MRS. JOE ED KETNER
Dallas, Texas

FRESH APPLE CAKE

1½ cup Lou Ana oil
2 eggs
2 cups sugar
2 cups apples chopped fine
2 cups (or less) chopped dates

1 cup pecans chopped fine or use blender
3 cups flour
1 teaspoon salt
1 teaspoon vanilla
1½ teaspoon soda

1½ teaspoon cinnamon

Beat eggs and oil well—add other ingredients. It's easier to beat if you add nuts and apples last. Bake 1½ hours at 300 degrees—glaze with apple juice and 1 cup confectioners sugar.

MRS. JAN WORTHY
Ruston, La.

AUNT SUSAN'S APPLE SAUCE CAKE

1 cup Lou-Ana shortening
2 cups brown sugar
2 cups thick, unsweetened
apple sauce
1 cup pecans

1 cup raisins
3 cups flour
1 teaspoon each
cinnamon and nutmeg
1 3/4 teaspoon soda

1 teaspoon vanilla

Cream butter and sugar, add alternately flour, applesauce and other ingredients. Pour into loaf cake pan and bake in 325 degree oven for 2 hours. Keeps indefinitely.

FROSTING

2 egg whites beaten stiff
1 cup sugar
½ cup water

1 teaspoon vanilla
1 tablespoon white
corn syrup

Boil water, sugar and corn sprup until it strings. Add slowly to beaten egg whites and beat until stiff.

MRS. M. M. LA CROIX

CREOLE CAKE

2 sticks butter or oleo
2 cups sugar
6 eggs
½ cup milk

1 12-ounce box vanilla
wafers crushed
1 small can flaked cocoanut
1 cup chopped pecans

Mix well and bake in tube pan at 325 degrees for one hour and forty-five minutes. Freezes well.

Submitted by
MRS. DOUGLAS MC GUIRE
of Ruston, La., to whom it was
given by Mrs. Bertie May
of Ruston.

OATMEAL CAKE

1½ cups hot water
1 cup oatmeal (minute)
1 cup light brown sugar
1 cup white sugar
½ cup butter

2 unbeaten eggs
1½ cups flour, sifted
1 teaspoon soda
1 teaspoon cinnamon
½ teaspoon salt

Pour water over oatmeal and set aside. Cream ⸱⸱er and both sugars with unbeaten eggs and mix well. ⸱⸱ ingredients and add to shortening mixture. Add ⸱⸱our into 12 X 8" pan greased and floured.

Bake at 325 degrees for 40 minutes.

TOPPING

1 stick butter	1 cup angel flake
3/4 cup brown sugar	cocoanut
1 tablespoon milk	½ cup chopped pecans

Mix butter, sugar and milk and boil for 1 minute. Take off fire and add cocoanut and pecans. Spread over cake. Brown under broiler and let cool.

MRS. JOE DURRETT
Monroe, La.

PRUNELLA CAKE

½ cup butter.	2/3 cup buttermilk
1 cup sugar	Stir 1 teaspoon soda
2 eggs	into milk
1½ cups flour	2/3 cup pitted stewed
½ teaspoon salt	prunes

Mix cake and add prunes last. Bake 350 degrees— 30 minutes. While cake is baking, make icing:

½ stick butter	2 tablespoons prune juice
2 tablespoons lemon juice	1 teaspoon cinnamon

Add about 2½ cups XXX sugar. Put icing on cake while it is hot. Sprinkle chopped pecans on top.

MRS. JOHN S. WHITE, JR.

LEMON SQUARES

½ cup butter	¼ cup confectioners
1 cup flour	sugar

Mix and spread in greased 8 inch pan. Bake 15 minutes at 350 degrees.

Then:

2 eggs well beaten	2 teaspoons lemon juice
Grated rind of 1 lemon	2 tablespoons flour
1 cup sugar	½ teaspoon baking powder

Spread on crust made with butter, confectioners sugar, and flour and bake 25 minutes at 350 degrees.

MRS. J. P. GRIFFON

POT CAKE

1 cup butter	3 squares unsweetened
2 cups sugar	chocolate
2 cups flour	1 cup water
2 eggs, unbeaten	1 teaspoon vanilla

Combine butter, chocolate and water in heavy saucepan and let come to a boil. Add sugar and flour. Add the two eggs and vanilla. Bake in greased 10" X 14" pan 35 minutes in a 350 degree oven.

ICING

½ cup butter	½ cup milk
2 squares unsweetened	1 pound box confectioners
chocolate	sugar

Combine butter, chocolate and milk. Let come to a boil, then add the box of confectioners sugar. Spread on cake when it is removed from oven.

MRS. SAM B. SHORT

7-UP CAKE

2 sticks oleo	5 eggs
½ cup shortening	3 cups sifted cake flour
3 cups sugar	1 small bottle 7-Up

1 teaspoon vanilla

Cream together oleo, shortening and sugar. Add eggs, one at a time and beat thoroughly. Add flour and 7-Up alternately to batter. Add vanilla. Pour into well greased tube pan and bake in a 325 degree oven for 1 hour and 15 minutes.

MRS. ALVIN POKORNY

ORANGE-DATE-NUT CAKE

1 cup butter	1 cup chopped nuts
2 cups sugar	1 cup candied pineapple,
4 eggs	diced
3½ cups cake flour	1 cup fresh grated
1 1/3 cups buttermilk	cocoanut
1 teaspoon soda	1 8-ounce package
1 tablespoon grated	chopped dates
orange rind	1 teaspoon lemon flavoring

SAUCE

1 cup fresh orange juice   2 cups sugar

Cream butter and sugar. Add eggs, one at a time. Mix flour alternately with buttermilk to which soda has been added. Add lemon flavoring and orange rind. Flour fruit and nuts. (Stir well then flour). Add nuts and fruit last. Put wax paper in bottom of greased tube pan and let extend slightly up sides of pan. Bake at 300 degrees for about 2 hours. Heat orange juice and 2 cups sugar. Pour over hot cake while still in pan. Let stay in pan for several hours.

MRS. C. B. TURNER

PRUNE CAKE

2 cups flour	3 eggs
1½ cups sugar	1 cup Lou Ana oil
1 teaspoon soda	1 cup buttermilk
1 teaspoon cinnamon	1 teaspoon vanilla
1 teaspoon allspice	1 cup cooked prunes
1 teaspoon salt	(cut up)

1 cup pecans

Mix all dry ingredients in one bowl. In another beat eggs, then add oil and buttermilk to egg mixture and mix with dry ingredients. Add vanilla and prunes. Bake at 300-325 degrees for about 45 minutes. Pour sauce over cake.

SAUCE:

1 cup sugar	1 tablespoon white
½ cup buttermilk	corn syrup
1 teaspoon soda	3/4 stick butter

2 teaspoons vanilla

Mix in pan and bring almost to soft ball stage. Let cool some, then pour over warm cake while still in pan.

MRS. EGERIA BARNETT

SYRUP CAKE

1 teaspoon soda	3 eggs, beaten
1 cup syrup	Pinch salt
½ cup softened butter	Flour enough to pour

Maybe ginger

Add soda to syrup and beat until foamy. Add other ingredients. Pour into oiled and floured pan, 13 inches-9 inches-2 inches, and bake at 350 degrees for 25 minutes. Test with a straw. Very old recipe.

MRS. JAMES PERCY HOYT
Cheneyville, La.

TROPICAL GINGERBREAD WITH CREAM CHEESE FILLING

½ cup butter	1 3/4 cups flour
½ cup sugar	1 teaspoon ginger
2 eggs	1 teaspoon cinnamon
½ cup molasses	¼ teaspoon salt
1 teaspoon soda	½ cup water.

1 cup cocoanut

Cream butter and sugar, add unbeaten eggs and blend. Into the molasses beat the soda until smooth. Sift the flour, salt and spices together. Add alternately to the creamed mixture the liquids and flour and lastly add the cocoanut. Pour into a buttered baking pan and bake in a moderate oven (375 degrees F.) for 25 minutes. Upon removal from the oven the cake may be split in two with a sharp knife and served with the following cream cheese filling between layers and on top:

1 cup whipped cream	3 tablespoons orange
1¼ ounces cream cheese	marmalade

Work the cheese until creamy with the marmalade. Fold in the whipped cream.

THE EDITORS

MRS. WREN'S ANGEL FOOD CUSTARD CAKE

1 Angel Food Cake	2½ pints whipped cream
2 cups scalded milk	4 egg yolks
3½ tablespoons flour	1 teaspoon vanilla
½ cup sugar	Grated rind of 1 orange

Rum for flavoring

Cream sugar, eggs and flour. Gradually add hot milk. Cook over boiling water until thick. Add flavoring. Slice Angel Food cake forming two layers. Put cake together with custard and ice with whipped cream. Variation: Fill with frozen strawberries, peaches, or chocolate pudding.

Submitted by
MRS. DONALD MC ANDREW

JELLY ROLL

4 eggs	1 teaspoon baking powder
1 cup sugar	¼ cup water
1½ cups flour	1 teaspoon vanilla

Separate eggs and thoroughly beat yolks. Add sugar gradually while beating. Add flavoring, water and 1 cup flour. Sift baking powder with ½ cup flour and fold into the batter. Beat whites of eggs very stiff; fold into batter. Pour batter evenly into pan and bake 10 to 15 minutes in moderate oven (350 degrees F.). Remove from pan and invert on moist towel. Spread grape or currant jelly over cake. Roll cake into desired form by using the towel and allow to set in rolled condition for a few minutes. After taking towel off, cut in equal lengths and dust with icing sugar.

From the files of
MRS. FRED ANDERSON
Gloster, Miss.

CHOCOLATE DATE CAKE

1 cup dates soaked in	1 cup butter
1 cup boiling water	1 cup sugar
½ teaspoon salt	1 3/4 cup unsifted flour
2 heaping teaspoons cocoa	1 teaspoon soda
1 teaspoon vanilla	2 eggs
Chocolate chips	Nuts

Cream oleo, sugar, add dates with water, add eggs one at a time, then add flour, salt, soda, cocoa and vanilla. Spread in greased 9-inch X 13-inch pan. Sprinkle chocolate chips and pecans on top and bake at 350 degrees for 30-35 minutes. Cut in squares.

AYLEIN ECKLES KONRAD

CHOCOLATE TART

8 crackers	1 teaspoon baking powder
2 tablespoons cocoa	1 cup pecans, chopped
1½ cups brown sugar	1 cup milk
6 eggs	1 teaspoon vanilla

Crumble crackers finely. You must have ½ pint. Add baking powder and sift into well beaten egg yolks. Add sugar and beat. Add nuts, cocoa and milk lastly. Put mixture in oiled pan, 11 inches X 7 inches X ½ inch and bake at 350 degrees for 15 minutes. Remove from oven. Cover with meringue made with the 6 egg whites and 2 tablespoons of granulated or powdered sugar for each egg. Return to oven and bake 10 minutes longer.

VIRGINIA W. TUCKER

This recipe came from the file of Miss Virgie's mother.

LEMON JELLY CAKE

½ cup butter
1 cup sugar
2½ eggs (beaten well
　　together)

1½ cups flour
1 teaspoon baking powder
1/8 teaspoon salt
1/3 cup milk

½ teaspoon vanilla

Combine by butter cake method beating well at end. Bake in 2 layer pans at 375 degrees F. Cool.

FILLING

Combine juice and rind of 2 lemons with

1 cup sugar
2 tablespoons butter

4 egg yolks (or 2 whole
　　eggs) well beaten.

Cook in double boiler stirring constantly till smooth and slightly thickened. Cool and spread between layers with powdered sugar on top.

From the files of
MRS. FRED ANDERSON
Gloster, Miss.

CHOCOLATE ICE BOX CAKE

¼ pound butter (or oleo)
2 cups powdered sugar
1 bar German sweet
　　chocolate
2 eggs

1 teaspoon vanilla
1 cup pecans cut in
　　small pieces
Lady fingers or
　　vanilla wafers

3 tablespoons hot water

Cream butter and sugar. Melt chocolate in hot water and add to butter and sugar mixture. Add slightly beaten eggs, vanilla and pecans. Line bottom of glass dish with vanilla wafers or lady fingers, pour chocolate layer on cakes, then add another layer of wafers and another layer of chocolate. Chill in ice box several hours. Serve with whipped cream and a cherry.

MRS. BERLIN E. PERKINS, JR.

FLOSSIE'S BUTTERMILK CAKE

2 sticks butter
　　(no substitute)
3 cups sugar
5 eggs

½ cup buttermilk
1/3 teaspoon soda
½ cup buttermilk
¼ teaspoon salt

3 cups sifted flour

Cream butter and sugar until mixture is like mayonnaise. Separate eggs. Beat yolks until light and creamy.

Add to butter-sugar mixture. Add soda to ½ cup of the buttermilk; add salt to the other half. Add this liquid to the butter-sugar mixure, alternately with the flour. Beat egg whites until stiff but not dry. Fold into the cake. Bake in an angel food pan greased on the bottom only. Bake at 350 degrees for 1 hour 20 minutes. Let cake remain in pan for 10 minutes. Remove and wrap in large cloth. This helps to keep cake moist. There is no extract used in the cake. You get the full flavor of the butter and buttermilk. This cake keeps so well and gets mellower with time.

MRS. CHARLES GARRETSON
Monroe, La.

RICH FRUIT CAKE

1 pound powdered sugar
1 pound butter
1 pound flour, sifted

1 pound raisins, chopped
1 pound currents
½ pound citron cut into bits

Mix all fruit together and dredge thoroughly with flour. Beat separately the yolks and whites of 1 dozen eggs, 1 tablespoon cinnamon, 2 tablespoons cloves and nutmeg. Beat butter and sugar to a light cream, stir in the beaten yolks and beat for several minutes. Now add half the flour then the spices, the rest of the flour and the dredged fruit. Fold in the stiffened whites and last of all add a wineglassful of brandy. This will make a very large cake or two small ones. Bake 1½ hours (or more) at 250 degrees.

MRS. CAMILLE WADDELL
Natchitoches, La.

WHITE FRUIT CAKE

1 pound butter
2¼ cups sugar
12 eggs
4 cups flour, sifted once
2 teaspoons vanilla
2 teaspoons lemon extract
2 teaspoons almond extract

2 pounds shelled pecans
  or 1 pound each
  pecans and walnuts
2 pounds each crystalled
  pineapple and cherries
  (no salt or baking
  powder)

Cream butter and sugar well. Add whole eggs, one at a time. Add flour gradually. Mix well. Add extracts, and lastly, fruits and nuts, which have been dredged with extra flour. Bake in slow oven (275 degrees) about 2½ hours to 3 hours, according to pan size. Makes 4 loaves.

MRS. JAMES W. MCLAURIN

COCOA CAKE

½ cup butter	2 cups flour
1 cup sugar	1 teaspoon soda
1 egg	1/3 cup cocoa
1 cup buttermilk	Pinch salt

1 teaspoon vanilla

Cream butter and sugar. Add egg and vanilla. Then add dry ingredients that have been sifted together, alternately with buttermilk. Pour into two greased and floured layer pans. Bake in moderate oven 325 degrees for 30 minutes.

FROSTING FOR COCOA CAKE

2 cups sugar	2 tablespoons butter
1/3 cup cocoa	5-7 tablespoons evaporated
Pinch salt	milk
2 tablespoons corn syrup	1 teaspoon vanilla

Mix well. Stir and cook until soft ball stage. Cool and beat until mixture loses its gloss. Add vanilla. Spread between layers and on cake.

Mrs. Oscar Voorhies
Alexandria, La.

OUR FAMILY'S OLD-FASHIONED DARK FRUIT CAKE

1 pound (4½ cups) cake flour	1 pound dates, seeded and sliced
1 teaspoon baking powder	1 pound raisins
½ teaspoon cloves	1 pound currants
½ teaspoon cinnamon	½ pound citron, thinly sliced
½ teaspoon mace	
1 pound butter	½ pound candied orange and lemon peel
1 pound brown sugar	
10 eggs well beaten	1 pound nuts chopped
½ pound candied cherries	1 cup honey
½ pound candied pineapple	1 cup molasses

½ cup cider

Sift flour once, add baking powder and spices and sift together well. Cream butter and sugar until light and fluffy. Add eggs, fruits, peel, nuts, honey, molasses, and cider. Add flour gradually. Turn into pans which have been greased, lined with brown paper and again greased. Bake 1½ hours at 250 degrees. This will make two large cakes.

Mrs. Robert Kennon, Jr.

DARK FRUIT CAKE

12 eggs well beaten
1 pound butter
3 pints watermelon
preserves and juice
3 pints fig preserves
and juice
2 packages dark,
seedless raisins
1 pound cut green
candied pineapple
1 pound cut red
candied pineapple

1 pound red candied
cherries
1 pound green candied
cherries
3 4 pints pecans
and/or walnuts
Ground grapefruit and
orange peel
2 cups white sugar.
Allspice, cinnamon, cloves
to taste and vanilla
2 pounds (or 6 cups) flour

Melt butter and add to eggs. Add all remaining ingredients, mix well, and put in pans which have been well greased and lined with wax paper. Heat oven to 275 degrees and bake cakes for 1 hour. Reduce heat to 250 degrees and bake another hour. Makes about 22 pounds.

From the files of
MRS. ELIZA PERKINS REDDEN

ICE BOX FRUIT CAKE

1 pound butter or
oleomargerine
1 pound marshmallows,
chopped
1 pound graham crackers
1 pound shelled pecans
¼ pound white raisins
¼ pound dark raisins
½ pound dates

¼ pound red candied
cherries
¼ pound green candied
cherries
¼ pound red candied
pineapple
¼ pound green candied
pineapple

Put the butter and chopped marshmallows in a large mixing bowl and place over boiler with hot water in it. Let heat until butter is melted and marshmallows will whip. Add crumbled graham crackers and other ingredients which have been diced. Set aside a few cherry halves, pineapple pieces and pecan halves to decorate top, if desired. Knead with hands. Place in two 2 quart pyrex casserole dishes that have been lined with wax paper or foil. Press tightly and place in refrigerator overnight. Keeps indefinitely. When ready to serve, cut in 1½ inch wide blocks, then slice very thin. Makes two 3 pound cakes.

MRS. MARTIN BRODERICK, JR.

FRUIT CAKE

½ pound almonds	½ pound butter
½ pound sugar	6 eggs
(1 1/3 cups)	¼ teaspoon allspice
2 cups flour	1 pound red cherries
1½ teaspoons cinnamon	½ pound chopped citron
1 pound green pineapple	1 box white raisins
1 pound pecans	¼ cup whiskey

Pour 2 cups of boiling water over almonds and let stand 10 minutes. Skin almonds and let dry. Cream butter and sugar and mix in 1 egg at a time. Grind or finely chop almonds. Sift together flour and dry spices and pour over chopped fruit. Mix well. Pour in egg mixture and mix well. Pour in ¼ cup whiskey and mix. Bake at 250 degrees for 1½ hours. Makes 1-5 pound cake.

MRS. MILLARD BEASON
Alexandria, La.

POUND CAKE

2 cups sugar	3½ cups cake flour
1 cup butter	3 teaspoons baking powder
4 eggs	1 cup milk
2 teaspoons vanilla	

Cream butter and sugar until light and very fluffy. Add eggs, one at a time, beating well after each addition. Sift together flour and baking powder. Add alternately with milk. Beat thoroughly. Add vanilla and blend. Bake in 350 degree oven about 40 minutes in two greased loaf pans.

MRS. CHARLES W. AUSTIN

SOUR CREAM POUND CAKE

½ pound butter	¼ teaspoon baking powder
3 cups sifted sugar	½ cup commercial sour
6 large eggs	cream
3 cups sifted cake flour	2 teaspoons vanilla
1 teaspoon almond flavoring	

Cream butter and sugar well. Add eggs, one at a time, beating well after each addition. Sift flour and baking powder together. Add to batter alternately with the sour cream. Fold in flavoring. Put in large tube pan—preferably Bundt—that has been well greased and floured. Bake at 325 degrees for 1½ hours.

MRS. RALPH M. FORD

CHOCOLATE POUND CAKE

1 cup butter	1 teaspoon vanilla
½ cup other shortening	½ teaspoon salt
3 cups sugar	½ teaspoon baking powder
5 eggs	1 cup milk
3 cups flour	4 tablespoons cocoa

Cream fat, add sugar. Continue creaming. Add eggs, one at a time, beating well after each. Add the vanilla, then the sifted dry ingredients alternately with the milk. Bake 1 hour and 20 minutes at 325°. Frosting optional.

FROSTING FOR CHOCOLATE POUND CAKE

2 squares of chocolate	Confectioners sugar
½ stick of butter	1 teaspoon vanilla
Milk or cream if needed	

Melt the chocolate and butter. Mix well and add sugar to right consistancy. Add vanilla and spread.

MRS. CHARLES KEAN

SPONGE CAKE I

1 1/3 cups sifted cake flour	½ cup sugar
½ teaspoon baking powder	¼ cup water
½ teaspoon salt	3/4 cup egg yolks
1 cup sugar	(6 large)
3/4 cup egg whites	½ teaspoon vanilla
(6 large)	1 teaspoon orange
1 teaspoon cream of tartar	flavoring

Beat egg whites until frothy, then sprinkle in cream of tartar and continue beating, gradually adding the ½ cup of sugar. Beat until the whites stand in peaks. Add water to egg yolks and beat well. Sift flour, baking powder, salt and 1 cup of sugar into mixing bowl, with egg yolks and beat until mixture is creamy and fluffy. Add flavorings and fold in beaten egg whites. Pour batter into pan and gently cut through batter to remove bubbles. Bake in 350 degree oven for 20 minutes, then bake 25 minutes longer at 375 degrees. Cool upside down. Remove from pan and spoon the following glaze over cake.

GLAZE FOR SPONGE CAKE

1 cup sifted confectioners sugar	1 tablespoon butter
	1½ tablespoons milk
5 tablespoons lemon juice	

Beat together, heat and spoon over cake.

MRS. ROY FIELD

SPONGE CAKE II

6 yolks of eggs
¼ cup water
1 cup sugar
½ teaspoon vanilla
½ teaspoon lemon extract

1 cup cake flour (sifted
    then measured)
6 whites of eggs
Pinch of salt
½ teaspoon cream of tartar

Beat yolks, sugar, water and flavoring until lemon colored—actually until consistency of whipped cream. Fold in flour carefully. Add little salt to egg whites and beat until foamy; add cream of tartar and beat until stiff enough to hold up in peaks, but not dry. Then fold carefully into cake mixture. Bake in ungreased angel food pan in cool oven for 1 hour, at 325 degrees. As you remove cake from oven, invert pan. Let stand upside down on rack until cool. Remove from pan. If oven cooks fast, bake at a little under 325 degrees. Serve with the following custard sauce.

CUSTARD SAUCE

4 cups scalded milk
1 cup sugar
4 tablespoons cornstarch

8 yolks of eggs
2 teaspoons vanilla
    extract

Mix sugar and cornstarch well together. Slowly pour hot milk over the mixture, stirring all the while. Beat yolks well, then pour hot milk mixture over yolks and stir until smooth. Place in double boiler over heat and stir constantly until as thick as desired. Remove from fire, cool, then add vanilla. Sauce should be almost consistency of whipped cream to serve on slice of sponge cake.

MRS. ROBERT B. WALLACE

SPONGE CAKE III

6 eggs
6 small tablespoons water
1½ teaspoon baking
    powder

1½ teaspoons flavoring or
1½ teaspoons grated
    lemon or orange peel
1½ cups sugar

1½ cups flour

Separate eggs. Beat yolks with water until light. Add sugar gradually. Add flour and baking powder that have been sifted together. Add flavoring. Fold in stiffly beaten egg whites. Pour into angel food, place in cold oven and bake at 325 degrees for about 55 or 60 minutes. Invert pan to cool.

MRS. FRANK LOWE

MARY'S BUTTER SPONGE

3 eggs (beaten together)
1 cup sugar
¼ cup warm water
1 cup flour

2 tablespoons butter
Pinch of salt
1 teaspoon baking powder
1 teaspoon vanilla

Mix eggs, sugar and flour together and beat well, add two tablespoons hot melted butter. Add other ingredients and mix well. Line baking pan with wax paper, pour in mixture and get in oven quickly. Bake at 350 degrees until brown.

MRS. FRANK M. WOMACK

PECAN CAKE FILLING

Any three layer yellow cake recipe.

FILLING

2½ cups sugar
3 egg whites
11 tablespoons water

4 tablespoons dark corn
syrup
1 teaspoon vanilla

3 cups pecans, ground

Mix water and corn syrup thoroughly and add sugar. Boil hard a few minutes stirring to dissolve. Cook on slow fire until syrup hardens in cold water—medium hard. Beat egg whites until stiff, but not dry. Pour syrup slowly over eggs beating constantly until eggs hold a peak. Add vanilla. Add ground pecans to egg whites and spread on cake.

MRS. GEORGE C. BRILEY
Natchitoches, La.

PECAN CAKE

1¼ cups sugar
½ stick butter
½ cup milk

2 eggs
2 cups flour
2 cups crushed pecans

2 teaspoons baking powder

The cake can be mixed in an electric mixer with all ingredients (except pecans) put in at once. Beat 3 minutes, fold in pecans, and bake in layer tins at 350 degrees for 25 or 30 minutes.

FROSTING & FILLING

2 cups sugar
1 cup water

2 egg whites
2 cups pecans crushed

Cook sugar and water until it strings, then add to egg whites. Beat until it begins to harden, add pecans, and spread at once.

MRS. LAWRENCE MOUTON SIMON

NUT CAKE

5 eggs
2 cups sugar
1 cup butter
3 cups flour
2 teaspoons baking powder
1 glass apple jelly
1 teaspoon nutmeg

1 cup milk
1 cup whiskey
1 quart pecans (chopped)
1 pound dates
1 package raisins
2 teaspoons coco
1 teaspoon allspice

1 teaspoon cinnamon

Cream butter and sugar, add the eggs one at a time, add all dry ingredients mixed together alternately with milk and whiskey. Stir in pecans and dates and raisins and then apple jelly. Pour in greased pound cake pan or three large loaf pans and bake for approximately 3 hours at 350 degrees. Makes 3 large loaf pans.

MRS. BENTON HARELSON

From the file of
MISS EFFIE DARDENNE
Plaquemine, La.

BLACK WALNUT CAKE

1 whole egg
6 eggs, separated
1 box confectioners
   sugar, sifted

1¼ cups walnuts, chopped
   medium coarse
3/4 cup almonds, chopped
1 cup sifted cake flour

Preheat oven to 325 degrees. Butter three 9" layer cake pans, lining bottom of each with brown paper, buttered. Beat egg yolks with 1 whole egg and sugar until mixture doubles in volume and sugar is dissolved. Beat egg whites stiff but not dry and add to egg mixture. Combine almonds, walnuts and flour. Add to egg mixture, 1/3 at a time, folding in gently. Pour into pans and bake 25-30 minutes. Cool pans on rack. When ready to serve, put layers together with: 2 cartons whipping cream, whipped 2 cups sifted confectioners sugar and 2 teaspoons vanilla.

Cakes may be prepared the day before serving; be sure to keep them covered tightly. The filling must be made on day needed, and cake should be put together not sooner than 3 hours before serving.

MRS. ROLAND B. HOWELL

FRUIT-PECAN CAKE

1 pound flour
1 pound sugar
½ pound butter
4 pieces of pineapple, cut
6 eggs unbeaten
1 pound pecans
½ pound black walnuts

1 teaspoon nutmeg
½ teaspoon allspice
½ teaspoon cinnamon
2 teaspoons baking powder
1 cup whiskey
1 cup tart jelly and
   1 teaspoon vanilla

2 pounds raisins cut fine

Cherries may be substituted for the pineapple. Mix all ingredients and bake 2½ hours in medium oven. Makes 2 small or 1 large cake.

MRS. WALTER E. HAWKINS
Shreveport, La.

CREOLE PECAN CAKE WITH BROWN SUGAR FROSTING

This has been a favorite with my family for many years. It is always served at Thanksgiving.

3/4 cup butter
2 cups sugar
3 cups flour
¼ teaspoon salt
2 teaspoons baking powder

3/4 cup milk
1 teaspoon vanilla
6 egg whites
1 1/4 cups pecans, chopped
1 teaspoon cinnamon

½ teaspoon cloves

Cream shortening, gradually add 2 cups sugar. Cream together well. Sift flour three times—the last time with the salt and baking powder. Add to mixture alternately with milk. Fold in stiffly beaten egg whites. Now, **divide** dough mixture in half. Add 1½ cups chopped pecans to one half dough. Add cinnamon and cloves to remaining half. Bake in two 9-inch round cake pans at 375 degrees until done. Frost when cool with the following:

BOILED BROWN SUGAR FROSTING

Boil 4 cups brown sugar and ½ cup water **just past** the soft ball stage. Beat into stiffly beaten whites of 2 eggs. Add 1 teaspoon vanilla. After frosting sprinkle top and sides of cake with finely chopped pecans.

MRS. KATHERINE H. LONG

PECAN BOURBON CAKE

1 pound pecans (chopped)
½ pound seeded raisins
1½ cups sifted flour
1 teaspoon baking powder
½ cup butter
1 cup plus 2 tablespoons sugar
3 eggs separated
2 teaspoons nutmeg
½ cup Bourbon
½ teaspoon salt

Mix pecans and raisins together and dredge with ½ cup flour. To other cup of flour add baking powder and sift again. Cream butter, gradually adding sugar, and beat until fluffy. Add egg yolks, one at a time, beating until lemon colored. Add nutmeg to whiskey and let stand for 10 minutes. Add it to the creamed mixture alternately with the sifted flour. Beat thoroughly. Mix in the raisins and nuts. Beat egg whites with salt until stiff. Then fold in. Pour batter into a tube pan (large enough to hold a 3 pound cake) that has been buttered and floured. Let the mixture stand for 10 minutes to settle. Bake in 325 degree oven for 1½ hours. Allow to stand for ½ hour before removing from pan.

ALINE VEAZIE PAVY
Opelousas, La.

SAD CAKE

1 package dry biscuit mix (6¼ ounces)
1/3 cup Lou Ana corn oil
1 box brown sugar (1 pound)
4 eggs
1 cup pecans, chopped

Mix sugar and biscuit mix until all lumps are gone from sugar. Add eggs, oil and pecans. Spread in either buttered pan or Teflon pan (9 inches-14 inches). Bake 45 minutes at 350 degrees. When done, cut in squares.

MRS. GEORGE HOFFPAUIR
Crowley, La.

Cookies

DATE BALLS

2 sticks oleo	1 cup dark brown sugar
1 pound chopped dates	1 cup light brown sugar
1 can cocoanut	4 cups rice krispies
2 cups of chopped pecans	

Cook oleo, dates, cocoanut, and sugar over low heat. Let come to a bubble and cook 6 minutes. Add 4 cups rice krispies and 2 cups chopped pecans. Make small balls and roll in powdered sugar.

MRS. L. J. BOURG

DATE NUT BARS

1 box dates	3/4 cup sugar
1 cup nuts	3 tablespoons flour
2 eggs	1 teaspoon allspice
1 teaspoon vanilla	

Chop dates and nuts. Add flour and allspice to nuts and dates and toss. Beat eggs and sugar. Add vanilla. Add dates and nuts to egg mixture. Mix well. Bake in slow oven, about 325 degrees until straw comes out clean. Cut in oblong pieces and roll in confectioners sugar.

MRS. H. F. BRADFORD

DAINTY OATMEAL LACE COOKIES

1 stick butter	1 egg
1 cup sugar	1 tablespoon vanilla
1 cup Quick Oatmeal	2 teaspoons flour
1 cup finely chopped pecans	

Cream butter and sugar well. Add egg, vanilla, and blend. Add oatmeal, flour and nuts. Mix well. Drop from demitasse spoon two inches apart on foil lined cookie sheet. Bake in preheated 350 degree oven for 12-15 minutes or until golden. Cool two minutes and slide off foil. Store in air-tight tins.

MRS. E. H. TAUSSIG
Lake Charles, La.

SCOTCH SHORT BREAD

1 cup butter	½ cup sugar
2 cups flour	Powdered sugar

Using your hands mix for a few minutes the butter, flour and granulated sugar. Shape like a small sausage, roll and chill. Slice about ¼ inch thick and prick each slice with a fork. Bake at 375 degrees until browned delicately. Remove and sprinkle with powdered sugar.

MRS. C. B. TURNER

DREAM BARS

½ cup butter   ½ cup brown sugar
1 cup flour

Cream above ingredients together. Put in 9 X 14 inch pan. Bake 10 minutes at 375 degrees. Cool.

2 eggs, well beaten   1½ cups cocoanut (can)
1 cup brown sugar   1 cup chopped nuts
1 teaspoon vanilla   2 tablespoons flour
1 teaspoon baking powder

Spread on above crust. Bake at 375 degrees for 20 minutes. Sprinkle with sugar. Cut in squares.

Submitted by
MRS. STEWART CHURCHILL
Belle Alliance Plantation

SUGAR COOKIES

3/4 pound butter   Vanilla
3/4 pound sugar   ¼ teaspoon salt
(1 2/3 cups)   ¼ teaspoon soda
1 1/8 pounds flour (4½ cups)   2 eggs
3 cups nuts (chopped)

Cream butter and add sugar. Combine flour, salt, and soda. Add 2 eggs, extract and nuts. Shape into rolls. Wrap in wax paper. Chill and cut into slices. Bake at 400 degrees.

MRS. WALTER GUINN
Cheneyville, La.

"OLE TIMEY" TEA CAKES

1 cup butter   1/8 teaspoon salt
1 3/4 cups sugar   Enough flour to roll and
2 eggs   cut. (Measure out 4
¼ cup buttermilk   cups, add gradually
1 teaspoon soda   until right consistency.
1½ teaspoons vanilla   Do not make too dry.)

Bake in moderate oven, 350 to 375 degrees.

MRS. GEORGE C. PURVIS
Rayville, La.

CHICKEN-FAT COOKIES

1 cup chicken fat	2 eggs
2 cups sugar	3½ cups flour
2 tablespoons milk	½ teaspoon salt

1 teaspoon soda

Sift flour, soda and salt. Remove chicken fat from hen and render for measuring. To the fat add sugar, milk, eggs and the flour mixture. Knead and put thru cookie press on to cookie sheet. Bake at 350 degrees for 10 to 12 minutes, or until light brown.

MRS. FRED C. TAYLOR
New Orleans, La.

SWISS-FRENCH COOKIES
Six dozen 2½ inch cookies

½ pound butter or margarine	1 egg yolk
1 cup sugar	2½ teaspoons cinnamon
2 cups sifted all-purpose flour	1 egg white
	Colored candies or ground nuts

Cream butter and sugar thoroughly. Beat in egg yolk. Add flour and cinnamon and blend well. Roll pieces of the dough into 1-inch balls between buttered palms. Place balls on ungreased sheet about 2 inches apart. Press out paper thin with a floured spatula. Paint with egg white and then sprinkle with colored candies or ground nuts. Bake at 350 degrees F. for 10 to 12 minutes.

MRS. FRANCIS W. HOFFPAUIR

BROWN SUGAR BROWNIES

1 cup melted butter	2 eggs
1 pound brown sugar (dark or light)	3 cups flour
	1 teaspoon soda

1 cup chopped pecans

Mix melted butter, sugar and eggs until creamy. Add flour and soda which have been sifted together. Stir in pecans. Spread batter, which is very stiff, in a greased 15½" X 10½" X 1" pan. Bake in a preheated 350 degree oven for 25 minutes. Cut into squares immediately, but allow to cool before removing from pan. These brownies are very chewy and delicious.

MRS. ROBERT E. BARROW, JR.
St. Francisville, La.

SKILLET COOKIES

1 stick butter	1 3/4 cups rice krispies
3/4 cup sugar	1 cup nuts
2 egg yolks	1 cup flaked Cocoanut
1 cup chopped dates	1 teaspoon vanilla

Combine and cook butter, sugar, egg yolks and dates about ten minutes in heavy skillet, stirring and mashing dates while cooking. Put into bowl and mix with the above the rice krispies, nuts, cocoanut and vanilla. Make into small balls and roll in cocoanut.

MRS. W. P. TREGRE
Shreveport, La.

SPICED ALMOND WAFERS
Makes 6 dozen

2 cups flour	1/4 teaspoon baking soda
1 teaspoon cinnamon	1/4 cup sour cream
1/4 teaspoon nutmeg	2 cups slivered, blanched
1 cup soft butter	almonds

1 cup light brown sugar

Sift together flour, cinnamon and nutmeg. Cream butter and sugar. Combine the two mixtures and stir in the soda and sour cream. Blend dough well and add almonds. Shape dough into 2-inch thick rolls, wrap in wax paper and chill 3 hours or more. Cut into slices 1/8-inch thick and bake on ungreased baking sheets at 325 degrees for 10 minutes. Cool on racks, then store in air-tight containers to keep crisp.

MRS. TROYE SVENDSON

PECAN PRALINE COOKIES

1 cup light brown sugar packed	1/2 teaspoon salt
1 tablespoon flour	1 egg white stiffly beaten
	1 teaspoon vanilla

2 1/2 to 3 cups pecans

Add 1 teaspoon vanilla to stiffly beaten egg white, fold in the sugar and add the nuts. Place small clusters on well greased baking sheet and bake at 275 degrees for 20 to 30 minutes. Remove from baking sheet immediately and let cool on rack or buttered platter. After they are cool, pack in covered jar or tin. They keep crisp for about 2 weeks.

MRS. BEN MILLER
MRS. RATCLIFFE ANDERSON

BROWNIES

1¼ cups sifted flour	1 cup sugar
½ teaspoon baking powder	2 eggs well beaten
½ teaspoon salt	½ teaspoon vanilla
1 cup chopped pecans	2 squares unsweetened
½ cup shortening	chocolate, melted

Mix and sift flour, baking powder and salt. Stir in nuts. Cream shortening until soft and gradually beat in sugar, eggs, vanilla and melted chocolate. Stir in flour mixture and turn into a greased, shallow 8-inch pan. Bake in moderate oven 30 to 35 minutes.

ICING

1 egg	3 heaping tablespoons cocoa
1 tablespoon butter	1 teaspoon vanilla
2 cups powdered sugar	Thin with Cognac

MRS. PHILIP R. FARNSWORTH
New Orleans, La.

LEMON BARS
CRUST

1 stick butter   1 cup flour
1/4 cup powdered sugar

Cut in all ingredients and press to the bottom of 9" square pan. Bake at 350 degrees for 15 minutes.

FILLING

2 eggs	½ teaspoon baking powder
2 tablespoons lemon juice	1 cup sugar
¼ teaspoon lemon rind	2 tablespoons flour

Mix and spread in above pie crust. Bake at 350 degrees for 25 minutes, remove from oven and sprinkle with powdered sugar. Cut into bars.

MRS. DANIEL COHN

SOUR CREAM TEA CAKES

1 cup butter	2 teaspoons baking powder
2½ cups sugar	1 teaspoon soda (scant)
3 eggs	1 teaspoon orange extract

1 cup sour cream

Cream butter and sugar. Add beaten eggs. Add cream and extract. Add enough flour to roll out. Keep as soft as possible to handle and add soda and baking powder to last addition of flour. After rolling out, cut with biscuit cutter or in desired shapes. Bake in 350 degree oven about 15-20 minutes.

MRS. ROBERT KENNON

FRUITCAKE COOKIES

1 pound red cherries	3 tablespoons milk
1 pound green cherries	1 cup Bourbon
1 pound white raisins	1 teaspoon allspice
1 pound pineapple	1 teaspoon cinnamon
8 cups pecans—chopped	1 teaspoon nutmeg
1 stick butter	1 teaspoon cloves
1½ cups brown sugar	3 teaspoons soda
4 eggs	4 cups flour

The cherries and pineapple are crystallized fruit. Chop and dredge in ½ cup flour—or a little more—the first five ingredients. Cream butter and sugar. Add eggs —one at a time—then the dry ingredients, that have been sifted together, alternately with the milk and Bourbon.

Pour batter over the cut fruit and nuts. Mix together. Drop by spoonfulls on well-greased cookie sheet. Bake at 275 degrees for 30 minutes.

MRS. J. F. ROCKHOLT

APRICOT WINKS

½ cup dried apricots	1 cup sifted flour
2/3 cup sugar	½ teaspoon salt
½ cup butter	1 egg white, unbeaten
1 egg yolk	½ cup pecans, very
½ teaspoon vanilla	finely chopped

Rinse apricots, cover with water and 1/3 cup of the sugar. Boil 10 minutes or until thick. Drain, cool and mash. Cream butter and remaining 1/3 cup sugar. Add egg yolk, vanilla and flour sifted with salt. Shape into small balls the size of marbles, approximately 30 in number. Dip balls into unbeaten white of egg. Roll in very finely chopped pecans. Place on greased cookie sheet. Make dent in center of each ball using handle on wooden spoon. Bake in slow oven at 300 degrees for 30 minutes. Remove to large waxed paper tray. Add cooked apricot filling.

MRS. GEORGE H. JONES

OATMEAL COOKIES

1 cup shortening	½ cup chopped nuts
1 cup brown sugar	1 teaspoon vanilla
1 cup granulated sugar	1½ cups flour
2 eggs beaten	1 teaspoon salt
3 cups quick cooking oatmeal	1 teaspoon soda
	1 cup raisins (optional)

Cream sugar and shortening, add eggs and vanilla, beat well, add sifted flour, salt, soda, nuts and raisins. Add oatmeal and mix well. Form into 3 rolls. Wrap in wax paper and chill overnight. Slice ¼ inch thick and bake on a greased cookie sheet in moderate oven (350) for about 10 minutes.

MRS. RALPH BURGE
MRS. HERBERT J. McGRATH
Beaumont, Texas

BUTTERSCOTCH SQUARES

2½ cups light brown sugar	1 3/4 cups flour
1¼ sticks butter	3 teaspoons baking powder
2 eggs, lightly beaten	2 cups chopped pecans
1 teaspoon vanilla	

In a double boiler, melt the sugar and butter, then add the eggs. Next sift together the flour and baking powder, add the pecans and vanilla. Combine the mixtures and bake in a shallow rectangular pan for 40 minutes at 325 degrees. Remove from pan (8 X 12) and cover with

FROSTING

½ cup butter	¼ cup milk
1 cup light brown sugar	Confectioner's sugar

Melt butter, add sugar, and boil for two minutes. Add milk and let come to a boil. Remove from heat and cool. Add enough confectioners sugar to bring to right consistency to spread on cake. Cut in squares.

MRS. R. L. SEEGERS
Ruston, La.

PECAN NOUGAT

6 cups pecans crushed with mortar & pestle	3 cups sugar
	6 tablespoons melted butter
6 egg whites (not beaten)	

Mix, spread in large well buttered biscuit pan, and bake at 400 degrees for 30 minutes. While still warm, cut into squares and remove from pan.

This is the original recipe handed down from Eloise Mouton from her mother Madam Voohries who was Princess Gradnigo.

MRS. GEORGE M. SIMON

BUTTER FINGERS

5 tablespoons confectioners   3 cups flour
   sugar   3 cups nuts, chopped

½ pound butter

Mix butter, sugar and flour well. Add pecans and shape it into fingers. Place on brown paper and bake at 350 degrees until light brown. Roll in confectioner's sugar while hot.

MRS. BESSIE MILLS SAMUEL
Fairhaven Plantation

ENGLISH TOFFEE SQUARES
Serves 6

16 vanilla wafers (1 cup   1 cup powdered sugar
   rolled)   ¼ pound butter
3 eggs, separated   1½ squares bitter chocolate
1 cup pecans, chopped ½ teaspoon vanilla

Roll vanilla wafers into crumbs and mix together with chopped nuts. Using half the mixture, cover the bottom of a buttered pan, 9 inches X 9 inches. Cream butter and sugar, add beaten egg yolks, melted chocolate and vanilla. Fold in beaten whites. Pour over wafers and spread remaining crumbs on top. Put in refrigerator over night. Cut in square and serve with whipped cream.

MRS. NORMAN SAURAGE, JR.

COCOANUT KISSES

1 can condensed milk   1 can dry cocoanut
       4 cups corn flakes

Mix well and drop by teaspoons on greased cookie sheet. Bake in slow oven about 250 degrees until a delicate brown.

From the recipe files of
COLLINGSBURG PLANTATION
Bossier Parish

RUSSIAN ROCKS

1 stick butter	2 tablespoons water
12 teaspoons sugar (6 brown, 6 white)	3 cups nuts
	1 pound raisins
3 eggs	2 teaspoons cinnamon
2 cups flour	1 teaspoon vanilla
½ teaspoon soda	1 teaspoon nutmeg

Cream sugar and butter, add eggs. Sift flour, cinnamon, nutmeg. Mix water and soda, add to butter mixture with flour. Add nuts and raisins and vanilla. Drop by teaspoon on greased cookie sheet. Bake at 350 degrees for 15 minutes. These get better the longer you keep them.

                                          MRS. L. J. BOURG

LEMON SQUARES

1 cup flour	1 cup shredded cocoanut
1 cup sugar	1 tablespoon baking powder
1 3/4 cups rolled saltines	3/4 cup butter or margarine

Mix above ingredients and cut in the butter. Reserve ¼ cup for topping and press the remaining mixture in a 12 X 12 cake pan. Now prepare the following:

1 cup sugar	3 well beaten eggs
2 lemons (juice and rind)	¼ cup butter

Cook the above in a double boiler until medium thick. Speard over the mixture in the cake pan. Sprinkle the reserved crumbs over the filling and bake 20 minutes (or until light brown) in a 350 degree oven. Cut into squares.

                                          MRS. ROBERT JENNINGS

DELICIOUS SQUARES

2 sticks butter or oleo	1 tablespoon water
½ cup white sugar	1 teaspoon vanilla
½ cup light brown sugar, packed	2 cups flour
	1 teaspoon baking powder
2 egg yolks	½ teaspoon soda
½ teaspoon salt	

Blend oleo and both sugars. Add remaining ingredients and mix well. Press this into bottom of 9 X 12 pan. Cover with 6 ounces of chocolate chips and cover this with meringue of 2 egg whites and 1 cup of brown sugar. Bake at 375 degrees for 15 minutes, then turn oven down to 250 degrees and bake 15 minutes more. Cut when cool.

                                          MRS. MARVIN STUCKEY

Pies

FAVORITE PIE CRUST
(2 pie shells)

1½ cups flour
½ teaspoon salt
½ teaspoon sugar

1 pinch baking powder
½ cup shortening
¼ cup hot water

Sift dry ingredients together. Make a well in center and pour in shortening and hot water which have been blended together. Stir quickly till flour is all moist. Turn ½ of this mixture at once onto waxed paper which has been dusted with 1 tablespoon flour. Fold over 3 times and pat round with hands. Cover with another piece of waxed paper and roll out to desired size. Transfer to pie plate. Flute edges. Prick several places with fork. This amount makes 2 pie shells. Remaining dough may be stored in waxed paper in refrigerator and brought to room temperature before shaping for next pie.

MRS. OSCAR E. VOORHIES
Alexandria, La.

PIE CRUST
Makes four pie shells

3 cups all purpose flour
1 cup shortening
1 teaspoon salt

1 egg
3 tablespoons water
1 teaspoon vinegar

Mix flour and shortening well. Beat egg adding water and vinegar, then add to flour and shortening. Add salt and mix to cornmeal consistency. Keep well in refrigerator until ready for use.

MRS. ORDA MCKENZIE
Natchitoches, La.

SHERRY CHIFFON PIE

1 baked pie shell
1 envelope unflavored
   gelatin
3/4 cup cold water

4 eggs separated
1 cup sugar
2/3 cup sherry
¼ teaspoon salt

½ pint whipping cream

Soften gelatine in the cold water 5 minutes. Beat egg yolks until light, add ½ cup of sugar. Add sherry and cook over hot water until thick. Add gelatine, cook a few minutes and cool. Beat egg whites and add rest of sugar and salt. Mix with custard and pour into pie shell. Chill until firm, about 3 hours. When chilled top with whipped cream and a dash of nutmeg.

MRS. LOYD HUVAL

PARTY GRASSHOPPER PIE

1½ teaspoons gelatine
1/3 cup cream, chilled
4 egg yolks
¼ cup sugar
¼ cup white creme
  de cacao

¼ cup green creme de
  menthe
1 cup heavy cream
1 baked pie shell or bite-size
  baked pie shells
¼ teaspoon salt

Mix gelatine in 1/3 cream, dissolve over low heat, stirring constantly. Beat 3 egg yolks, and gradually beat into egg yolks sugar and salt. Add gelatine mixture to yolks, along with creme de cocao and creme de menthe. Chill until slightly thickened. Beat until stiff 1 cup heavy cream and fold into chilled mixture. Pour into baked pie crust and chill until firm. For parties, make the miniature, bite-size shells, fill with grasshopper filling, and garnish with a sliver of green or red cherry or crushed mints. If your crusts and fillings don't come out even, the filling is great served as a pudding.

MRS. CHARLES D. BALDRIDGE, JR.

PECAN PIE

3 eggs
3/4 cup white sugar
1 cup white corn syrup
1 teaspoon vanilla

Butter, size of an egg
2 cups pecans
Pinch of salt

Beat eggs lightly and add all other ingredients. Put into uncooked pastry shell and cook at 350 degrees for about 45 minutes.

MRS. HENRY Y. BENNETT

CHERRY PIE DELIGHT

1 9-inch pie shell
1 can cherry pie filling, plus
  ¼ cup sugar

1 cup coarsely chopped
  pecans
1 teaspoon almond extract

Mix above and pour into pie shell, cover with following topping:

1 cup flour
1 stick butter

½ cup light brown sugar
½ cup finely chopped pecans

Mix flour, butter and sugar until crumbs are formed. Sprinkle over top of pie. Bake at 350 degrees for 30-35 minutes. Sprinkle with chopped pecans and bake until top is brown. Serve with whipped cream.

MARY BRIDGES
Monroe, La.

FRENCH CHERRY PIE

2 3-ounce packages cream cheese
1 cup confectioner's sugar

1 pint heavy cream
1/4 teaspoon almond extract
1 teaspoon vanilla extract

1 can instant pie cherries

Cream sugar and cream cheese. Whip cream slightly and add to cheese mixture, continuing to beat. Add flavorings, spread in graham cracker crust and spread cherries on top. Chill. (The graham cracker crust recipe is always on the package of graham crackers crumbs)

MRS. G. W. JAMES
Ruston, La.

SHOO FLY PIE

Pastry for 3 8" pie shells
or 2 9" shells

CRUMB MIXTURE

4 cups flour

1 cup sugar

3/4 cups margarine

LIQUID

1 cup molasses

1 teaspoon soda

1 cup boiling water

Line 3 8" pans with pastry (prepared pie shells may be used). Combine ingredients for crumb mixture, using hands to blend well. Save 1½ cups of the crumb mixture. Combine ingredients for liquid and mix with crumb mixture. Pour into pie shells. Top with crumbs previously set aside. Bake at 350 degrees F for about 25 minutes.

MRS. A. C. PRINCE
Mount Hope, West Virginia

This is an old Pennsylvania Dutch molasses pie. This recipe has been handed down for three generations.

SOUR CREAM PUMPKIN PIE

3/4 cup light brown sugar
1 envelope plain gelatine
1 teaspoon cinnamon
½ teaspoon cloves
¼ teaspoon nutmeg
½ teaspoon salt

3 eggs, separated
½ cup milk
1 No. 303 can pumpkin
1 cup dairy sour cream
(½ pint)
¼ cup granulated sugar

1 10-inch baked pie shell

Combine brown sugar, gelatine, spices and salt in a

saucepan. Add beaten egg yolks, milk and pumpkin. Mix well. Cook over medium heat, stirring constantly, until gelatin dissolves—about 8 minutes. Remove from heat and allow to cool slightly. Add sour cream and mix well. Beat egg whites until slightly stiff and gradually add granulated sugar, a tablespoon at a time, beating after each addition. Continue beating until stiff. Fold into cooled pumpkin mixture, put into baked pie shell and chill about 4 hours before serving.

MRS. ALMA STROUBE CUMMINGS
Miami, Florida

FUDGE PIE

1 stick butter	½ cup pecans (optional)
1 cup sugar	2 squares chocolate
¼ cup flour	2 eggs

1 teaspoon vanilla

Melt butter and chocolate together. Remove from heat; add sugar, flour and eggs. Beat well. Add vanilla and nuts. Pour in buttered pie plate and bake at 350 degrees for 25 minutes. Serve warm topped with ice cream.

MRS. DANIEL W. SARTOR
Rayville, La.

CORN SYRUP PIE

1½ cups sugar	1 cup dark corn syrup
4 eggs	small lump butter

Beat sugar into eggs. Add syrup and butter. Bake in uncooked pie shell about 45 minutes—400 degrees for 10 minutes, then 300 degrees until done. DO NOT UNDERCOOK. Chopped pecans may be added to the custard before baking

MRS. NEIL BENNETT
Lenoke, Arkansas

JELLY PIE

1 cup jelly (tart)	1½ cup sugar
(May be Damson	6 eggs
plum preserves)	1 teaspoon vanilla

3/4 cup butter

Cream butter and sugar. Add beaten egg yolks. Beat well. Add jelly. Fold in whites of beaten eggs, and add vanilla. Place in uncooked pie shell and bake in 350 degree oven for 40 minutes or until firm when pressed.

MRS. ROBERT KENNON

BEST EVER PUMPKIN PIE

3/4 cup brown sugar
½ teaspoon salt
1 tablespoon flour
½ teaspoon cinnamon
1 cup milk

¼ teaspoon ginger
1/8 teaspoon cloves
¼ teaspoon nutmeg
2 eggs slightly beaten
1 3/4 cup pumpkin

½ cup cream

Mix together and pour into and unbaked pastry shell. Bake 10 minutes at 450 degrees. Reduce to 325 degrees and bake 35 minutes.

Mrs. William L. Mott
Cheneyville, La.

PEACH CUSTARD PIE

1 large can sliced peaches, well drained, or 6 to 8 fresh peaches
3 eggs
1 cup plus 2 tablespoons sugar

¼ cup flour
1 stick butter or oleomargarine
2 teaspoons vanilla
¼ teaspoon salt
9-inch unbaked pie shell

Arrange peach slices in pie shell. Combine eggs, sugar, flour, oleomargarine, vanilla and salt. Pour mixture over peaches and bake at 350 degrees for 1 hour, or until lightly brown.

Mrs. Steve Alford

ICE CREAM PIE

1 baked 9 inch pastry shell, cooled
1 pt. chocolate ice cream softened
½ cup sugar

1 pt. vanilla ice cream, softened
4 egg whites
½ teaspoon vanilla
¼ teaspoon cream of tartar

CHOCOLATE SAUCE

3 squares chocolate or 6 tablespoons cocoa
3/4 cup water

1 cup sugar
6 tablespoons butter
1 teaspoon vanilla

Pinch of salt

Spread chocolate ice cream in pie shell, top with layer of vanilla ice cream and place in freezer. Beat egg whites with vanilla and cream of tartar until soft peaks form. Gradually add sugar, beating until very stiff and glossy. Spread meringue over ice cream, carefully sealing to edge of pastry. Bake under broiler for 1 to 2 minutes or until meringue is lightly browned.

Freeze pie several hours or overnight. To serve, cut in wedges and drizzle with chocolate sauce.

CHOCOLATE SAUCE

In a saucepan combine ingredients for sauce and cook until thick (consistency to pour). Serve warm over wedges of pie.

MRS. JACK ABRAUGH
Rayville, La.

FRESH PEACH PIE

CRUST

1 cup flour	Salt
½ cup shortening	3 tablespoons ice water

Mix and put in 11-inch pie plate. Bake at 400 degrees until done.

FILLING

Cook until clear and thick:

1 cup crushed peaches	3 teaspoons cornstarch
½ cup water	1 cup sugar

Line baked pie shell with freshly sliced peaches. Sprinkle with sugar. Cover with cooked peach mixture. Cool. Cover with whipped cream, sweetened with 2 tablespoons sugar and 1 tablespoon vanilla. Place in refrigerator to set.

MRS. J. F. ROCKHOLT

BLUEBERRY BAVARIAN CREAM PIE

1 9-inch baked pie shell	1 cup sugar
2 bananas	1 8-ounce package soft
1 cup whipping cream	cream cheese
1 can blueberry pie filling	

Line bottom of pie shell with sliced bananas. Whip cream, adding sugar gradually. Add cream cheese to whipped cream and spread mixture over banana slices. Then top with blueberries and chill.

MRS. ERNEST D. WILSON

KISS PIE

6 egg whites (at
   room temperature)
2 cups sugar
1½ teaspoons vinegar

2½ pints whipping cream
1 cup chopped pecans
½ cup cherries chopped
   one at a time

Beat egg whites until very stiff and glossy. Gradually beat in 1 cup of sugar. With second cup of sugar, alternate vinegar and sugar a little at a time. Spread in two 9-inch round layer pans lined with brown paper (bottom and sides)) and bake in preheated 275 degree oven for 60 minutes. Cool. Frost as you would a cake with whipped cream, chopped pecans and cherries, between layers, on top, and on sides. Sprinkle a little cherry juice here and there with a coffee spoon.

MRS. WILLIAM MIDDLETON, JR.
Plaquemine, La.

SUSAN'S PIE

Large cream cheese
1 tablespoon lemon juice

½ cup sugar
2 slightly beaten eggs

1 teaspoon vanilla

Cream. Pour in crust. Bake 15 minutes at 350 degrees. Use graham cracker crust. Cook 5 minutes. Cover with:

1 cup sour cream

2 tablespoons sugar

1 teaspoon vanilla

Bake at 300 degrees 5 minutes. Has to sit in refrigerator 6 hours.

MRS. GEORGE WHITE
New Orleans, La.

GERMAINE ARNAUD'S APPLE PIE

6 to 9 tart apples
¼ cup raisins
½ cup chopped pecans
1 teaspoon grated orange

3 tablespoons cherry
   preserves or jam
½ cup sugar
3 tablespoons red wine

Combine all of the above ingredients and put in a sauce pan and cook for 15 minutes stirring frequently. Pour into unbaked shell and cover top with another crust. Bake at 450 degrees 15 minutes and then 350 degrees until crust is golden.

MRS. BENTON HARELSON

LEMON MERINGUE PIE

1 cup sugar
½ cup water
5 scant tablespoons corn-
   starch dissolved in ½
   cup water

2 well beaten egg yolks
¼ teaspoon salt
1 tablespoon butter
1 teaspoon grated
   lemon rind

6 tablespoons lemon juice

Put all ingredients in boiler and slowly cook over direct heat, stirring until thick. Pour into baked pie shell.

MERINGUE

4 egg whites   8 tablespoons sugar
¼ teaspoon cream of tartar

Beat together. When whites hold a peak, add 1 teaspoon lemon juice and beat until stiff. Cover baked pie with meringue and bake at 325 degrees about 15 minutes.

MRS. W. U. GAINES
Rayville, La.

LEMON REFRIGERATOR PIE

4 egg yolks
½ cup sugar
Juice of 2 lemons
1 envelope gelatine

½ cup cold water
4 egg whites
½ teaspoon salt
½ cup sugar

Beat together, until light and lemon colored, egg yolks, ½ cup sugar, lemon juice. Cook in double boiler until thick.

Dissolve gelatine in ½ cup cold water, stir into hot mixture and cool. Beat egg whites, salt and sugar until thick but not dry. Fold into egg yolk mixture. Pour into baked pie crust and place in refrigerator. When ready to serve, top with whipped cream or cool whip.

MRS. T. LUSTER JAMES

FRENCH MACAROON PIE

15 saltine crackers
14 dates, cut fine
1 cup sugar

½ cup chopped pecans
1 teaspoon almond extract
3 egg whites, beaten stiff

Crush crackers until fine. Add dates, sugar, pecans, and almond extract. Mix well, then fold in stiffly beaten egg whites. Put into buttered 8-inch pie pan and bake at 300 degrees for 45 minutes. Serve cold with whipped cream.

MRS. A. L. POSTLETHWAITE

LEMON PIE

1½ cups milk, scalded	Pinch of salt
1 cup sugar	4 eggs separated
2 tablespoons cornstarch	Juice of 2 lemons

Grated rind of 1 lemon

Sift sugar, cornstarch and salt together and add scalded milk. Cook over medium heat until thickened. Remove from fire and add a small amount of this custard to 3 egg yolks, beaten slightly, and then add lemon juice and rind to yolks. Return to remainder of custard and cook until it bubbles. Remove from heat and pour into baked pie shell, cover with meringue and brown in 325 degree oven.

MERINGUE

Beat egg whites and add 8 tablespoons sugar gradually.

ORANGE PIE

Same as lemon pie, except use juice of 1 orange and ind of one orange, 3 or 4 tablespoons cornstarch, and omit lemon juice and rind.

CHOCOLATE PIE

Same as lemon pie, except use 2 tablespoons cocoa, 3 or 4 tablespoons cornstarch and 1 teaspoon vanilla. Omit lemon and orange.

COCOANUT PIE

Same as lemon pie, except use 3 or 4 tablespoons cornstarch, and add 1 cup flaked cocoanut to cooked filling, add 1 teaspoon vanilla and sprinkle layer of cocoanut on top before browning. Omit lemon, orange and cocoa.

MRS. ETHEL BOWMAN
Ruston, La.

COCOANUT PIE

3 eggs	¼ teaspoon salt
1 1/3 cups sugar	¼ teaspoon vanilla
¼ cup milk	1½ cups shredded cocoanut
2 tablespoons butter	Unbaked pie shell

Beat eggs until foamy and add the other ingredients gradually while continuing to beat. Pour into unbaked pie shell and bake at 350 degrees for about 1 hour, or until light brown and firm.

MRS. ROBERT S. WYNN
Ruston, La.

COCOANUT BUTTERSCOTCH PIE

1 cooked pastry shell	3 tablespoons butter
2 cups milk	¼ teaspoon salt
2 eggs plus 2 egg whites	1 teaspoon vanilla
3 tablespoons flour	1 can cocoanut
1 cup dark brown sugar	(Southern style)

Scald milk in double boiler. Mix sugar and flour and add to milk, cook 15 minutes, stirring constantly until thickened. Add butter, half can of cocoanut and salt. Stir into the egg yolks, lightly beaten. Return to double boiler and cook one minute. When cool, add vanilla. Make meringue of the egg whites, spread thickly with remainder of cocoanut and brown slightly.

MRS. R. M. THOMAS

CHESS PIE (UNORTHODOX)

4 egg yokes	4 egg whites
1 cup sugar	8 tablespoons sugar
1 cup butter	1/8 teaspoon cream
1/8 teaspoon salt	of tartar

1/8 teaspoon salt

Cream first 4 ingredients thoroughly for custard. Make a very thick meringue by beating egg whites and adding last 3 ingredients. Make favorite pie crust and place in 8-9 inch pie plate. Cook for about 20 minutes in a 260 degree oven before adding custard. Then bake 1 hour. Remove from oven, let cool and sprinkle very lightly with nutmeg. Cover with meringue and brown slightly.

MRS. RONALD A. COCO

CHESS PIE

1 stick butter	2 tablespoons corn meal
1½ cups sugar	(mix with flour)
3 unbeaten eggs	1 teaspoon vanilla
2 tablespoons flour	1 tablespoon lemon juice
½ cup cream	Pinch of salt

Cream butter, add sugar and cream together. Add other ingredients in order given. Pour into half baked pastry shell and bake for 45minutes in 325 degree oven.

MRS. W. A. COOPER

STRAWBERRY PIE
Serves 6

8 inch prebaked pie shell   2 tablespoons lemon juice
3 ounce package cream   3 cups strawberries
     cheese   3 tablespoons cornstarch
1 cup whipping cream   1 cup sugar

Use enough of the cream to soften cheese and spread evenly over the bottom of baked pie shell. Wash, hull and drain the berries and place half of them in the cheese-coated pie shell. Wash remaining berries, cover and bring to a boil. Mix sugar and cornstarch and stir into the hot berries, cooking over reduced heat and stir until the juice is clear; about ten minutes. Stir in lemon juice. Cool and spread over the uncooked berries. Chill in refrigerator until 10 minutes before serving time. Top with sweetened whipped cream and a few uncooked berries for color.

MRS. LEWIS O. WHITE

OLD FASHIONED MINCEMEAT
Yields 5 quarts

2 pounds beef-neck   1 pound sultana raisins
    meat, ground   1/2 pound citron, chopped
1 pound suet, finely ground   1/2 pound orange peel,
2 pounds sugar   chopped
5 pounds tart apples,   1 tablespoon salt
    pared, cored and   1 teaspoon cinnamon
    chopped   1 teaspoon allspice
2 pounds muscat raisins   1 teaspoon mace
1 pound currants   1 quart boiled cider
Brandy to taste

Combine beef, suet, sugar, fruits, salt, spices and 1 quart cider in large kettle. Cover. Simmer, stirring occasionally for 2 hours. Add more cider during cooking if necessary. Add brandy. Pack into hot sterilized jars. Seal. Store in cool place.

MRS. MARTIN P. BRODERICK

Candy

DIVINITY

3 cups sugar	1 pinch salt
½ cup white corn syrup	1 teaspoon vanilla or
1 cup water	almond extract
2 egg whites, beaten stiff	1 cup chopped pecans

Cook first 3 ingredients to stiff soft ball, but not stringy. Pour syrup into stiffly beaten egg whites, beating continuously. Add flavoring, nuts (and coloring, if desired) and when it loses its sheen, it can be dropped from a spoon onto a greased table or poured into a greased plate.

MRS. HENRY Y. BENNETT

FUDGE

1/8 pound plus 1	2 cups chopped nuts
tablespoon butter	4½ cups sugar
3 8-ounce packages semi-	1 large can evaporated
sweet chocolate	milk

Mix the first three ingredients in a bowl. In heavy sauce pan, combine sugar and milk and boil slowly for 6 minutes, stirring constantly. Mix all ingredients and blend well. Pour into buttered pan to cool.

MRS. CHARLES CROOK

PECAN PRALINES

3 cups sugar (1 brown, 2	½ stick butter
white optional)	Pinch of salt
1 cup evaporated milk	1 teaspoon vanilla

Toasted pecans—2 to 3 cups

Boil gently over a very low heat the milk, sugar, salt, and a small portion of the butter in a large saucepan. (about three quarts in size). Stir occasionally. When the mixture forms a firm ball in cold water remove from the fire. Add remainder of the butter, the vanilla, and toasted pecans. Beat all together until mixture starts hardening around the edge of the saucepan. Drop teaspoonful at a time on to waxed paper. If larger size pralines are desired, use a tablespoon.

From the file of
MRS. FRANK PERCY, SR.
Greenwood Plantation

PECAN PRALINES

1 cup white granulated sugar	1 cup evaporated milk

1 cup white granulated
sugar
1 cup light brown sugar
1 cup pecan halves (or more)

1 cup evaporated milk
1 teaspoon butter
1 teaspoon vanilla extract

Mix first four ingredients, bring to boil, stirring constantly. Add butter and extract and cook until forms soft ball in cold water. Add pecans and beat until begins to harden. Pour into buttered dish and break into pieces.

MRS. ALEX SOMPAYRAC
Natchitoches, La.

PEANUT BRITTLE

Cup for cup of sugar and roasted peanuts. Use clean dish towel and wooden mallet to pound peanuts very fine. Caramelize sugar in heavy iron skillet. Remove from fire and stir in peanuts. Pour on marble slab saturated with cold water. Roll, paper thin, with rolling pin saturated with cold water. Break in small pieces.

From the files of
MRS. J. HEREFORD PERCY

GRAHAM CRACKER PRALINES

Cover cookie sheet 12 inches X 15 inches with graham crackers. Sprinkle with 1½ cups pecans. Bring to a boil and boil for 3 minutes:

1 cup brown sugar   2 sticks butter

Pour over graham crackers. Bake in oven (350 degrees) for 10 minutes. Cut while warm.

MRS. ROY RHYMES
Monroe, La.

BLACKBERRY JAM

4 cups prepared fruit   ½ bottle Certo
7 cups sugar   fruit pectin

Crush berries (if desired sieve half of pulp to remove some of the seeds). Measure 4 cups into large saucepan. Add sugar. Place over high heat, bring to a full rolling boil and boil hard 1 minute stirring constantly. Remove from heat at once stir in pectin. Skim off foam with metal spoon. Stir and skim for 5 minutes. Cool slightly to prevent fruit from floating to top.

MRS. A. F. ORTIZ

CANDIED ORANGE PEEL

Remove peel from orange in 4 sections; put in cold water. Bring to boiling point. Pour off water. Put in cold water and bring to boiling point again. Pour off water and add cold water. Cook until tender in 3rd water.

Scrape out white part of peel (not all). Cut in strips with scissors.

Make syrup of 1 cup sugar and ½ cup water. Stir until it boils; boil until forms thread. Add orange peel and let **boil** 5 minutes. Strain and put peels on plate covered with granulated sugar. Roll.

MRS. FRED ANDERSON
Gloster, Miss.

GUAVA JELLY

1½ cups guava juice   1 tablespoon lemon juice
      1½ cups sugar

Wash and cut ripe strawberry guava fruit into pieces. Cut off stem ends, but do not not peel. Cover with water and boil 5 minutes. Strain through a cheese cloth bag—strain twice. Measure juice and bring to a boil then add lemon juice and sugar and boil rapidly until the jelly stage is reached. Pour into sterilized jars.

MRS. BEN R. MILLER

STRAWBERRY JAM
(Uncooked—6 medium jars)

1 3/4 cup prepared fruit   ½ bottle of Certo Fruit
4 cups sugar   Pectin
    2 tablespoons lemon juice

Prepare fruit—crush completely. Put into large bowl. Add sugar and mix well. Mix lemon juice and Certo well and stir into fruit. Stir about 3 minutes. Pour quickly into jar and cover with lid. Let sit at room temperature 24 hours. Store in freezer.

MRS. A. F. ORTIZ

WATERMELON RIND PRESERVES

5 pounds melon rind   5 to 6 large oranges
5 pounds sugar   or lemons cut into
5 quarts water   thick slices

Peel melon rind leaving no trace of pink. Cut into

2-3 inch strips. Soak overnight in solution of 2 ounces powdered lime (from drug store) and water to cover. Next morning rinse well and cover in solution of 2 table-spoons alum (powdered) and enough water to cover rind for 5 minutes. Mix sugar and water for syrup and heat before adding rind. Dip rind directly into syrup, from alum solution, without rinsing. Cook for about an hour before adding fruit slices. Make more syrup if needed.

MRS. RONALD COCO

Beverages
and
Party Foods

EGG NOG

6 eggs	6 tablespoons whiskey
6 tablespoons sugar	Pinch salt

1 pint cream (whipping)

Mix sugar with egg yolks and beat until thick. Beat egg whites until stiff. Add whiskey to egg yolks stirring well. Fold in whites. Serve each portion with 2 tablespoons of whipped cream. More whiskey may be added if desired. Whipped cream may be sweetened or left unsweetened. Serve immediately.

THE EDITORS

SENTELL NECTAR SODA

3 cups sugar	1 teaspoon almond extract
1½ cups water	Red food coloring (just a
1 can condensed milk	drop or two to make
1 teaspoon vanilla	pink)

Dissolve sugar in water, add condensed milk, vanilla and food coloring. Keep covered in a jar in refrigerator until ready to serve. Put several spoonsful in a glass and pour in carbonated water. Stir well and add ice. Add vanilla ice cream to make extra delicious.

MRS. STERLING GLADDEN, JR.

This is an old family favorite.

COFFEE PUNCH

1 gallon strong coffee	3 teaspoons vanilla
Enough sugar to barely sweeten	1 quart coffee or vanilla ice cream

1 pint whipped cream

Serve over ice in punch bowl.

MRS. OMER HEBERT
Plaquemine, La.

CRANBERRY PUNCH

3 quarts cranberry juice	½ cup lemon juice
1 quart orange juice	4 quarts ginger ale

Mix juices and freeze, if desired, in cartons you would like for one mixing. Remove from freezer soon enough for it to become mushy before serving. Add ginger ale just before serving. Makes 50 to 60 cups (2 gallons).

MRS. BEN DOWNING, JR.

PUNCH
Makes 1½ gallons (plus 1 pint)

1 large can orange juice (46 ounces)	1 large bottle real lemon (1 quart)
1 large can pineapple juice (46 ounces)	2½ quarts water
2 large bottles ginger ale	30 sprigs of mint
	2 cups sugar

Boil 2½ quarts of water plus 30 sprigs of mint for ten minutes. Strain and cool. Add 2 cups sugar. Mix with juices. Freeze. Take out ½ hour before serving (have mushy). Add two large bottles of ginger ale.

MRS. JOHN R. MCKINNIE

GOLDEN WEDDING PUNCH
50-60 cups

30 sprigs fresh mint	2 quarts orange juice
2 cups sugar	2 cups pineapple juice
2 quarts boiling water	2 quarts ginger ale or champagne
2 cups lemon juice	

Boil mint, sugar and water for 15 minutes. Strain and let cool. Add all juices. Add ginger ale or champagne just before serving.

From the files of
MRS. W. R. EIDSON

COMBINATION PUNCH
35-40 punch cups

1 quart pineapple juice	1 quart apple juice
1 quart can orange juice	1 quart ginger ale

Mix the juices and let stand for about two hours to blend flavors. Pour in ginger ale and serve over ice. A delicious and refreshing summer drink.

BESS HAWSEY

HOT SPICED APPLE JUICE

5 quart size cans apple juice	2 sticks cinnamon
1 box whole cloves	½ cup sugar (or to taste)

Put 4 cans of juice in container. Bring to a hard boil. Drop in bag of cloves and broken cinnamon. Add sugar. Boil together for five minutes, stirring frequently. Turn fire low and let simmer. After you have served half of juice, add other can of apple juice. Turn fire up for a few minutes. Lift out spice bag and let simmer until party is over.

MRS. A. E. MONTGOMERY, JR.
Monroe, La.

EASY PUNCH

3 envelopes of unsweetened
   Kool-Aid all one flavor
½ cup lemon juice
   (real lemon)
3 cups of pineapple
   juice. Use ½ of
   14 ounce canned pine-
   apple juice
3 cups sugar

Put ingredients in order given into a gallon jar. Stir well until sugar has dissolved. Add water to make a gallon. Chill (if possible) before pouring over ice into a punch bowl. This recipe makes 30 cups. The punch can be made up ahead of time or fixed as needed. It is wonderful for children's parties, benefits or large gatherings. It is inexpensive and very good.

I usually make up several gallons and chill them, then I make up the rest as needed. Flavors that are popular are cherry, raspberry,orange and lime.

MRS. E. V. FASCE

PINEAPPLE CRANBERRY HOT PUNCH

1 large can pineapple juice
1 pint cranberry juice
¼ cup honey
2 cups water
1 lemon sliced
12 whole cloves

Heat all of the above ingredients and serve.

THE EDITORS

HOT CRAB CANAPES

1 cup (lump) crab meat
1 cup heavy cream sauce
   or ½ can cream of
   celery soup
¼ teaspoon celery salt
¼ teaspoon pepper
1 tablespoon
   Worcestershire sauce
3 drops Tabasco
½ teaspoon salt
¼ cup parsley flakes

Mix all ingredients. Pile mixture on triscuits, melba toast, or grilled tiny bread squares. Sprinkle with parsley. Bake in hot (400 degree) oven for about five minutes or until lightly browned. Serve at once.

MRS. LEWIS O. WHITE

DEVILED HAM TURNOVERS

1 stick oleomargarine	½ teaspoon prepared
1 small package soft	mustard
cream cheese	Red pepper sauce
1 cup flour	½ teaspoon
1 can deviled ham	Worcestershire sauce
1 clove garlic, pressed	

Make pastry by mixing together oleomargarine, flour and cream cheese. Chill at least 1 hour. Blend deviled ham with remaining ingredients. Add no salt because ham is salty. Roll pastry thin and cut into 2 inch rounds. Take ½ of after dinner coffee spoon of ham mixture and put on halves of pastry circles. Fold over, pinch edges and prick twice with fork. Bake in 350 degree oven about 12 minutes. May be frozen before or after baking.

MRS. ASHER WHITLEY

Crab meat, chicken or mince meat (at Christmas time) may be substituted for the deviled ham.

CRAB MEAT DIP

1 bunch green onions	1 can cream of mushroom
1 bell pepper	soup
1 cup diced celery	2 cans King crab meat
1 stick butter	2 cans water chestnuts
Salt and pepper to taste	sliced

Saute onions, pepper and celery in butter. Add rest of the ingredients and cook for 20 minutes over low heat. Serve on melba toast from chafing dish.

MRS. CHARLES BARHAM
Ruston, La.

CAVIAR MOUSSE
Serves 40

4 ounces caviar	2 tablespoons lime juice
3 small packages Yogurt	1 package gelatine softened
2 cups (or less) mayonnaise	in ¼ cup water and
1 tablespoon	dissolved over hot
Worcestershire sauce	water
2 tablespoons onion juice	

Mix all ingredients and pour into ring mold which has been rinsed in cold water. Chill until firm. If this should fail to jell, pour into pan and heat until very hot.

It will not hurt it. Chill again. A bit expensive, but goes a long way as a spread for crackers at cocktail parties. Also freezes well for a short time.

MRS. L. M. DAVIS

ORANGE BALLS
3-4 dozen

One 12-16 ounce package vanilla wafers
¼ cup chopped nuts
1 cup powdered sugar
¼ cup melted butter
1 cup undiluted frozen orange juice

Crush vanilla wafers and mix with other ingredients. Make balls and roll in remaining powdered sugar. Store and freeze in tins. Remove shortly before using.

MRS. ROBERT PARISH

SHRIMP BUTTER

¼ pound soft butter
8-ounce package cream cheese
4 tablespoons mayonnaise
1 small onion grated
Salt, pepper and garlic salt to taste
2 cans deveined shrimp (or fresh)
Juice of 1 lemon

Put all ingredients in electric beater and mix well. Chop shrimp very fine and add to mixture. Serve on crackers. Try garnishing molded shrimp salad with this.

MRS. WALLACE PEARSON
Lafayette, La.

SHRIMP TAPAS
Serves 10-15

1½ pounds tiny shelled raw shrimp
6 tablespoons olive oil
1 garlic clove, peeled
½ teaspoon salt
3/4 cup dry sherry
1 tablespoon parsley minced

Combine all ingredients. Pour over shrimp in deep bowl and marinate 4 to 5 hours. Remove garlic clove. Now turn all into electric skillet and cook quickly just until shrimp turn pink. Serve hot with picks.

MRS. SAM JONES
Lake Charles, La.

ANTIPASTO

1 can tuna fish	4 ribs finely chopped celery
1 can chopped, black olives	1 jar marinated hearts of artichokes
1 jar antipasto mixture	¼ teaspoon red pepper

Finely chop all ingredients, mix and serve with crackers.

MRS. RICHARD MAESTRI

MACKEREL BALLS

½ pound mackerel	3 tablespoons parsley
3 medium size Irish potatoes	½ teaspoon salt
2 eggs	½ teaspoon cayenne
6 green onions	pepper
3 large cloves garlic	¼ cups flour

¼ cup white cornmeal

From a large piece of skinned and boned King Mackerel that is frozen, scrape about ½ pound of meat off with a teaspoon. You can do this as the fish is thawing, and still firm. Return unused portion of mackerel to the freezer to be used later.

Boil and mash the potatoes. Add the grated fish, seasonings and finally the beaten eggs. Roll into balls about the size of an agate marble. Roll the balls in the mixture of flour and cornmeal and return to the refrigerator until time to be fried. Fry in deep fat only long enough to brown and serve immediately as an appetizer.

The same recipe can be used by making the mixture into the usual size of fish cakes and serve as an entree.

MRS. H. H. HOLLOWAY, JR.

REUBEN SANDWICH

Corn beef, cooked, thinly sliced	Sauerkraut
Swiss cheese	Mustard
Rye bread	Mayonnaise
	Butter

Garnish

The quanity of ingredients will depend on taste and number of sandwiches to be made. Butter outside of each slice of bread. Spread inside of each with mustard and mayonnaise. Layer corn beef, sauerkraut and swiss cheese on one slice of bread for each sandwich, cover with second slice of bread and brown on griddle, in skillet or under broiler. Garnish plates.

MEREDITH JOAN ROBINSON

PICKLED MUSHROOMS

1 clove garlic	¼ teaspoon pepper
3/4 cup salad oil	½ teaspoon dry mustard
¼ cup olive oil	3 bay .leaves
½ cup lemon juice	2 (4 ounce) cans button
1 onion (chopped)	mushrooms

1 teaspoon salt

Put all ingredients into refrigerator jar. Drain mushrooms and add to sauce. Cover and let stand in refrigerator 24 hours. Before serving, drain mushrooms on paper towel, insert toothpicks for easier eating.

MRS. T. M. SAYRE
Rayville, La.

STUFFED MUSHROOMS
Serves 50

1 pound lump crabmeat, fresh	2 tablespoons chopped parsley
½ cup chopped celery	½ cup capers
¼ cup chopped green pepper	Homemade mayonnaise
	Salt, pepper and red pepper to taste

Mix all ingredients and stuff mushrooms. Serve cold, topped with a rose of mayonnaise.

NOTE: For cocktail parties, use the bite-size mushrooms; for luncheon, the bigger the better. You may also stuff them with all sorts of things—ham, fowl, or fish.

MRS. WILLIAM SLACK

CURRIED OLIVES

1 tablespoon instant minced onion or ¼ cup finely chopped onion	1 tablespoon curry powder
	½ cup salad oil
	1½ cups drained, stuffed olives

2 tablespoons lemon juice

Combine onions and lemon juice. (If using instant minced onions, allow to stand in juice 5 minutes) Add curry powder. With electric or rotary beater, slowly beat in the salad oil. Put olives in jar; pour mixture over olives. Cover and refrigerate 3 days. Drain before serving.

MRS. WILLIAM Y. LOBDELL

PICKLED OKRA

4 cups cider vinegar	Dill seed
6 cups water	Celery seed
1½ cups sugar	Mustard seed
½ cup salt	Hot peppers
Okra	Garlic

Bring vinegar, water, sugar and salt to boil. Pour over okra which has been packed into jars. (Do not seal). Next morning pour liquid back into pot and boil again. While heating liquid add to each jar of okra 1 teaspoon dill seed, 1 teaspoon celery seed, 1 hot pepper, ½ bud of garlic and 1 teaspoon mustard seed. Add boiling liquid and seal. Do not pack okra too tight in jars.

MRS. TED DUNHAM

SAUSAGE PINWHEELS

2 cups flour	½ cup oleomargarine
3 teaspoons baking powder	2/3 cup milk
1 teaspoon salt	1 pound bulk type hot sausage

Sift together flour, baking powder and salt. Cut in oleomargarine. Add milk and mix lightly. Knead twice and roll out half of biscuit in rectangle. Spread half the hot sausage (room temperature). Roll up the long way and cut thin like ice-box cookies. Repeat for other half. Bake 400 degrees for 15 minutes.

MRS. DELBERT A. LIPPS
MRS. JAMES ALTIC
Monroe, La.

TARTE A L' OIGNON

A portée de la main: 200 grs de beurre 250 grs de farine—3 ou 4 beaux oignons—100 grs de lard—2 verres de lait—poivre, sel.

Durée de la préparation: 1 heure.

Faites une pate à tarte (200 grs de farine, 100 grs d'Astra, ½ verre d'eau, 5 grs de sel fin) et dressez dans un moule à tarte.

Epluchez et émincez vos oignons. Faites-les jaunir dans une casserole avec 100 grs beurre. Mélangez-les ensuite avec environ le contenu d'un verre de sauce béchamel. Assaisonnez de sel, poivre et d'un peu de muscade.

Faites frire quelques minces bardes de lard dans du beurre. Egouttez-les et disposez-les au fond de la pate piquèe, que vous remplissez avec de la sauce. Faites cuire une demi-heure environ a four assez vif au début, modéré ensuite. Servez chaud.

ONION PIE

Have on hand: 3/4 cup butter—1 cup flour—3 or 4 good onions— 6 or 8 slices of bacon—2 cups of milk— pepper, salt.

Time needed: 1 hour.

Make a dough for pie crust out of butter, flour, half cup of water, and dash of salt. Place crust in pie plate.

Peel onions and slice thinly. Sauté in butter until light brown. Mix these with about 1 cup of white sauce. Season with salt, pepper and bit of nutmeg.

Fry bacon and drain. Place bacon on bottom of pie crust and fill with white sauce. Cook in moderate oven about half hour, having started in more-or-less hot oven. Serve hot.

NOTE: Cut in 1 inch wedges and serve as hors d'oeuvre.

DANIEL FAGAN WRIGHT
Hammond, La.
Formerly LeHavre and Paris

GLAZE FOR COLD MEATS

1 package unflavored gelatine—for cold beef, tongue
1¼ cups beef stock   or turkey
1 teaspoon tarragon vinegar
Add dry mustard to taste— for cold ham
Add saffron to taste— for cold chicken
Use chicken broth instead of beef stock.

Roll or fold slices of meat and arrange attractively. Garnish with black olives, tomato wedges, sliced hard cooked eggs, cucumber slices and dill pickles. Soak gelatine in ½ cup cold beef stock. Dissolve in remaining stock which has been heated. Add vinegar. When mixture is cool, spoon over meats and place in refrigerator. Repeat two or three times as glaze jells over meats. Pour remaining glaze in small, flat pan. Congeal in refrigerator and cut with small, fluted cutter. Place on edge of platter before serving. Ca c'est beau!

THE EDITORS

RIBBONED SANDWICH LOAF

½ pound baked ham
India relish to taste
Grated onion to taste
Mayonnaise

2 hard boiled eggs
1 cup lettuce, chopped fine
White bread
Brown bread

Butter for spreading

Grind ham and mix with relish, onion and only enough mayonnaise to hold ingredients together. In another bowl mash eggs and season with salt and pepper. Toss finely chopped lettuce with eggs and again add only enough mayonnaise to mix ingredients well. With an electric knife, if possible, trim edges off 3 slices of bread at a time, placing a piece of brown bread between 2 pieces of white. Brush inside of white bread with butter, both sides of brown. Place ham mixture on white, place brown bread on top, spread lettuce mixture on brown, place white bread on top. Wrap lightly in cellophane and chill thoroughly. These can be made the day before. Again using an electric knife, cut sandwiches into desired shape. Place on tray so the pink, yellow and brown colors show. The above makes up approximately 1 loaf of thin sliced white bread and 1 loaf of brown.

MRS. VERNON E. LaCOUR
Plaquemine, La.

PECAN BALLS

2 cups sugar
1 1/3 cups corn syrup—
  for chewy center
  If creamy center desired,
  use 3/4 cup

1/8 teaspoon salt
2 cups heavy cream
3/4 cups evaporated
  milk—one small can
4 tablespoons butter

2 teaspoons vanilla

Place in heavy saucepan, sugar, corn syrup, salt, ½ cream and ½ milk. Boil up slowly and add remaining cream and milk so slowly mixture never ceases boiling. Cook to softball (or 234 degrees F.) stage—add butter. Cook a minute or so longer. Remove from fire, add extract, and pour into well-greased platter. This scorches very easily.

When cool, and thoroughly set, cut into one-inch squares. Flatten out in palm of hand, put crushed pecans in the center and roll into ball. Press pecan halves around the caramel ball.

MRS. GEORGE PAULAT

CHINESE STEAKS
(Cocktail Hour Tidbits)

1 cup soy sauce
1 teaspoon garlic paste
3 pounds of steak, trimmed

3/4 teaspoon fresh ginger juice or ¼ cup thin slices of ginger

Add to the soy sauce garlic paste and fresh ginger juice or thin slices of ginger. Slice a beef tenderloin or sirloin steaks into 1-inch cubes (about 3 pounds of beef, trimmed). Put into a plastic bag or bowl and marinate over night. Turn occasionally to insure even distribution of marinade.

To serve, spear individual steaks with tooth picks and drop into hot deep Lou-Ana oil.

MRS. FONILLE WINANS

BROCCOLI DIP

2 packages frozen broccoli
1 small onion chopped
2 stalks celery chopped
1 can chopped mushrooms

1 stick butter
2 rolls garlic cheese
1 can cream of mushroom soup

Tabasco and red pepper

Sauté onion, celery and mushrooms in butter. Melt garlic cheese in top of double boiler with 1 can cream of mushroom soup. Cook broccoli according to instructions and drain. Combine all ingredients and season with dash of tabasco and red pepper. Serve from chafing dish with chips.

MRS. CHARLES CROOK

MISSIE'S CHEESE BALLS

¼ pound New York sharp cheese
1 cup flour
1 stick butter

¼ cup chopped pecans

Mix thoroughly and roll into balls the size of a walnut. Press with bottom of glass and bake at 325 degrees for 10-12 minutes.

MRS. W. L. McKEE

MISS FANNIE'S CHEESE BALLS

1½ cups sharp cheese	Red pepper to taste
1 tablespoon flour	3 egg whites
¼ teaspoon salt	Cracker meal

Grate cheese on fine grater. Mix with salt, flour and pepper. Whip eggs very stiff and add to cheese mixture. Form into small balls and roll in cracker meal. Place on a platter coated with cracker meal, store in refrigerator at least two hours. Fry in deep, hot, fresh oil and drain on brown paper. Makes about 25 balls, and they freeze very well.

From the file of
MRS. LEE HERZBERG

CHILI CHEESE LOG

1 3-ounce package cream cheese	1 tablespoon lemon juice
2 cups shredded New York cheese	Dash of red pepper
¼ teaspoon garlic powder or salt	¼ cup ground, toasted almonds
	1 teaspoon chili powder
	1 teaspoon paprika

Let cheese stand at room temperature to soften. Combine cheese, lemon juice, garlic powder and red pepper. Beat with electric beater until light and fluffy. Stir in ground almonds, shape into a roll about 1½ inches in diameter, sprinkle roll with mixture of chili and paprika. Chill several hours before using.

MRS. J. EMORY ADAMS
MRS. J. M. ARMSTRONG, JR.
Ruston, La.

CHEESE STRAWS

1 cup shortening	1 5-ounce jar sharp cheese spread
1 teaspoon salt	2 cups flour
¼ teaspoon red pepper	

Work together with hands shortening, salt, pepper and cheese spread. Add flour 1 cup at a time. Divide mixture into 2 balls, then work each ball into long roll about one inch in diameter. Wrap in wax paper and let stand until firm enough to slice very thin. Place on ungreased baking sheet and bake at 350 degrees for about 10 minutes. If a cookie press is available, put soft mixture in this and cut in 2 inch or longer lengths.

MRS. SANDERS BASKIN
Ruston, La.

CHEESE ROCKET

2 3-ounce wedges Bleu cheese	2 tablespoons grated onion 1½ teaspoons
2 5-ounce jars very sharp cheese	Worcestershire sauce ½ cup minced parsley
4 3-ounce packages soft cream cheese	Red pepper and garlic salt to taste

1 cup pecans, finely chopped

Mix all ingredients, using only half the pecans and parsley. Put into well-buttered mold and chill overnight. Unmold and garnish with rest of pecans and parsley.

MRS. AGRIPPA G. ROBERT

HOT CHEESE SANDWICHES

1 pound very sharp cheese grated fine	Parsley chopped fine Salt, Tabasco, monosodium
½ stick butter or oleo	glutamate, and
1 small bell pepper chopped fine	Worcestershire sauce to taste

2 green onions chopped fine

Remove crust from 2 loaves of sliced pullman bread. (All of this may not be needed). Put cheese and butter into mixing bowl and mix with an electric blender. Add seasonings and blend again. Add bell pepper, onions and parsley and mix this by hand with spoon. Spread slices of bread with this mixture and roll each slice, as for jelly roll, and secure with toothpicks. Cover sandwich rolls with wax paper, then a very damp cloth, and store in refrigerator until needed. Run under broiler until slightly brown, turning once. Serve hot.

MRS. E. V. FASCE
MRS. R. J. HUMMEL

KIPFULS

1 cup butter	1 tablespoon thick
1 cup cream cheese	sour cream
2 cups flour	1 big pinch salt

Mix butter and cream cheese; add sour cream and salt; add flour and knead into a ball. Wrap in wax paper and place in ice box 3 hours. Roll paper thin and cut into small squares. Fill each with 1 teaspoon apricot or raspberry jam. Roll from corner and shape into half moons. Bake in brisk oven 20 minutes and cool before serving.

THE EDITORS

ARTICHOKE BALLS

1 can hearts of artichokes	2 tablespoons Italian
1 cup seasoned bread	cheese
crumbs	2 cloves garlic
2 eggs	5 tablespoons olive oil

Put garlic through press and add to olive oil. Beat eggs slightly and add to oil mixture. Mash artichokes and add cheese and crumbs. Shape in balls the size of marbles and roll in extra cheese and seasoned bread crumbs—2 parts cheese to 1 part bread crumbs. Let stand in ice box before using. These freeze beautifully.

MRS. J. EMORY ADAMS

CHILI DIP

1 medium onion, chopped	½ pound grated
1 tomato, chopped	sharp cheese
2 tablespoons flour	1 teaspoon cumin
2 tablespoons oleo	1 tablespoon
1 can chili (without beans)	Worcestershire sauce

Red pepper to taste

Sauté onion and tomato in oleo until onion is limp. Add flour and stir well. Add other ingredients and heat thoroughly before pouring into chafing dish. Fritos are excellent with this dip. For a chafing dish full, double the recipe.

MRS. AGRIPPA G. ROBERT

TAMALE-CHILI DIP

1 large onion	1 can chili, without beans
1 can tamales, mashed	Sharp cheese to taste

Saute one large onion, and add remainder of ingredients. Add a little garlic, chili powder, Worcestershire sauce, and liquid smoke. Serve with king-size fritos.

MRS. BOYD J. BEADLES
Shreveport, La.

ROYAL PLUM PUDDING

1 1-pound jar purple plums	1 cup chopped walnuts
1 package ginger bread mix	¼ cup sugar
½ teaspoon salt	2 tablespoons cornstarch
2 cups light raisins	1 tablespoon lemon juice

Drain plums, reserving juice for sauce. Remove pits and cut plums in pieces. Prepare gingerbread mix ac-

cording to directions on box, adding salt and plum pieces
Stir in raisins and walnuts. Transfer batter to well-
greased 6 cup mold or spring bottom pan. Bake uncovered in moderate (375 degree) oven about 1 hour.
Loosen mold and immediately unmold on serving platter.
Meanwhile, prepare plum sauce: Add water to reserved
plum syrup to make 1½ cups. Combine sugar and cornstarch in small saucepan. Stir in plum syrup and cook
over medium heat, stirring constantly until mixture
thickens. Add lemon juice and serve warm over pudding
or use as a glaze. Fluffy hard sauce: Cream together ½
cup butter and 2 cups sifted confectioners sugar. Stir in 1
beaten egg yoke and 1 teaspoon vanilla. Fold in 1 stiffly
beaten egg white. Serve with plum pudding.

MRS. GARNER MOORE

TAPENADE

1/3 pound chopped, black French olives
1 teaspoon Dijon mustard
18 anchovy filets
½ cup capers
½ cup olive oil
Touch of ground cloves
Touch of ground ginger
Black pepper
Dash of Cognac

Mix all together and serve on Melba toast.

MRS. FRANK GRIGSBY
Shreveport, La.

EGGS MAGNIFIQUE

3 hard boiled eggs
1 can cream of mushroom soup
½ teaspoon Worcestershire sauce
1 pinch oregano
½ teaspoon chopped parsley
Salt and pepper to taste
Milk (only if needed to thin)
Dash monosodium glutamate
Paprika
Melba toast

Put soup in pot and simmer, stirring to get out all
lumps. Add all seasonings and continue to simmer; stir
until completely smooth. Thinly slice eggs (put aside 1
yolk, grated, for later use). Add sliced eggs to mixture.
Serve hot on Melba toast. Put grated yolk on top of
each serving and sprinkle with paprika. Magnifique for
brunch or supper, served with crisp bacon or boiled ham
slices, and green salad.

MRS. HUBERT N. WAX

VEAL PICATTO

6 thin veal cutlets (cut from sirloin tip roast)	2 ounces dry, white wine (preferably Chablis)
4 tablespoons butter	½ cup water
1 tablespoon flour	1 tablespoon lemon juice
Minced parsley	Salt and pepper to taste

Melt butter slowly; do not brown. Add (unsalted and unpeppered) veal cutlets. Cook gently without browning. When red appearance of veal disappears, turn and cook other side in same manner. Remove from skillet, being sure to save any juices that leave the meat after taking it out onto platter. To remaining butter, blend in flour. Add slowly the wine, water and lemon juice. Add salt and pepper to taste; also salt and pepper cutlets. Return cutlets and juices to sauce, which is set at a very low temperature. Turn cutlets to fully coat with sauce. Leave cutlets in mixture, heating only long enough for them to be hot through and through. Sprinkle with minced parsley (fresh or dried) and serve immediately. (This dish can be prepared early, and at the point of returning the cutlets to the sauce, can be finished at the last minute before serving)

MRS. WILLIAM E. DAVIS

Cut veal into bite-size pieces and serve in chafing dish as hors d'oeuvres.

THE EDITORS

TOASTED MUSHROOM SANDWICHES

½ pound fresh mushrooms	¼ teaspoon monosodium glutamate
¼ cup butter	
3 tablespoons flour	1 cup light cream
3/4 teaspoon salt	2 teaspoons minced chives
1 loaf of bread sliced thin	1 teaspoon lemon juice

Chop mushrooms, saute in butter 5 minutes. Blend in flour, salt and monosodium glutamate. Stir in cream and cook, stirring constantly, until thickened. Add chives and lemon juice, remove from heat and cool. Remove crusts from bread, flatten with rolling pin, spread with filling and roll. Place in pan with seam side down. Pack in layers with wax paper between each layer, place in refrigerator or freezer. Each sandwich may be cut in half if smaller ones are desired. Toast on all sides and serve.

MRS. HENRY GUERRIERO
Monroe, La.

HAM BALLS

1 cup minced ham	1 tablespoon butter
2 cups mashed potatoes	2 eggs

2 tablespoons cream

Mix potatoes, ham and cream. Add eggs, butter and a little milk. Form into firm balls. Roll in dried bread crumbs and fry in Lou Ana shortening. Eat hot.

VIRGINIA W. TUCKER

Note from the editors: Also try 1 cup sharp, grated cheese added to the above. These are good rolled into bite-size balls and served hot as appetizers.

ORANGE PECANS

1 cup sugar	1 tablespoon lemon juice
¼ cup evaporated milk	1 tablespoon grated
1 tablespoon white	orange rind
corn syrup	¼ teaspoon salt
2 tablespoons orange juice	2 tablespoons butter
1 teaspoon orange flavoring	2 cups pecan halves

Boil together sugar, evaporated milk, corn syrup, orange juice, orange peel, and salt until it makes a soft ball in cold water. Add pecans, butter and orange flavoring and cook 2 minutes longer. Set sauce pan in ice water in sink. Stir vigorously until very thick. Drop out on wax paper and separate halves. If directions are followed, pecans will be creamy, not sugary. After ingredients are assembled, this can be made in about 15 minutes.

MRS. EUGENE FLOURNOY
Monroe, La.

SHRIMP SPREAD

1 pound fresh shrimp	Mayonnaise
½ rib celery	Worcestershire sauce
1 green onion (tops also)	Tabasco

Boil shrimp for 10 to 15 minutes, depending on size, in well seasoned water containing celery leaves, salt, pepper and red pepper. Peel. Grind (on coarse grind) shrimp, celery and onion. Mix with only enough mayonnaise for a spread for crackers. Add Worcestershire and Tabasco to taste.

MRS. NORMAN S. SAURAGE, JR.

PATÉ DE LA MAISON D'ABADIE

½ pound liverwurst
1 8-ounce package
 cream cheese
3/4 teaspoon salt
¼ teaspoon (or more)
 cayenne pepper
1 teaspoon curry powder
Dash celery salt
Dash seasoned salt

½ cup cream (fresh
 or canned)
1 tablespoon
 Worcestershire sauce
3 4-oz. cans mushrooms,
 stems and pieces,
 drained, sauteed in 1
 stick melted butter or
 margarine.

1 tablespoon sherry

Mix in above order, adding mushroom-butter mixture while still hot. Blend well. Pour into plastic molds which have been lightly greased with olive oil. Freeze. Unmold while still frozen by dipping for one second in hot water. Allow to thaw on serving tray in refrigerator. Good with any type of cracker or Melba toast (particularly rye Melba).

MRS. ROY DABADIE

MINIATURE SHRIMP BOATS

Scoop out cherry tomatoes and drain well. Fill each with home made mayonnaise and shrimp salad. It is best to chop the shrimp fine as tomatoes are very small. Nice for afternoon tea or cocktail party.

MRS. RALPH PERLMAN

SAUSAGE BALLS

1 pound bulk hot sausage
1 pound extra sharp cheese, grated

3 cups biscuit mix

Mix all ingredients. Shape into small balls. Bake on cookie sheet at 425 degrees. Excellent for coffees or cocktail parties.

MRS. ALVIN BERTRAND

NUT ROLL

1 pound pecan halves
1 pound graham crackers
1 pound marshmallows

1 small jar cherries
1 8 ounce can grated
 cocoanut

1 stick butter

Crush graham crackers, add nuts and cocoanut. Melt butter in double boiler add marshmellows, stir until melted. Chop cherries and add to butter mixture with juice. Pour this into first mixture and mix thoroughly. Pour onto wax paper and roll very fast. Put in refrigerator in aluminum foil to chill. Slice into ½ inch slices when ready to serve.

MERIDITH JOAN ROBINSON

HOT MUSTARD

2 cans dry mustard	3 tablespoons sugar
1 jar hot mustard	1 teaspoon salt
1 jar plain mustard	½ cup imported olive oil

Mix dry ingredients in bowl. Add enough cold water to make a thick paste. Add remainder of mustard and olive oil. Blend well. Jar and refrigerate. Keeps well and improves with age.

MRS. GORDON M. RONALDSON

CRISP ICE BOX PICKLES

1 gallon sour pickles	5 pounds sugar
5 toes garlic	

Two gallon crock. Pour off all the vinegar from the sour pickles—you won't need any of it. Slice pickles cross wise. Use layer of pickles, sugar, one toe of garlic; repeat until all pickles, sugar and garlic are used. If you have some sugar left over, pile it on top. Be sure to use all the sugar. It makes the juice. Cover the top of crock with foil or its own top if it has one. Place it in a cool place. After about 2 days, stir with wooden spoon. Stir again in a couple of days. By the seventh day all sugar is melted and your pickles are ready to put in jars and kept in the refrigerator. Throw garlic away. Pickles keep for months.

AYLEIN ECKLES KONRAD

ARTICHOKE PICKLES

Scrape Jerusalem, or ground, artichokes, put in cold water, washing well. Drain off water, cover with salt then pour boiling water over artichokes. When water cools dry each artichoke, put in jars, add whole cloves, black pepper, sliced garlic, all-spice, fresh ground red-pepper. Fill jars with boiling vinegar and seal. Let stand about three weeks before using.

MISS CARMEN BREAZEALE
Natchitoches, La.

BREAD AND BUTTER PICKLES

1 gallon cucumbers, sliced   2 green peppers, shredded
8 small white onions   ½ cup salt

Wash cucumbers, but do not peel. Slice cucumbers, onions, and shred peppers. Mix with salt and bury in one quart of cracked ice. Let stand three hours. Drain well.

5 cups sugar   2 tablespoons mustard seed
1½ teaspoons turmeric   1 teaspoon celery seed
½ teaspoon ground cloves   5 cups vinegar

Pour over sliced pickle, and place over slow heat. Stir. Heat to scalding, but do not boil. Seal while hot.

From the file of
MRS. JUDITH MAJOR
MRS. JOHN MCKOWEN

GREEN TOMATO PICKLES

1 gallon green tomatoes,   1 cup green hot peppers,
    quartered   chopped
1 quart onions, chopped   ½ cup salt
1 quart bell peppers, chopped   1 quart red vinegar
5 cups sugar

Into a galvenized pan put the vinegar, sugar, salt and hot pepper. Bring to a boil. Add tomatoes, onions and bell peppers. When mixture boils, put in jars and let stand for 4 to 6 weeks. Chill before serving.

MRS. SAM B. SHORT

INDEX

339

CUPS PER POUND

flour .... 4 cups
cake flour .... 4 3/4 cups
sugar, granulated .... 2¼ cups
brown sugar .... (firmly packed) 2 cups
cornstarch .... 3 cups
rice .... 2 1/8 cups
butter, margarine, lard .. .. 2 cups
hydrogenated fat .... 2¼ cups
eggs (without shells) .... 2 cups
cheese, grated .... 4 cups
walnuts, shelled .... 4 cups
almonds (California), shelled .... 3 cups

EQUIVALENT SUBSTITUTIONS

1 lb. flour .... ½ lbs. cornstarch
1 cup cake flour .... 7/8 cup all purpose flour
1 oz. chocolate .... 3 tbs. cocoa plus 1 tsp. fat
1 cup honey ...... 1 to 1¼ cups sugar & ¼ cup liquid
1 cup light cream   3 tbs. butter & 7/8 cup milk
1 cup heavy cream   1/3 cup butter & 3/4 cup milk
1 cup sour milk .... 1 cup buttermilk
1 cup milk plus 1 tbs· vinegar .... 1 cup sour milk
1 tsp. baking powder .... ½ tsp. baking soda plus
                        1 cup sour milk or molasses
1 tsp. double acting baking powder ...... equals 2 tsp.
                        quick acting baking powder

NOTES

NOTES

NOTES

NOTES

NOTES

NOTES

NOTES

NOTES

C'EST SI BON
THE YOUNG WOMEN'S
CHRISTIAN ORGANIZATION
201 ST. CHARLES ST.
BATON ROUGE, LA. 70802

Send......copies of C'Est Si Bon at $4.25 per copy, postpaid.*

Enclosed is my check or money order for $.............................

Send to ....

Street ....

City .... State .... Zip Code ....

Check if gift wrapping is desired. ☐
*Includes 30¢ for Postage & Handling

C'EST SI BON
THE YOUNG WOMEN'S
CHRISTIAN ORGANIZATION
201 ST. CHARLES ST.
BATON ROUGE, LA. 70802

Send......copies of C'Est Si Bon at $4.25 per copy, postpaid.*

Enclosed is my check or money order for $.............................

Send to ....

Street ....

City .... State .... Zip Code ....

Check if gift wrapping is desired. ☐
*Includes 30¢ for Postage & Handling

C'EST SI BON
THE YOUNG WOMEN'S
CHRISTIAN ORGANIZATION
201 ST. CHARLES ST.
BATON ROUGE, LA. 70802

Send......copies of C'Est Si Bon at $4.25 per copy, postpaid.*

Enclosed is my check or money order for $.............................

Send to ....

Street ....

City .... State .... Zip Code ....

Check if gift wrapping is desired. ☐
*Includes 30¢ for Postage & Handling